OXFORD MONOGRAPHS ON
CLASSICAL ARCHAEOLOGY

Edited by

JOHN BOARDMAN
J. J. COULTON
DONNA KURTZ
MARTIN ROBERTSON
R. R. R. SMITH
MARGARETA STEINBY

FRONTISPIECE: London, British Museum E 279

Dionysian Imagery in Fifth-Century Athens

THOMAS H. CARPENTER

CLARENDON PRESS · OXFORD
1997

Oxford University Press, Great Clarendon Street, Oxford OX2 6DP

Oxford New York
Athens Auckland Bangkok Bogota Bombay
Buenos Aires Calcutta Cape Town Dar es Salaam
Delhi Florence Hong Kong Istanbul Karachi
Kuala Lumpur Madras Madrid Melbourne
Mexico City Nairobi Paris Singapore
Taipei Tokyo Toronto
and associated companies in
Berlin Ibadan

Oxford is a trade mark of Oxford University Press

Published in the United States
by Oxford University Press Inc., New York

British Library Cataloguing in Publication Data
Data available

Library of Congress Cataloging in Publication Data
Data available
ISBN 0–19–815038–5

1 3 5 7 9 10 8 6 4 2

Typeset by Hope Services (Abingdon) Ltd.
Printed in Great Britain on acid-free paper by
Biddles Ltd., Guildford & King's Lynn

To R. J. Gula, L. H. Sackett
and R. V. Scudder

Preface

A GREAT deal has been written about Dionysos during the past decade; so much, in fact, that a colleague has recently dubbed the subject 'a growth industry'. None the less, I think there is room for yet another book on the god primarily because the approach here is different from those of most of the others. Rather than texts, the primary sources here are the more than 4,000 extant representations of Dionysos and his companions from fifth-century Athens; the central question addressed is, what can these images reveal about fifth-century Attic perceptions of Dionysos? Other types of evidence from the same period, including texts, are used to broaden the perspective gained from the images rather than vice versa.

Dionysos in the fifth century was the subject I thought I was ready to write on more than a decade ago when John Boardman rightly convinced me that to do that effectively I first had to look at the god's place in archaic art. The present book is based on the foundations built in my *Dionysian Imagery in Archaic Greek Art*, but in many ways it is a very different book; the question addressed is much broader, made possible by the much larger body of extant textual, epigraphic and archaeological evidence for fifth century Attic culture. As in the previous book, however, I have not embraced a particular theoretical premise nor have I been dissuaded from the cautious use of common sense.

The list of works cited at the end of the text gives a rough idea of my debt to the work of other scholars. In addition I have benefited greatly from conversations with innumerable colleagues and students. From the start John Boardman's willingness to read and discuss chapters as they developed, his critical comments and insights, and his encouragement have been invaluable. Chris Faraone's critical reading of an early draft of the manuscript has made it a better book than it otherwise would have been, as have later readings by Martin Robertson, Donna Kurtz, and Brian Sparkes. Discussions with Brian Shefton, Maria Pipili, Terry Papillon, Andy Becker, Glenn Bugh, Nick Smith, Jenny Clay, Jon Mikalson, Lynn Roller, Andy Reyes, Kathleen Lynch, and Meg Miller have helped me to clarify many difficult points. Much of the book was written in the Ashmolean Library at Oxford where I had access both to the superb collection of books on ancient art and archaeology and to the resources of the Beazley Archive which Donna Kurtz kindly made available to me. Thomas Mannack and Melanie Mendoça helped me with searches of the Archive database, but I also benefited from their acute observations on the complexities of Attic imagery during many lively conversations. My greatest debt, however, is to my wife, Lynne Lancaster, who has been, in ways too numerous to tell, my daily source of inspiration.

The first draft of this book was written during a year in Oxford made possible by a Fellowship from the National Endowment for the Humanities. Travel grants from Virginia Tech helped me make subsequent visits to Oxford for additional work, and I am grateful to Robert Landen, former director of the Center for Programs in the Humanities and Robert Bates, Dean of the College of Arts and Sciences for their continued support of my work.

Of the many people who helped me to assemble the photographs for the book, I particularly want to thank Lucilla Burn, John Oakley, Bob Wilkins, Jenny Lowe, Michael Vickers, Henry Kim, Brian Sparkes, Marion True, François Lissarrague, and Alan Pasquier.

The book is dedicated to three extraordinary schoolmaster-scholars at Groton, who as colleagues early in my career were wise and gentle *ciceroni* whose guidance was fundamental in setting me on the course I have taken.

For each object mentioned in the text, a source where an illustration can be found is listed in a note. For these sources I have tried to cite works accessible in most good research libraries, and have used *LIMC* or the *CVA* when possible. For Attic vases an index at the end of the book includes references to the Beazley apparatus (*ABV*, *ARV*, *Para*, and *Add*) or to Haspel's *ABL*.

All statistics are based on the vases in the Beazley Archive Database. In addition to vases listed in Beazley's *ABV*, *ARV*, and *Para*, the Database includes other vases for which photographs have been published in books, periodicals, and catalogues in the collection of the Ashmolean Library. The statistics are only intended to show relative values based on the fairly substantial sample of 53,000 vases (May 1995). All dates are BC unless otherwise noted.

T.H.C.

Blacksburg
October 1995

Contents

List of Plates

42A & B	Once Toronto, Borowski
43	London, British Museum E 140 (*ARV* 459.3)
44A	Brussels, Musée Royaux d'Art et d'Histoire R 255 (*ARV* 670.4)
44B	Paris, Cabinet des Médailles 357 (*ARV* 987.2)
45A	London, British Museum E 775 (*ARV* 1328.92)
45B	Munich, Antikensammlungen 2654 (*ARV* 462.47)
46A	Boston, Museum of Fine Arts 10.211 (*ARV* 16.14)
46B	Paris, Louvre G 69 (*ARV* 133.21)
47A & B	Oxford, Ashmolean Museum 1912.1165 (*ARV* 208.144)

Photographic Credits

Abbreviations

ABL   C. H. E. Haspels, *Attic Black-Figured Lekythoi* (Paris, 1936).

ABV   J. D. Beazley, *Attic Black-Figure Vase-Painters* (Oxford, 1956).

Add   T. H. Carpenter *et al.*, *Beazley Addenda* (Oxford, 1989).

AJA   *American Journal of Archaeology.*

AK   *Antike Kunst.*

AM   *Mitteilungen des Deutschen Archäologischen Instituts, Athenische Abteilung.*

Anz   *Archäologischer Anzeiger.*

ARV   J. D. Beazley, *Attic Red-Figure Vase-Painters*, 2nd edn. (Oxford, 1963).

BABesch   *Bulletin antieke beschaving. Annual Papers on Classical Archaeology.*

BCH   *Bulletin de correspondance hellénique.*

BICS   *Bulletin of the Institute of Classical Studies of the University of London.*

BSA   *Annual of the British School at Athens.*

CV   *Corpus vasorum antiquorum.*

GRBS   *Greek, Roman and Byzantine Studies.*

JdI   *Jahrbuch des Deutschen Archäologischen Instituts.*

JHS   *Journal of Hellenic Studies.*

LIMC   *Lexicon Iconographicum Mythologiae Classicae.*

ML   *Monumenti antichi pubblicati per cura della Reale Accademia dei Lincei.*

NSc   *Notizie degli scavi di antichità.*

Para   J. D. Beazley, *Paralipomena* (Oxford, 1971).

RA   *Revue archéologique.*

RM   *Mitteilungen des Deutschen Archäologischen Instituts, Römische Abteilung.*

I

Sources

THE body of visual evidence available for a study of Dionysos in fifth-century Athens is much richer than the contemporary textual sources; it has the added advantages of being quite datable and of not suffering corruptions at the hands of careless copyists. The god himself appears on more than 900 surviving fifth-century Attic vases, something over 3.5 per cent of the known total, which is more than any other god;[1] he figures prominently in the sculpture from the east pediment, east frieze, and east metopes of the Parthenon; and he was the subject of monumental paintings in Athens of which we have written accounts. Yet, in spite of the volume of the evidence, its authenticity, and its datability, remarkably little effective use has been made of it in attempts to understand the nature and place of Dionysos in Athens. This study is intended to be a partial response to the question, what can surviving visual sources reveal about fifth-century Attic perceptions of Dionysos?

The study is limited to the Attic Dionysos for two reasons. The most obvious is that the bulk of surviving visual imagery for Dionysos was produced in Attica. Equally important, however, is the need for a limited focus when discussing perceptions. The question, how did the Greeks perceive Dionysos is unanswerable. The response must be, which Greeks? Even limiting the study to Athens is only a first step, and now we need to ask, which Athenians and when? The time period for the study is limited to the century and a quarter (some four generations of Athenians) between about 525, when the red-figure technique of vase painting came into its own, and about 400, soon after *Bacchae* and *Frogs* were first performed in Athens; this is the period for which the visual evidence is richest.[2] Some objects studied here, like the sculpture from the Parthenon, can be dated with a high

---

[1] Recently some rather exaggerated claims have been made about the occurrences of Dionysian subjects on Attic vases (e.g. Hoffmann (1988: 158)). Searches of the 53,100 black- and red-figure vases in the Beazley Archive Database (May 1995) produced the following results: Dionysos appears on 4,343 vases (8.2 per cent); satyrs and/or 'maenads' without Dionysos appear on an additional 5470 (10.3 per cent). The total of Dionysian scenes is 9813 (18.5 per cent). These figures are significant only as they show that most Attic vases do not, in fact, have Dionysian subjects on them.

[2] In T. Carpenter (1986), I have discussed the development of Dionysian imagery prior to the last quarter of the 6th cent.

degree of precision on the basis of external evidence; other objects, like painted vases, can be organized on the basis of stylistic development into relative chronologies which can be pegged to a few firm dates allowing most individual pieces to be assigned to a quarter-century at the least.[3]

In spite of these limits on time and place, the subject remains extremely complex, not least because at any one point in the fifth century most Athenians would have had several different coexisting perceptions of Dionysos. For example, the Dionysos of Euripides' *Bacchae* and the Dionysos of Aristophanes' *Frogs* probably appeared in the theatre of Dionysos in the same year, while above the theatre on the Acropolis a nude, athletic Dionysos reclined in the east pediment of the Parthenon. At the same time on different red-figure vases produced in the nearby Kerameikos a beardless, half-naked Dionysos romped with Ariadne, a stately, bearded Dionysos in long chiton and himation stood amongst satyrs, and a bearded mask of the god attached to a column was flanked by dancing women. (This is to say nothing of the cult statues and paintings, nor of dithyrambs or other hymns sung in his honour.) Surely each of these images conveyed a different perception of the god, or a perception of a different dimension of the god; yet they are all Dionysos. Without doubt part of the mystery and power of the god was expressed by the multitude of personalities and forms signified by his name.[4]

In what follows I attempt to define some of these different perceptions of the god and to describe how they develop; that is, how they change and how their importance over time seems to grow or diminish. In writing about human perceptions of a god I am, of course, considering ways humans found to express their understanding or awareness or experience of him. Just as the visual is only one kind of expression, so the human was only one of many forms Dionysos was said to take. But human is the form he is almost always given in visual representations, so this study is further limited to an examination of perceptions of the anthropomorphic Dionysos.

There are many reasons why this visual evidence has not been used more effectively in the past. Large among them are the lack of clarity about the kinds of authority the various types of imagery (particularly vase painting) have, and the concomitant confusion over the validity of the various methods used to draw conclusions from it. These matters need to be addressed briefly before turning to the evidence which is the basis of this study.

---

[3] In what follows here, I rely upon the chronological framework established by Beazley and most recently discussed by Robertson (1992: 41–2). I am aware of problems with this dating, but I still believe it is closer to the truth than others proposed to replace it. For the most part I place vases in quarter-centuries. For a broader discussion of the dating of Greek pottery, see Biers (1992: 82–5) and Sparkes (1991: 28–59).

[4] For discussions of various dimensions of Dionysos see Carpenter and Faraone (1993).

Figure-decorated vases and architectural sculpture provide most of the evidence in the following chapters. One obvious difference between these two types, which is particularly important for this study, is that one was usually produced for private use while the other was designed for public display. The subjects of architectural sculpture were, presumably, determined by civic officials, and the same could probably be said for monumental painting. Painted vases, on the other hand, were usually purchased by individuals for private use, whether the symposion or the grave, and the choices of subjects and elements of imagery were probably made by the painter or workshop owner, sometimes, perhaps, in consultation with a client. The market must have had considerable influence on imagery on vases, but we can have no idea whether the average purchaser at one time or another was more interested in quality of drawing, overall decoration, treatment of subject, or even shape. Where the choice of subject and even details for architectural sculpture may well have had civic and political implications, the same is less likely to have been true of most vase paintings.

A further distinction between types of objects might be made on the basis of the labour required for their production. Where a life-sized human figure carved from marble might take a sculptor a year to produce, a red-figure amphora might take a potter and painter a matter of hours to throw and decorate.[5] Experimentation, whimsy, and idiosyncrasies are obviously more likely to occur in imagery on inexpensive, private objects than in monumental public ones. On the other hand, monumental images commissioned for public space are more likely to reflect (or shape) commonly held perceptions.

The ambiguous status in Athens of vase painting, our largest source of images, is a serious obstacle to the use of those images as evidence for Attic attitudes and perceptions. Relatively little is known about the people who made the pots and drew the pictures or the people who bought them, or even how Athenians used them.[6] So the question arises, whose Dionysos do the vase paintings show?

Textual sources say little about the potters and nothing about the people who decorated the vases. Signatures on some vases give us names of people involved in the production of them, but there is disagreement on just what these names mean, and there is little external evidence to help identify the named people, whatever their roles.[7] However, from internal evidence—

---

[5] On potting and painting see Sparkes (1991: 8–27); Noble (1988).

[6] For an overview and bibliography for some of these problems see Arafat and Morgan (1989). See also Scheibler (1983).

[7] For a recent discussion of names see Robertson (1992: 3–4). For a summary of evidence for potters and painters, Johnston (1991: 212).

from the study of the vases themselves—we do know something about some vase painters.

Sir John Beazley, adapting a method originally developed for the identification of hands for unsigned Renaissance paintings,[8] identified more than 1,000 individual painters and groups of painters of fifth-century vases and assigned more than 20,000 works to them. A study of the corpus of surviving images from one influential group of painters can highlight particular areas of interest and reveal aspects of what might be called the painters' professional personae. Of course, it would be foolish to draw any broad conclusions about a painter from such evidence, but the treatment of an old subject can demonstrate wit and ingenuity, and the appearance of a new scene can demonstrate a capacity for invention or adaptation. In what follows, this knowledge is particularly useful, since most changes in Dionysian imagery can be traced to a few groups of painters. It might be added that the most inventive vase painters are often not the best at drawing—there is no necessary correlation between aesthetic pleasure and iconographic interest provoked by a piece.

This last point brings up one further issue worth mentioning, that there is a great discrepancy in technical competence between the best and the worst of the Attic vase painters, and even the best are still decorators of ceramic vessels, not Renaissance masters! As Martin Robertson has recently written, 'I see the best Greek vase painters as artists; but the majority were craftsmen producing pottery vessels with more or less mechanical decoration; and even the artists spent much of their time doing just that; they too were primarily workers in a utilitarian craft.'[9]

We know even less about the particular people who bought the vases than we know of the producers.[10] The fact is that the majority of surviving Attic red-figure vases were found in Italy in Etruscan tombs, and there is evidence to suggest that some vases were specifically designed for the export market.[11] It has been suggested that at least some were bought by Athenians for special occasions and then perhaps sold on the second-hand market for export.[12] Through finds we know that Attic vases were exported to many parts of the Mediterranean world and even to areas bordering the Black Sea, and through trademarks we know something about the trade in vases,[13] but we still know little about the actual markets at home or abroad. Recently a few scholars have argued, if unconvincingly, that the vases were seen in

---

[8] See Kurtz (1985).   [9] Robertson (1992: 3).

[10] For a recent discussion, Johnston (1991).

[11] Spivey (1991). For recent discussions of Etruscan use of Attic vases see Arafat and Morgan (1994: esp. 113–21) and Small (1994), who argues that many (and perhaps the majority) of Attic vases found in Etruria were bought specifically for the tomb.

[12] Webster (1972: 42–62).   [13] Johnston (1979).

Athens as little more than cheap imitations of gold and silver vessels owned by the wealthy.[14] In short, for relatively few vases can we say with any certainty for what buyer (culture, class, or gender) a vase painting was originally produced.[15] Furthermore, since most surviving vases were found in tombs, we can say little about their intended use (unless we want to take the unlikely position that most were made for the tomb). What we can say with some confidence is that the vases were made and decorated in Athens and that the shapes of a high proportion of surviving vases, particularly from the first half of the century, were designed for the storage and consumption of wine, particularly at the symposion. What should also be said again is that all Attic pots were not created equal and the range in quality of drawing and design must at all times point to broad-based markets. The care Euphronios, Phintias, Douris, and Makron, to name a few, put into some of their drawings is inexplicable unless there was a market which appreciated that high quality of execution. That barely intelligible vase paintings could be produced at the same time, perhaps in the same workshops, should be kept in mind.

Even admitting that we can know very little about specific vase painters aside from what we can glean from their drawings, we still can say something about the types of external sources that might have influenced choices of stories and choices of imagery in Dionysian scenes. For the purposes of discussion possible sources might be sorted into five groups: (1) traditional tales; (2) literature (written or performed); (3) other visual imagery; (4) patrons' requests; (5) whimsy. There is very little evidence for the influence of actual cult practices on vase paintings during the fifth century.[16]

Most if not all stories about the gods and heroes must have existed as traditional tales which were passed on orally before they took on literary or visual forms. In fact, visual and literary forms can most productively be seen as two independent manifestations of a story. To express the meaning of the visual narrative one must use a linear verbal form, but that does not necessarily imply the existence of a formal literary source or that the imagist knew the literary source when one did exist.

[14] e.g. Gill and Vickers (1990: 1–30).

[15] It seems self-evident to me that the nature of the market for painted vases, even in Athens, would have changed in many ways during the century and a quarter that is the focal period of this study. Sutton (1992: 28) following Webster (1972), argues on the basis of shapes and subjects that during the course of the 5th cent. 'vase painters discovered and cultivated a feminine market'.

[16] Possible reflections of cult on Attic vases are discussed below in Ch. 5. The unconscious has sometimes been cited as a source of imagery, and while it may well have been an influence, I see no reliable way of determining the role of the artisan's unconscious in his or her choice of imagery. Though entertaining, such speculation is ultimately fruitless and has the added danger of being an open door for the introduction of new sets of culturally determined assumptions and expectations.

Literary sources are essential to the study of ancient visual narratives for the obvious reason that they tell us the stories that we would not otherwise know or even be able to guess in many instances. However, to assume or hope that surviving scraps of literary evidence match up with surviving scraps of visual evidence, given the tiny proportions of each that have come down to us, is unproductive; such pursuits seldom contribute much to the study of either philology or archaeology.

Whether or not most vase painters were literate is unclear. Literate inscriptions on vases probably show that some were; nonsense inscriptions on others show that some were not; the absence of inscriptions from most vases leaves the question open. That vase painters attended festivals where literary works (dithyramb, lyric, epic) were performed and theatrical productions were staged seems highly likely. That some vase painters remembered what they heard sung or recited or saw in the theatre seems obvious. How these influences might have affected the imagery they put on pots, however, is a different question.[17] None the less, the relation between visual images of Dionysos and literary descriptions of him are of interest here because both would have contributed to Athenian perceptions of him.

Theatre may at times have served as link between literary narrative and visual narrative on vases; for some vases we can demonstrate that images do refer to the theatre.[18] For example, theatrical performances are the most likely sources for an aulos player in full costume (long chiton, *phorbeia*) performing in the presence of satyrs carrying bits of disassembled furniture (Pl. 16B);[19] for a satyr wearing shorts with an artificial phallos and tail attached in a depiction of the return of Hephaistos (Pl. 14A);[20] for the peculiar depiction of Andromeda's captivity on several other vases.[21] Yet it is easy to overemphasize the influence of the theatre on the iconography of vases without clarifying anything. The depictions of most of the thousands upon thousands of figures that appear on Attic vases show no demonstrable connection with the theatre, and it is worth remembering that the audiences of most tragedies knew the basic plots before they saw the plays.

Images by peers were, without any doubt, the most important sources for most vase painters. Those images can be from sculpture or monumental painting, but more often than not they are demonstrably from other vases. This is not to say that vase painters copied each others' works; there are, in

---

[17] For a useful discussion of this problem as it relates to depictions of events included in the poems of the Epic Cycle, see Cook (1983).

[18] See recently Green (1991).   [19] Boston 03.788, *ARV* 571.75, Boardman (1975: fig. 325).

[20] Vienna 985, *ARV* 591.20, *LIMC* III pl. 362, Dionysos 555.

[21] e.g. Sophocles' *Andromeda*, see Trendall and Webster (1971: 63 III,2,1–3).

fact, remarkably few duplicates among Attic vases.[22] Rather, the subject, the moment or moments of an episode chosen for the depiction or the ways the central figures are shown is often repeated. Indeed, conventions are often the means by which a figure or scene is made recognizable, and this is an extremely important point to keep in mind when studying the iconography of Attic vases. Most vase paintings were composed of images that were instantly intelligible from some distance; it is difficult to imagine that many people in fifth-century Athens spent much time examining the 'average' vase in much detail.

A caveat is in order here. A preconception that underlies many discussions of iconography is the assumption that all vase paintings are of equal value as evidence. The unspoken implication is that the breadth of knowledge and depth of thought that went into each image is essentially the same and therefore each can be used in the same way. Given the facelessness of Greek vase painters, this is perhaps a natural development; since we have no external evidence about their knowledge in any area (literature, festivals, cults, athletics, military equipment) we might as well assume they have equal authority in all. The numbingly repetitive nature of so much Greek vase painting suggests that this assumption is almost certainly wrong. As it can be demonstrated that some vase painters are better at drafting than others, so it can be demonstrated that some are more inventive with their imagery. As already noted, some vase painters are much more likely than others to include new imagery in their works, and it seems sensible to conclude that new imagery on a finely crafted work by one of these vase painters was probably intended for a closer look than was most imagery on most Attic vases. But the very act of looking closely at the imagery on some vases poses the same problems now that it must have posed then. From a practical standpoint it is difficult to get a close view of the imagery on the curved surfaces of many forms without manipulating them. Good light coming at a particular angle is often necessary to see inscriptions and some details in dilute glaze. In the best of light most red-figure inscriptions are difficult to read, even with good eyes, at a distance of much more than two feet. That at least a few images on vases, particularly cups, were intended for close inspection seems likely, and more often than not it is probably to symposia that we should look for the viewers and perhaps the occasions.

There is evidence that some vases were special orders. This is obviously the case with Panathenaic amphorae which were filled with oil and used as

---

[22] See Oakley (1992, 201–3 and nn. 33–5); Noble (1988: 107–8); Connor (1981: 37–42); Schauenburg (1977: 194–204).

prizes for the contests at the Panathenaia every four years.[23] However, there is also evidence that individual pieces were special orders as well.[24] There are several ways a patron might influence the imagery on a vase he orders: he could request a specific subject; he could request new elements in an old subject or specific elements in a new subject; or he could request the inclusion of inscriptions in the scene. Since the majority of the vases under consideration in this study have shapes appropriate for the symposion, the possibility that some scenes were made for specific symposia and had imagery of special meaning to the members of specific groups will be explored below.

Finally, I should admit that I am fully prepared to believe that some images are included in scenes simply because they are decorative or entertaining, rather than because the painter intended them to have a specific meaning. Shield devices are a case in point. There are hundreds of them on warriors' shields on black and red-figure vases. They are so clear and often so unusual that it seems they should mean something, and Aeschylus' use of them in *Seven Against Thebes* (387–676) would seem to confirm this conclusion. Yet after having looked at many hundreds of them and having tried to find correlations between devices and specific characters or types of devices and types of characters, I am convinced that they are, with rare exceptions, whimsically decorative.[25]

In spite of problems over the identities of potters, painters of pots, and patrons, the fact remains that there exists a very large body of images on Attic vases to which most scholars have easy access, and a word is in order, I believe, about appropriate methods for the use of these images. While the design-based choice of a vase painting for the cover of a book is relatively harmless (and often quite pleasing), the indiscriminate use of images as evidence for Greek religious or social attitudes, without an awareness of the visual tradition of which they are a part, can only lead to weak conclusions and at the same time undermine the value of such images as evidence for anything else. An image is open to an almost infinite number of interpretations by a viewer unfamiliar with the culture *or* the visual tradition.

I believe that any attempt to pursue the meanings an image had for the people who made it or for those who chose to buy it must be undertaken in what might be described as two complementary stages. First the image must be defined as part of a visual tradition, then it must be interpreted

---

[23] See Neils (1992: 29–51 and bibliography). It has been estimated that more than 1,400 of these vases were produced every four years. See Johnston (1987: 125–9).

[24] Webster (1972, 42–62).

[25] For a recent discussion of this problem see Spier (1990), who considers shield devices along with devices on gems and types on coins.

within the context of the culture that produced it. Whatever method is used to interpret the image, the first step remains the same and involves a process that can be independently repeated and confirmed. In short, no matter how theoretical the ultimate approach may be, it must start with a process that is unambiguously empirical.[26]

Fundamental to everything else that follows is a close examination and identification of all the elements that make up the image; as long as any element remains unnoticed or unidentified, this step remains incomplete.[27] The process of identification depends upon comparisons with images on contemporary vases. For this process a useful analogy might be drawn between learning to translate an ancient language and learning to 'read' imagery on Greek vases. Where the simple dictionary translation of a word in a text or the general naming of an image is often quite straightforward, an awareness of the more subtle implications of the word or image only comes with increased experience of its various occurrences. As an attentive reader of words or images becomes more familiar with the language, subtle changes and variations stand out more clearly.

The definition of relationships between elements of imagery in a scene can be more problematic. Here too comparison with contemporary images can be productive, but the precise nature of the relationship often remains obscure, and the possibility must always be entertained that in some scenes no explicit connection between the elements of imagery was intended. One can productively speculate on the nature of a relationship or the meaning of an ambiguous gesture, but this is part of a different process and should remain separate from the initial definition of the visual context. In short, we should make clear those things we do know through this empirical approach before we turn to speculation on those things we do not know.

As etymology contributes to definition, so the original use of an image can shed light on its later occurrences; thus, another part of this empirical stage of exploration is to trace the sources of various elements of imagery and to note variations in use over time. As in all aspects of this process, the

[26] The term 'empirical' has had a bad press of late, e.g. Sourvinou-Inwood (1991: 3–23). With Sourvinou-Inwood I believe that objects and texts should be read within their own contexts and that we must find ways to circumvent our own 'culturally determined assumptions and expectations' in our study of these objects and texts. However, given the mere scraps of visual and textual evidence that have survived from 5th-cent. Athens, I do not believe it is possible 'to reconstruct all the relevant ancient assumptions and expectations and fashion perceptual filters out of them'. This idea strikes me as more of a mantra than a possibility.

[27] This is not to imply that we can always give names to all of the figures in a scene. In fact, the majority of vases have figures on them whose specific identity is unclear. In many scenes, such as warriors fighting or quarrelling, none of the figures can be named, but given the conventional nature of the form, they can be identified as types and their attributes described. It is possible that some of these generic scenes were painted to allow the viewer to provide his or her own identification.

broader one's experience of the imagery, the clearer one can be about the significance of the variations.

Relative chronology is always important in any comparative statements about vases. The nature of the imagery rarely remains static for long, and during the fifth century the changes are rapid and often quite dramatic as each new generation of vase painters modifies the imagery of the preceding generation. In fact, the century and a quarter which is the subject of this study includes at least four generations of Athenians. A young man painting vases or writing plays in 400 could be the great, great grandson of a man who painted vases or wrote verse in 525; to suggest his perceptions of Dionysos would be the same as those of his great, great grandfather is, of course, absurd. To note that only one or two generations separate works is to emphasize distance rather than proximity.[28]

Yet another part of this 'empirical stage' is to consider the image in relation to the various larger groups of which it is a part. So, in this study an unusual red-figure Dionysian scene by the Niobid Painter might be considered with reference to: all red-figure Dionysian scenes by the Niobid Painter; all scenes by the Niobid Painter; all red-figure Dionysian scenes; all fifth-century depictions of Dionysos. Throughout this whole process each comparison helps to define the parameters of possible interpretations. In short, the comparative process helps to set limits on what an image can or cannot mean.

Having established the visual context through comparisons with contemporary images and groups of images, a broader meaning for the scene, admittedly, often seems little closer than it did at the start. However, the essential groundwork has been laid, and the challenge for students of ancient imagery is to find reliable ways to move from the image to the culture or from the culture to the image. How does the image relate to other types of contemporary imagery? What is the historical context and how precisely can we define it? What evidence is there for a social context? Are anthropological models useful? Are there theoretical approaches that help to make sense of the evidence? While it is clear to me that no single method can be appropriate for the interpretation of all imagery, I do believe some new approaches elaborated during the past several years have yielded promising results. But whatever the method, the quality of the results are dependent on the quality of the evidence.

In what follows here, I have not adopted a theoretical premiss but, rather, have tried to let the images lead where they will. Having analysed them in the context of their visual tradition, I have attempted to consider them in

---

[28] To be assured that 'generation gaps' are not exclusively modern phenomena, one need only recall the debate between *Kreitton logos* and *Etton logos* in Aristophanes *Clouds* (889-1106).

relation to other types of evidence to move out of what can become a closed circle of reasoning. So, I have sought references to subjects and images in contemporary literature and its scholia, in later literature and in contemporary and later epigraphical evidence. As with visual comparisons, I have paid close attention to chronology, and unless there is convincing evidence that a later textual source is based on a source contemporary with or earlier than the image under consideration, I have rarely relied on it. The composite, a-temporal (synchronic) nature of many modern descriptions of Greek cult practices and festivals tends to be one of their great weaknesses (and one that I have been determined to avoid in these pages).[29]

The following chapters are essays on some significant developments in Dionysian imagery in fifth-century Athens. Since Dionysos had appeared in scenes on Attic vases for more than a half a century before the earliest images included here were produced, some comments may be useful on the earlier developments of Dionysian imagery. Also, since most of the vase paintings discussed here are in the red-figure technique, some observations on the iconographic implications of the change from black-figure to red-figure as they apply to Dionysos are in order.

The Dionysos who first appears in Greek art on an Attic black-figure dinos during the first quarter of the sixth century represents little more than his function as bringer-of-wine.[30] There he is one of the lesser deities in a procession of gods and goddesses on their way to celebrate the wedding of Peleus and Thetis. Humbly dressed, he walks barefoot and carries a branch of a grapevine while the grander gods wearing elegant cloaks ride in four-horse chariots. Within three decades, however, Dionysos had become one of the most common subjects on Attic black-figure vases, and 'canonical' imagery had been developed to depict him.

On black-figure vases he is always a bearded figure with long hair, usually dressed in a chiton and himation. This description, of course, fits black-figure depictions of most of the senior Olympians, but Dionysos is distinguished by the larger size of his beard, by the ivy wreath on his head and by the kantharos or drinking horn, ivy sprig or grape vine he carries. Often he is accompanied by satyrs and nymphs. Nymphs without satyrs rarely accompany him on black-figure vases before the last quarter of the century.[31]

The imagery for depicting Dionysos seems to have been created in Athens and more than 2,000 surviving depictions of him on archaic Attic

---

[29] Hamilton (1992), has recently called attention to this problem in relation to the Anthesteria. See particularly 59–62.

[30] London 1971.1–1.1, *Para* 19.16*bis*, T. Carpenter (1986: pls. 1A, 2, 3B).

[31] For a partial list of black-figure Dionysian scenes see Christopulu-Mortoja (1964).

vases are the main source for knowledge of the god during the sixth century. During that century he only rarely appears in sculpture or on vases from other areas, and in surviving literature from before the classical period he is only occasionally mentioned. The *Homeric Hymn to Dionysos* (VII), if it is archaic, provides the only clear description of him, and that image, ironically, bears little relation to the surviving images of him from the visual arts.[32]

In the vast majority of black-figure depictions of the god he simply stands, walks or sits amongst satyrs and nymphs. His appearances in narrative scenes that show recognizable myths are relatively rare, and he plays a central role only in the Return of Hephaistos and the Gigantomachy. Throughout the history of Attic black-figure—from his first appearance during the first quarter of the sixth century down into the early decades of the fifth century—his physical appearance and attributes remain essentially the same.

The introduction of the red-figure technique in Athens at the end of the third quarter of the sixth century brought with it strikingly new imagery along with innovations in drawing. Early on red-figure painters established a new canon of Dionysian imagery. Through new narrative scenes and new, more specific imagery in old scenes, they gave the god a much more complex, more fully developed persona than he had in black-figure. Even in their generic scenes the god tends to be more sharply defined.

While late black-figure painters sometimes adopted elements of the new style of drawing pioneered by the early red-figure painters, they seldom adopted the new imagery or the new 'tone' that came with it. They continued to produce old-fashioned pictures while the early red-figure painters showed new stories and new imagery in some old scenes.[33] During the decades on either side of 500 large numbers of black-figure vases continued to be made, and it is perhaps significant that some newly popular subjects and elements of imagery in them rarely appear on contemporary red-figure. Depictions of the thyrsos and the goat are useful in illustrating this point as it relates to Dionysian imagery.[34]

The thyrsos, which is one of Dionysos' most distinctive attributes, first appears on vases by the early red-figure painters and was never adopted by

[32] For the archaic Dionysos see Carpenter 1986; also *LIMC* III s.v. Dionysos.

[33] e.g. compare the imagery by vase painters from the Leagros Group with imagery from the Pioneers, some of whom may have worked together in the same workshop. See Beazley (1986: 74–5). Cf. Robertson (1992: 36–7).

[34] Another image that should be mentioned in this context is the balding satyr, who does not appear on black-figure vases, but does appear on later (but not earlier) cups by Oltos, on cups by Epiktetos, and on vases by Phintias and Euthymides. Thereafter he is commonplace.

black-figure painters.[35] Composed of ivy leaves attached to the top of a giant fennel stalk (or narthex)[36] the thyrsos is a distinctive, artificial creation quite unlike the vines and branches sometimes carried in Dionysian scenes both before and after its first appearance. It does not appear in Dionysian scenes by the earliest red-figure painters such as the Andokides Painter or Psiax, nor does it appear in early Dionysian scenes by Oltos. However, it does appear on two of Oltos' later cups and on cups by Epiktetos,[37] on a hydria by Euthymides and on a stamnos by the younger Pioneer, Smikros.[38] Thus, in relative terms, we can point with some accuracy to the moment it first appears on vases, though neither why it was introduced nor where it came from is at all clear.[39]

On the other hand a goat appears with Dionysos on more than one hundred black-figure vases contemporary with early red-figure, while it appears with him on fewer than a dozen red-figure vases from the same period.[40] As with the thyrsos in red-figure, the significance of the goat in black-figure is not at all clear. The Dionysian scenes by the Eucharides Painter, who worked in both techniques, show clearly that the two traditions required different iconographic models. The thyrsos appears in his red, but not in his black-figure scenes; the opposite is true for the goat. The same is true for his elder colleague the Nikoxenos Painter.[41]

The exclusion of a very distinctive object like the thyrsos (which later became a canonical Dionysian image) from black-figure scenes and of the goat from most red-figure scenes could suggest that the vases painted in the different techniques had different types of markets, which could imply different uses. The fact that the geographical distribution of find-spots for early red-figure and contemporary black-figure vases seems to be quite similar points to the complexity of the markets and serves as another warning of the care we must take in placing images in their visual context before considering their broader implications.

What follows here is neither a survey of all fifth-century Attic Dionysian

[35] For the few late black-figure vases with thyrsoi see Edwards (1960: 84 n. 51); Coche de la Ferté (1951: 15 n. 6). Add: Wellington (NZ) C34, *CV* 1, pl. 24.9–10; Naples 128333, *ABV* 367.93, *RM* 27 (1912) pl. 8; Athens 647, *ABV* 562.547; Delos 568, Dugas (1928: pls. 41, 69); London Market, Sotheby 1 December 1913, pl. 1. 70.

[36] Beazley (1933: 400–3).

[37] Oltos: Rome, Vatican, Ast. 763, *ARV* 60.64*bis*; Tarquinia RC 6848, ARV 60.66, Arias, Hirmer, and Shefton (1962: pl. 100). A branch which might be called a 'proto-thyrsos' appears on some of his earlier vases, e.g. London E 437, *ARV* 54.5, *CV* 3 pl. 19. Epiktetos: Paris, Louvre G 6, *ARV* 72.21, *CV* 10 pl. 10; Providence 25.077, *ARV* 73.34, *CV* pl. 14; Paris, Louvre C 10472, *ARV* 72.23.

[38] St Petersburg 624, *ARV* 28.15; Paris, Louvre G 43, *ARV* 20.2

[39] It first appears in surviving literature much later. See Henrichs (1987: 121 n. 71).

[40] For a partial list of Dionysian scenes with a goat on black-figure vases see Burkert (1966: 99 n. 25).

[41] For both painters see Robertson (1992: 118–21).

imagery nor an exhaustive study of all issues raised by the images; either undertaking would require many volumes. Rather, the following chapters are essays on what I believe to be some of the more significant developments in Dionysian imagery in fifth-century Athens. I will consider it successful if some scholars find my analysis of the evidence useful and if new solutions are stimulated by the problems raised. Ultimately the pursuit of Dionysos in ancient Greece requires the joint efforts of philologists and papyrologists, epigraphers and iconographers if the results are to be broadly significant.

2

The Gigantomachy

THE Parthenon on the Acropolis in Athens, more than any other monument, embodies the meaning of the word 'classical', and as such, its sculpture is an appropriate place to begin a consideration of Dionysian imagery in fifth-century Athens. Images of Dionysos appeared three times on the east end of the building above the entrance to the cella that housed the chryselephantine statue of Athena Parthenos. He may also have appeared in the Gigantomachy painted or engraved inside Athena's shield and at the birth of Pandora on the statue's base. In the pediment he was a beardless youth of athletic build reclining on a leopard skin with his back to the marvellous happenings in the centre of the scene. In the frieze, again a beardless youth if Carrey's drawings are to be believed, he sat on a stool with a himation about his waist and rested his right arm on Hermes' shoulder.[1] In the second metope from the left he fought a giant.

The Gigantomachy is the subject of all fourteen metopes on the east end of the Parthenon, and the identification of Dionysos in metope 2 is certain.[2] Though the head is missing, the pose, dress, and companions of the figure can be distinguished. The god faces right with his left leg advanced and his left arm stretched out in front of him toward a fleeing giant. He wears an animal skin over a chiton. The attachment holes remain for a snake (which was probably bronze) that wrapped around the giant's right leg, and much remains of a large feline that stands on its hind legs and bites the giant's side. Parts of the giant's right leg, left foot, torso, and helmet also remain.

Praschniker, in his reconstruction of the metope, gives the god a knee-length chiton, boots, and a thyrsos and makes him beardless (Pl. IA). The chiton, boots, and thyrsos are likely on the basis of many other depictions of the Gigantomachy on vases; however, the absence of a beard is less certain.[3] The closest parallels for the figure in the metope are from earlier Attic red–figure vases where the god is regularly aided by snakes and felines.

---

[1] For a discussion of Dionysos in the pediment and frieze, see below, Ch. 6.

[2] See Berger (1986: 56, 59 and pls. 37, 40–1).

[3] For different views on the length of the chiton see Brommer (1967: 24) and Schwab (1989: 25). For the beard see Praschniker (1928: 192–3 and fig. 119). 'Nach dem Muster des Parthenonfrieses wurde der Gott bartlos gezeichnet.' He compares the god of the metope with a figure on a 4th-cent. relief

Dionysos is a regular participant in the Gigantomachy from the first depiction of the subject on vases before the middle of the sixth century, but prior to the end of that century he is only one of many deities in the fight and is rarely depicted in duels. Then, with early red-figure painters he suddenly becomes the most frequently depicted figure in that battle. At the same time he takes on new attributes that define his role there more precisely. Before focusing on the god, however, some words should be said about the place of the Gigantomachy itself in archaic and classical imagery.

Hundreds of depictions of the battle (or parts of the battle) have survived. They are lively scenes and often include curious details that seem as if they should allude to specific events and places, yet the surviving literary sources are so late and mundane that they provide little or no help in discovering that 'meaning'. The earliest extant account of it is from the second century AD in Apollodorus (1. 6. 1–2); however, references to the battle appear in literature by the beginning of the fifth century. The existence of a sixth-century epic about it has been sensibly posited, but the traditional tale on which it would have been based must have been much earlier.[4] By all accounts the giants were offspring of Gaia and Ouranos who challenged the power of the gods and were defeated only with the help of the hero Herakles. The battle was said to have taken place in Phlegra or Pallene. Herodotus (7. 123) called Phlegra the old name for Pallene, the westernmost finger of the Chalcidice.[5]

The Gigantomachy was the subject of architectural sculpture at Delphi and Olympia from the last quarter of the sixth century with groups of gods and giants fighting, and during the first half of the fifth century duels were carved in metopes on temples E and F at Selinus. However, the majority of the evidence for the Gigantomachy comes from Attica where the story had particular significance. In addition to appearing on hundreds of Attic black- and red-figure vases, it was the subject of architectural sculpture on the Acropolis in the sixth and fifth centuries, and possibly of a frieze in the fifth-century temple of Poseidon at Sounion.[6] From the Parthenon itself it was

amphora in St Petersburg (KAB 6a, Schefold (1934: 161, pl. 28.1–2). Vian (1952: 139) prefers a comparison with a figure in a Gigantomachy on a 4th-cent. Apulian krater, Bari 4399, Vian (1951: 395, pl. 47). These are odd choices. The St Petersburg vase does not show a Gigantomachy, and the Bari vase is one of very few South Italian depictions of the subject. Neither scene includes either felines or snakes. In fact, the Gigantomachy appears only rarely on any vases after the middle of the 5th cent.

[4] See Vian (1952: 169–83). For extant literary sources see Arafat (1990: 9–11).

[5] In his discussion of the Athenian Acropolis, Pausanias (1. 25. 2) mentions a depiction of the war with the giants 'who once dwelt about Thrace and on the Isthmus of Pallene'. However, in his discussion of Arcadia (8. 29. 1) he writes 'the Arcadians say that the fabled battle between giants and gods took place here (by a spring called Olympias) and not at Pallene in Thrace'.

[6] For a catalogue of sculpture and vases see Vian (1951). For a new interpretation of the Sounion frieze see Felten and Hoffelner (1987).

the subject of the east metopes and of a painting inside the shield of Athena Parthenos, but perhaps as important was its appearance on the peplos carried in the Panathenaic procession which was itself the subject of the frieze around the cella of the Parthenon.[7] One version of the origin of the Panathenaia has it founded by Erichthonios to commemorate Athena's part in the war against the giants, which would help to explain why the battle was chosen as the subject to be woven into the peplos.[8]

Depictions of the Gigantomachy first appear on a small group of large vases from before the middle of the sixth century. Several of these were found on the Acropolis in Athens, where some were dedications. The early scenes show the assembled gods together fighting the giants, and Dionysos is a regular participant in these group scenes.[9] Most depictions of the battle show only a part of it, and of the well over 200 Attic black-figure depictions of some part of the Gigantomachy, nearly 90 per cent include Athena. On a large majority of those, mostly undistinguished works from the last quarter of the century or later, she fights alone. Aside from these, duels between a god and a giant or giants are relatively rare in black-figure.[10]

There is a renewed interest in group scenes with red-figure painters at the end of the sixth century and beginning of the fifth, but duels are more common, and then Dionysos is by far the most popular fighter. Of more than fifty surviving depictions of duels from the first half of the fifth century, he is the subject of more than one third, while Poseidon and Athena each accounts for less than one quarter.

Thus, while large numbers of conventional depictions of Athena and a giant were mass-produced by black-figure painters on into the fifth century, red-figure painters also took up the subject of the Gigantomachy and, while maintaining most of the conventional forms, they added new elements of imagery that changed the focus of some in subtle ways. For red-figure painters Dionysos, not Athena or Poseidon, became the most popular single figure.

The scenes on both sides of a late archaic stamnos in London by the Tyszkiewicz Painter[11] provide a good starting point for a discussion of Dionysos in red-figure depictions of the Gigantomachy (Pl. 2A & B). Though not the earliest to show the new elements of imagery, the scenes incorporate them and show clearly the connection between the imagery on vases and on two metopes from the Parthenon.

---

[7] For a summary of recent interpretations of the frieze see Jenkins (1994: 25–30).

[8] For a bibliography on the alleged origins of the festival see Neils (1992: 194 n. 1). See also Mansfield (1985: 51–4).

[9] For Dionysos in early Gigantomachies, see T. Carpenter (1986: ch. 4).

[10] See Vian (1951: 36–71). After Athena, Poseidon is most common in duels, with more than twenty, while Dionysos duelling appears on fewer than ten.

[11] London E 443, *ARV* 292.29, *CV* 3 pl. 21. 3.

On one side, Dionysos, facing right, fights two giants who are dressed as hoplites. He wears a short chiton, boots, and a leopard skin tied by the paws at his throat. With his right hand he holds a spear, with his outstretched left a kantharos and ivy sprigs. A small leopard attacks one of the giants who falls before the god's assault. On the other side Apollo, facing left, fights two giants who are naked except for leopard skins tied by the paws at their throats. The god wears a himation over a long chiton, swings a single-edged sword back over his head with his right hand, ready to slash, and holds its scabbard with his left. One of the giants wears a helmet and prepares to throw a rock as he falls back, the other holds a boulder above his uncovered head.

From the first depictions of the Gigantomachy in the mid-sixth century, Dionysos is usually aided by snakes and felines. Red-figure painters, however, tend to choose one or the other,[12] though sometimes they exclude both. The god's pose on the London stamnos—left arm extended, right arm behind him holding a spear or thyrsos ready for a thrust—is the pose used in most red-figure depictions of him in the Gigantomachy—there are more than thirty[13]—and is, as already noted, the pose and orientation used on the Parthenon metope. The pose, however, is not uniquely his; it is also used for other deities in contemporary Gigantomachies. For example, Athena's aegis often hangs over her outstretched left arm, and Poseidon often carries the island of Nisyros on his. A scene by the Niobid Painter on a krater in Ferrara [14] is particularly instructive because Apollo, Athena, and Poseidon are shown in precisely this pose—Athena with her aegis and Apollo and Poseidon with cloaks. It is essentially the aggressive pose of a hoplite, who would wear a shield on his left arm instead of a skin or an aegis, and it is only the lack of the shield or other armour that makes it distinctive.

From the outset the short chiton is Dionysos' normal dress in the Gigantomachy on Attic vases, and it is a garment he seldom wears in scenes not in some way connected with that subject. Likewise, the leopard skin is a common attribute for him in this scene, though it also appears in a broader Dionysian context.

The boots Dionysos wears on the London stamnos are of particular interest and deserve some comment here. Soft and close-fitting, they reach up above the middle of his calf. Flaps hang down from the tops of the boots, and spots on those flaps make clear that they are made of leopard fur. The

---

[12] For red-figure exceptions, see Berlin F 2321, *ARV* 333.3, *LIMC* IV pl. 148, Gigantes 369 (leopard and snake); Ancona, *ARV* 595.66, *LIMC* IV pl. 149, Gigantes 377 (lion and snake); Athens, Acr. 760, *ARV* 552.20, Boardman (1975: fig. 337. 2 (lion, leopard, and snake)).

[13] For a list see Brommer (1980: 19–20); T. Carpenter (1986: 55 n. 1) for additions and corrections.

[14] Ferrara 2891, *ARV* 602.24, *LIMC* IV pl. 141, Gigantes 311.

irregularly shaped flaps at the top are the distinguishing characteristics of these boots and are clearly made of animal skins, which are either part of the lining or are kinds of socks (*piloi*) worn inside the boots.[15] In any case, the boots are obviously more appropriate for northern winters than for Athenian summers. In fact, these boots are probably called *embades* and are of Thracian origin—or, at least, Attic vase painters thought they were Thracian.

Boots of this type first appear on Attic vases by the last quarter of the sixth century, worn by Thracian horsemen who also wear an animal-skin cap (usually called an *alopekis*) and a distinctive patterned cloak (*zeira*).[16] From the late sixth century on through most of the fifth these boots, along with other elements of Thracian dress, seem to have been adopted, on occasion, by Athenian horsemen, as attested by vase paintings and, most notably, by the frieze from the Parthenon where at least a dozen horsemen wear the distinctive boots.[17]

Dionysos first wears the boots in an early red-figure scene by Oltos, the first red-figure depiction of the god in the Gigantomachy (Pl. 1B).[18] This is also the first inclusion on an Attic vase of the leopard skin draped over his outstretched left arm, though it does appear somewhat earlier on the north frieze of the Siphnian Treasury at Delphi.[19]

The god does not wear these boots on black-figure vases, and during the first half of the fifth century, he wears them only in a small group of narrative scenes including the Gigantomachy, the Return of Hephaistos and depictions of his madness (*mainomenos*). Soon after they first appear on the god, satyrs are sometimes also shown wearing them, often in the Return of Hephaistos and mostly from the first quarter of the century. The only other

[15] Pickard-Cambridge (1988: 205 n. 3 and 206–7) following Webster (1972, 37), sees the primary distinction between boots as laced vs. loose. Some of the Thracian boots are clearly laced, others are bound on with straps; none is loose. Morrow (1985: 64–6) notes that laces are not indicated on the boots of the Parthenon horsemen and suggests that they could have been added in paint. As evidence, she points to a depiction of Dionysos (London E 439, *ARV* 298, *LIMC* III pl. 312 Dionysos 151), but she could just as well have pointed to our contemporary depiction of Dionysos wearing boots without laces (London E 443, *ARV* 292.29, see above, n. 11) to prove the opposite. Surely the boots the god wears on these two vases are of the same type, and the animal skin flaps, not the laces, are the distinguishing elements.

[16] e.g. Brescia, *ABV* 292.1, Arias, Hirmer, and Shefton (1962: pl. 66); Munich 2620, *ARV* 16.17, Boardman (1975: fig. 26. 1); Harvard 1959.219, *CV* Robinson 2 pl. 10. The animal skin of the cap is often spotted or striped and is therefore unlikely to be fox.

[17] Miller (1991: 65); Lissarrague (1990d: 210–31); Raeck (1981); Zimmermann (1980); Cahn (1973: 13–15); Bovon (1963: 579–602).

[18] London E 8, *ARV* 63.88, *LIMC* IV pl. 148, Gigantes 365. In a nearly identical scene by Oltos (Rome, Villa Giulia 50388, *ARV* 65.114, *LIMC* III pl. 370, Dionysos 615) the boots do not appear.

[19] Dionysos in a similar pose on a black-figure lekythos in Cambridge (G 123, *ABL* 234.41) by the Diosphos Painter, is later.

god to wear them during the first half of the century is Hephaistos, occasionally in the Return where Dionysos is also present. Apollo, Artemis, and
Hermes are often shown wearing boots, but theirs are of distinctly different
types.[20] On two vases from before the middle of the fifth century Orpheus
wears these boots as he is attacked by Thracian women, and on a vase not
much later than these, Lykourgos, king of the Thracian Edonians, wears
them as he kills his son.[21] The Thracian musician Thamyras can also wear
them, and on two vases from the second half of the century the Thracian
goddess Bendis is shown wearing them.[22] From a vase painter's perspective,
their Thracian pedigree seems clear.

When Dionysos wears boots, they are almost always of the Thracian type
with flaps at the top.[23] These are horsemen's boots and have nothing to do
with the loose, cuffed boots that belong to the symposion and the woman's
bath, which must be more like bedroom slippers than a sturdy walking or
riding type.[24] Though the Thracian boots become a relatively common
attribute for Dionysos during the second half of the fifth century (and in the
fourth century on South Italian vases), they are first associated with him in
depictions of the Gigantomachy. Their principal purpose seems to be to signal his Thracian connections, and as such, they are the god's first distinctly
Thracian attribute.

To return to the London stamnos, Apollo's pose and sword on the
reverse are also part of the new red-figure imagery for the Gigantomachy
(Pl. 2B). The pose is appropriate for the type of sword he wields, probably
known as a *machaira*, which was designed for slashing rather than for stab-
bing.[25] Introduced on vases by early red-figure painters—Oltos, Epiktetos,

---

[20] There are a few exceptions, e.g. Apollo wears the Thracian boots in a Gigantomachy in Basle (Lu
51, *ARV* 609.7*bis*, *LIMC* IV pl. 141, Gigantes 312), probably a careless mistake (see below note 86 for
further discussion of this problem), and Atalanta (or Artemis?) wears them on Giessen 46, *ARV* 768.35,
LIMC II pl. 700, Atalante 96.

[21] Orpheus in boots: Ferrara 2795, *ARV* 541.7, Alfieri (1979: 27 fig. 66); Boston 90. 156, *ARV*
605.62, Caskey and Beazley (1954: pl. 57). Lykourgos: Cracow 1225, *ARV* 1121.17, Trendall and
Webster (1971: 49–50, III,1,13).

[22] Verona 52, *ARV* 1023.147, *LIMC* III pl. 73, Bendis 1; Tübingen S/10 1347, *CV* 5 pl. 21. On the
latter, Artemis appears on the reverse wearing Thracian boots. This is an obvious attempt to equate the
two. See also a gold medallion from Eretria with a similar Artemis *AK* 17(1974) pl. 16. 1–2. Robertson
(1967: 823) has suggested Bendis as a possible identification for the seated woman wearing similar boots
in the tondo of Ferrara 2462 (T 563, *ARV* 1286, Alfieri (1979: 29 fig. 216)). Martin Robertson kindly
called my attention to this piece.

[23] For a rare exception see London E 265, *ARV* 1594.49, *CV* 3 pl. 8.1.

[24] e.g. London E 201, *ARV* 189.77, *CV* 6 pl. 88. 1; London E 68, *ARV* 371.24, Boardman (1975:
fig. 253. 3); Harvard 1960. 346, *ARV* 563.8, Boardman (1975: fig. 321). For a discussion of these boots
see below, Ch. 7.

[25] For the weapon see Anderson (1991: 26, 32); Sanz (1990—I owe this reference to Brian Shefton);
Snodgrass (1967: 97).

Euphronios, and Euthymides[26]—the pose is best known for its use by Kritios and Nesiotes for Harmodios in their bronze Tyrannicide group set up in the Athenian Agora in 477 as a replacement for Antenor's group taken off by the Persians in 480.[27] What is noteworthy about the pose and weapon is that they replace an earlier convention for Apollo in the Gigantomachy in both sculpture and vase painting where he was accompanied by his sister Artemis, both of them drawing bows. In extant literary versions of the Gigantomachy as well, he uses a bow (Apollodorus 1. 6. 2; Pindar, *Pythian* 8. 12 ff.). In fact, whenever Apollo has a weapon on black- or red-figure vases—except when he fights a giant—it is almost invariably a bow.[28] In seven of nine depictions of Apollo in this 'new' Gigantomachy from before the middle of the fifth century he raises his sword in the Harmodios pose, the earliest example being on a fragment of a cup by Euthymides found on the Acropolis in Athens.[29]

To return to the Gigantomachy metopes on the east side of the Parthenon, the figures in metope 9 provide a close parallel for the 'new' red-figure depictions of Apollo and a giant (Pl. 3A).[30] The long-haired figure to the right facing left should be Apollo in the 'Harmodios' pose— sword raised in his right hand, left hand by his side holding a scabbard or bow. The giant wearing a cat skin and falling back provides a parallel for the giant fighting Apollo on both the London stamnos and a stamnos by the Kleophrades Painter in the Louvre (Pl. 3B).[31]

The figures of Dionysos and Apollo on the London stamnos show the conventional forms for representing these gods in the Gigantomachy (both in pose and attributes) on early red-figure vases, and these are the same conventions used to depict those two gods in the Gigantomachy on the Parthenon metopes half a century later. The fact that the poses for Apollo and Dionysos in the metopes are 'old fashioned' would suggest that they were based on images that had some type of authority, which would

[26] e.g. Arezzo 1465, *ARV* 15.6, Euphronios (1990: 113–22); London E 17, *ARV* 62.80; Rome, Forum Antiquarium, *ARV* 72.20, *NSc* 1900, 177 fig. 26; Athens, Acr. 211, *ARV* 29.20, Graef and Langlotz (1933: pl. 10). For a survey of some of the uses of the pose in Greek art see Suter (1975).

[27] For a discussion of possible connections between the use of the motif for Harmodios and Apollo, see T. Carpenter (forthcoming).

[28] In his fight with the giant Tityos he uses a bow on London E 278, *ARV* 226.2, *CV* 3 pl. 15. 1, a sword on Louvre G 164, *ARV* 504.1, *CV* 1 pl. 10. 2–3; Munich 2689, *ARV* 879.2, *LIMC* II, pl. 275, Apollon 1071.

[29] Harmodios pose: Athens Acr. 211, *ARV* 29.20, *LIMC* IV pl. 138, Gigantes 299; Louvre C 10748, *ARV* 187.55, *LIMC* IV pl. 145, Gigantes 324; London E 443, see above, n. 11; Ferrara 3095, *ARV* 490.125, *LIMC* IV, pl. 139, Gigantes 308; Paris, Cab.Méd. 573, *ARV* 417.1, Vian (1951: pl. 36. 335); London E 469, *ARV* 589.1, Prange (1989: pl. 52); Once Populonia, *NSc* 1908, 222, no. 29a; Aristogeiton pose: Ferrara 2891, see above, n. 14, Gigantes 311; Basle Lu 51, see above, n. 20.

[30] See Berger (1986: 57, 65, pls. 37, 58–60); Praschniker (1928: 168, 210, fig. 126).

[31] Louvre C 10748, see above, n. 29.

obviously exclude scenes on vases. The possibility that the Panathenaic peplos provided this model is worth considering.[32]

A main purpose of the Panathenaic procession, which is the subject of
the Parthenon frieze, was to bring a new peplos to the cult statue of Athena
on the Acropolis. Though most of the surviving evidence for it is from the
fifth century or later, the celebration of this festival in some form probably
dates back at least to the seventh century.[33] A new peplos was woven every
year. Various literary sources tell that at least from the fifth century a depiction of the Gigantomachy was woven into the peplos;[34] Euripides in his
Hecuba (466–74) tells that the robe was saffron and that the scenes were
woven 'with threads of every colour'.

Recently J. Mansfield has argued that the 'robe (peplos) of Athena and
the Panathenaic peplos are not the same thing'. Rather, he suggests, a
peplos was made every year for the statue of Athena, but the 'Panathenaic
peplos was a large tapestry, the work of professional weavers, decorated
with woven representations of the battle between the gods and Giants,
which was dedicated to Athena every four years at the Great Panathenaia,
at which time it was displayed in the procession as the sail of a wheeled
ship.' He proposes that both the ship and the peplos-sail commemorated
the Athenian role in the defeat of the Persians and that the first of these large
peploi was probably dedicated in 474/3 or 470/69.[35]

From an iconographic standpoint this is a particularly attractive proposal,
since the images on the peplos-sail, which was later displayed as a wall hanging in a temple on the Acropolis,[36] would have been easier to see and more
accessible than those on a life-sized peplos draped on a small cult statue. In
any case, the images of the Gigantomachy on the peplos were 'sacred representations'[37] and would have had the type of authority that might influence other major forms. Certainly there was a canon for the depiction of
the Gigantomachy on the peplos, but just as certainly, that canon must have
been modified on occasion as styles changed. That some changes in the

---

[32] That figure decoration on fabrics could be a vehicle for the transmission of narrative images from
as early as the 7th cent. is made clear by a daedalic 'tonrelief' in Naples, see Hampe (1936: 72, pl. 35).
There the images appear in panels. On the François Vase (Florence 4209, *ABV* 76.1) the images are in
a frieze as well. See *Bolletino d'arte* Serie Speciale 1, 99 fig. 16; 162, fig. 129. On a black-figure hydria in
Copenhagen (13536, *ABV* 714, *CV* 8, pls. 319, 321) from the second quarter of the 6th cent. women
wear figure-decorated peploi, one in panels and the other in friezes. Aristophanes, *Wasps* 1215 is an early
reference to woven fabrics as wall hangings (see MacDowell (1971: 288)). See also Barber (1991: esp.
ch. 16) and Vickers (forthcoming).

[33] Shapiro (1989: 18–21); for bibliography see Neils (1992: 194 n. 1).

[34] e.g. Euripides, *Iphigenia at Tauris* 222–4; Aristophanes, *Knights* 566, *Birds* 823–31; Plato, *Euthyphro*.
6b–c, *Republic* 378a–c.   [35] Mansfield (1985: 4, 51).

[36] Ibid. 55.   [37] Implied in Plato, *Euthyphro* 6b.

iconography of the Gigantomachy in sculpture and on vases first occurred in the imagery on the Panathenaic peplos seems possible.[38]

Two types of giants are depicted on the London stamnos; Dionysos fights civilized giants dressed and armed as hoplites while Apollo fights barbaric giants dressed in leopard skins and armed with rocks and boulders. Giants can use stones as weapons—surely appropriate for offspring of Gaia—from the first appearance of the Gigantomachy on black-figure vases before the middle of the sixth century, though early occurrences are relatively rare.[39] Giants on black-figure vases usually wear hoplite armour and fight with spears or swords. So, Hesiod (*Theogony* 185–6) tells of their gleaming armour and long spears. The earliest giant to wear an animal skin is on a fragment of the same red-figure cup where Apollo first wields a sword.[40] The earliest rock-throwing giant who wears only a leopard skin tied at the throat is on a fragmentary cup in London by Onesimos from not long after the first appearances of the sword-wielding Apollo and Dionysos in Thracian boots.[41] On one side Hephaistos and Ares fight two giants who wear only skins tied by the paws at their throats, while on the other side a fallen giant wearing a helmet and holding a shield draws a sword. The contrast between 'civilized' and 'barbarian' giants is made here as it is on the later stamnos and as it seems to be made on the Parthenon metopes.[42] At the end of the fifth century this distinction is still maintained in depictions of the Gigantomachy that have been said to reflect the painting on the inside of the shield of Athena Parthenos.[43]

To summarize, it seems likely that a new public depiction of the Gigantomachy was created in Athens around the end of the sixth century, which is reflected in early red-figure vase paintings and later in some of the Parthenon metopes. The new poses for Apollo and Dionysos, Apollo's sword, Dionysos' boots, and naked, rock-throwing giants should all be parts of the new imagery. While it is very tempting to try to attach these innovations to an historical event like Marathon, the relatively soft dating for the

---

[38] The changes in the depictions of both Dionysos and Apollo in the Gigantomachy seem to have occurred before the Persian sack of Athens in 480. If Mansfield is right in seeing the peplos-sail as a commemoration of the Athenian role in the defeat of the Persians, the Gigantomachy would probably have had to be woven into the smaller peplos as well if the peplos served as a model of any kind. Barber (1992: 112–17) supports the view that the Gigantomachy was the subject of both peploi.

[39] e.g. Athens, Acr. 2211, Graef and Langlotz (1925: pl. 94) and Acr. 607, *ABV* 107.1, Graef and Langlotz (1925: pl. 34).

[40] Athens, Acr. 211, see above, n. 29.   [41] London E 47, *ARV* 319.3, *CV* 9 pls. 7–8.

[42] Sparkes (1985: 27). Of ten giants on the Parthenon metopes, only two certainly wear skins (1, 9), those fighting Hermes and Apollo. The giant fighting Hermes holds a rock as a weapon, as may the giants on 12 and 13. At least five of the giants held shields, those fighting Dionysos, Ares, Athena, Poseidon, and Zeus (2, 3, 4, 6, 8).

[43] Athens, 1333, *ARV* 1337.8, Simon and Hirmer (1981: pl. 233). See below, n. 90.

vases makes this highly speculative.[44] All that can be said with any confidence about the dating of the vases in relation to Marathon is that the earliest surviving occurrences of the new Gigantomachy need not have been produced before 490.

That early red-figure depictions of the Gigantomachy reflect new civic imagery seems fairly clear, yet there is reason to think that the intent of the version on vases was often quite different from the intent behind the civic models. So, for example, though the figures of Apollo and Dionysos on the London stamnos (Pl. 2A & B)[45] certainly reflect the newly orthodox imagery, the details in the paintings and the juxtaposition of the figures are sure to be very different from the model. The painter has gone to some pains to link the two scenes on the vase through imagery.[46] The distinctive spotted leopard skin worn by the giants fighting Apollo on one side are identical to the one worn by Dionysos on the other, whose boots are lined with the same fur and who is aided in his fight by a similarly spotted leopard. Also, the *machaira* wielded by a giant fighting Dionysos is identical to Apollo's sword. Apollo fights distinctly Dionysian giants, while the reverse is true for Dionysos. The gods stand back to back in poses reminiscent of Harmodios and Aristogeiton. On the Parthenon there are six metopes between Apollo and Dionysos, and it is unlikely they could have been linked there by such specific imagery.

The relative infrequency of depictions of Athena in red-figure Gigantomachies also points to a different intention. Her role in the battle was almost certainly the focus of civic representations of it, so her poor showing on early red-figure Gigantomachies relative to Dionysos is odd, especially since she is virtually the only deity to appear in contemporary black-figure depictions of the subject.[47] The shapes on which most of the red-figure Gigantomachies appear are, of course, associated with the symposion, an additional link with Dionysos, and it is worth wondering whether this sympotic connection may have affected the nature and intent of some of the imagery. Did a sophisticated audience of symposiasts tend to look on the battle with an irreverent eye?

Depictions of the Gigantomachy on the Panathenaic peplos and on the east metopes of the Parthenon show unambiguously that the subject had a

[44] For an example of the problems of arriving at precise dates for an early painter, see Williams (1990: 33–7); Robertson (1992: 22), on the relationship between Oltos and Euphronios.

[45] London E 443, see above, n. 11.

[46] On some other occasions the Tyszkiewicz Painter seems to link scenes on either side of a vase through details of imagery. See e.g. Malibu, Getty 76.AE.206, *ARV* 290.6*bis* where Zeus with a thyrsos-like sceptre (enlarged finial) on one side pursues a woman, while on the other side a satyr with a thyrsos purses a woman whose pose is the same as the one directly in front of Zeus.

[47] See above, p. 17 and n. 10.

heroic dimension in public art of fifth-century Athens.[48] Menelaos' mention of it in Bakchylides' *First Dithyramb* (62-3) shows that defeat of the giants could be piously used in poetry as a warning against *hubris*; Plato's mention of its allegorical use (*Republic* 2. 378c–d) confirms its didactic potential. At the same time, Hegemon could produce a parody of the Gigantomachy in the theatre at Athens in 413:

> The man was famous chiefly for his parodies and made himself the talk of the town by his mischievous and theatrical recitation of epic lines . . . With his *Gigantomachy* he beguiled the Athenians to such an extraordinary degree that they laughed most heartily on that evil day when reports came to them in the theatre of the disaster in Sicily. (Athenaeus 9. 407a trans. C. B. Gulick (Loeb))

Perhaps we should understand some of the scenes on early vases more in the spirit of Hegemon than of Bakchylides.

Elements of imagery in scenes on related cups by Onesimos and the Brygos Painter may be equivalent to Hegemon's 'mischievous and theatrical recitations of epic lines'. Pictures on a fragment of a cup from Athens recently attributed to Onesimos hint at this (Pl. 4A & B).[49] The battle was in a frieze around the tondo, where Selene stood in her chariot. In the surviving fragment of the frieze Zeus mounts an elaborately decorated chariot while Herakles, wearing a lion skin and Scythian trousers, preceded by Athena, rushes along beside the horses in front of which a giant has fallen. On the outside of the fragment two satyrs pull a biga, the box of which is decorated with the silhouette of a phallos-bird, while a satyr with a trumpet (*salpinx*) and a scabbard follows. One of the satyrs pulling the biga wears a cat skin and Thracian boots. A satyr biga appears on a few late black-figure vases,[50] but it seems to have been a red-figure invention, and it appears almost exclusively on vases from before the middle of the fifth century.[51]

The conclusion that the satyr biga on the outside of the cup is a parody of Zeus' chariot on the inside seems almost inescapable. The one stands in relation to the other much as the satyrs in Euripides' *Cyclops* do to

[48] See Castriota (1992: 138–43) for speculation on the underlying civic meaning of the metopes on the Parthenon.

[49] Athens, from Marathon St., Boulter (1985: pl. 29). Attributed by Williams (1976: 12). For a comment on the connection between imagery on late archaic Gigantomachy cups, see Williams in *CV* London 9, p. 20 on 5.

[50] e.g. Munich 1389, *CV* 1, pls. 24. 3, 27. 1 (compare Boston 00. 342, *ARV* 598.4, Caskey and Beazley (1954: pls. 55–6)); Athens, Acr. 885, Graef and Langlotz (1933: pl. 54). See Caskey and Beazley (1954: II 71–2) and Brommer (1937: 55, Anm. 21).

[51] An exception is Boston 175. 1970, Buitron-Oliver (1972: 132–3. 73). One unpublished vase (Athens, Vlastos, *ARV* 291.24) is by the Tyszkiewicz Painter, the painter of the London stamnos. Cf. Cambridge 37. 17, *ARV* 133.4 Lissarrague (1987) and (1990d: 75, fig. 57A–B).

Odysseus' companions in Book 9 of the *Odyssey*, though in saying that I am not suggesting that a satyr play was the basis of the vase scene. Clearly we have here a distinctly humorous scene juxtaposed with a traditional depiction of the Gigantomachy, and while earlier depictions of the subject on vases, from its first appearance, were probably intended at least in part as entertainment, what might be called wit is difficult to find.

In addition to the satyr biga on the outside of the cup, Herakles' Scythian dress in the Gigantomachy on the inside may have been included as an ironic comment on the hero if, in fact, it refers to the official police force of public slaves known as Scythians in Athens.[52] On a slightly later cup by the Brygos Painter in Berlin,[53] the group of Zeus, Herakles in Scythian trousers, and Athena is repeated, and as on the fragment by Onesimos, Selene drives her chariot in the tondo. On the other side of the better preserved cup, Hephaistos, Poseidon, and Hermes fight giants. Aside from Herakles' costume, the iconography is quite traditional, though it is worth wondering if Zeus' oversize thunderbolt has mock-heroic overtones. The Brygos Painter also uses a similarly dressed Herakles on another cup where the subject is distinctly comic, involving satyrs in pursuit of Hera.[54] All three of these depictions of the Scythian Herakles are on cups, presumably intended for symposion use, and it seems possible that the ironic use of notably unheroic dress for Herakles might reflect the sophisticated tastes of the symposiast for whom they were made.

To speculate further, one might recall here John Boardman's argument that Herakles is the hero associated with the Peisistratids.[55] After the fall of the tyrants there is a marked decrease in the number of vases on which Herakles appears. In fact, he rarely appears in red-figure Gigantomachies— less than 10 per cent—even though the myth requires his presence. Without his help the giants could not have been defeated. To include the Peisistratid hero as a kind of flunky in the Onesimos and Brygos Painter versions of the fight humorously solves the problem of what to do with him.

These cups suggest that already in the first quarter of the fifth century red-figure vase painters could not only create satyr parodies of traditional stories, but could even include mocking elements within the traditional scenes themselves, which seems to suggest a private rather than a public

---

[52] Simon (1982: 126 n. 20). Miller (1991: 61) has recently questioned whether such a force ever existed. In any case, as Ferrari-Pinney (1983: 131) observes, Scythians on Attic vases are minor characters; 'they are not heroes, but companions of heroes'.

[53] Berlin F 2293, *ARV* 370.10, *CV* 2 pls. 67–8. See Sparkes (1985) on the relation between the cups.

[54] London E 65, *ARV* 370.13, Kurtz and Sparkes (1982: pl. 30).

[55] Boardman (1972).

type of humour, enjoyed perhaps by certain symposiasts on certain occasions.[56]

To return to the satyr biga, it is generally assumed that the warrior satyrs on early red-figure vases were inspired by satyr plays performed in Athens.[57] Supporting this hypothesis is the figure on the inside of a lost cup from the first quarter of the fifth century of which a drawing survives.[58] A satyr with a spear in his right hand and a leopard skin over his outstretched left arm moves to the right in precisely the pose used for Dionysos in most depictions of him in the Gigantomachy. The satyr wears satyr-shorts with an artificial phallos and tail attached, a costume associated with actors in satyr plays. He is a mock Dionysos going to war, presumably against the giants. On fragments of a contemporary amphora in Malibu at least one satyr wears similar satyr-shorts and carries a pelta with a phallos-bird in the round as a device and a leopard skin as an apron (Pl. 5B).[59] Satyrs with peltai, a characteristically Thracian shield, first appear on Attic vases during the last decades of the sixth century and seldom appear after about the middle of the fifth.[60] On a small group of black-figure lekythoi from early in the fifth century a satyr with a pelta dances a pyrrhic,[61] while on other vases by the same painter warriors with hoplite shields dance the same dance, suggesting that the painter found the foreign pelta a more appropriate shield for satyrs.

One obvious problem with the conclusion that warrior satyrs were inspired by an early satyr play about the Gigantomachy is the absence of any evidence (aside from vases) pointing to such a play. That some imagery on late sixth and early fifth century vases was influenced by productions of satyr plays in Athens seems clear.[62] However, it is also possible some vase painters invented their own satyr parodies which have nothing to do with the

[56] See also St Petersburg 679, *ARV* 382.188, Boardman (1975: fig. 258), a hound's head rhyton by the Brygos Painter, where pygmies fight cranes on the neck. One of the pygmies wears Thracian boots and a leopard skin over his outstretched left arm. Is he a mock Dionysos, a comic allusion to the Gigantomachy? See Dasen (1993: 186) who comments on the rarity of such clothing in the battle of the pygmies and cranes.

[57] Brommer (1959: 17; 1983: 115–19); Buschor (1943: 90–1).

[58] Once Aldibrandi, *ARV* 121.23, Hartwig (1893: 637).

[59] Malibu, Getty 86.AE.1190.6 + 575. Brommer (1983: 116–17, figs. 2A–C; B is upside down). For an additional fragment (with most of the phallos-bird) joining A, see Boardman (1992: 238, fig. 11).

[60] Snodgrass (1967: 78–9); Best (1969: 3). Sometimes the pelta carried by a satyr has an apron hanging from it (e.g. Athens 18567, *ABV* 522, no. 20, *BCH* 92 (1968) 584 fig. 34) similar to the apron that hangs, on occasion from hoplite shields carried by warriors (e.g. Palermo G 1283, *ARV* 599.2, Arias, Hirmer, and Shefton (1962: pl. 179)). Given its uselessness, this apron on a pelta must be a comic device. See Lissarrague (1990d: 151–89).

[61] Athens 18567, see previous note; London B 626, *ABV* 531.4, *BCH* 92 (1968) 584, fig. 35; Florence 4 B 28 and Louvre C 11255, *ARV* 133.10. See Poursat (1968: 583–6), also Karouzou (1972: 58–71).

[62] For the most convincing discussion of the connection between vase paintings and satyr plays see Simon (1982: 123–48).

theatre.⁶³ By 500, vase painters had been painting satyrs on vases for nearly a century, and during that time satyrs are hardly mentioned in literature and rarely appear in other arts.⁶⁴ At the same time, there is good reason to think that satyr imagery was included in rural festivals, perhaps even men dressed as satyrs.⁶⁵ It is no coincidence that the sudden appearance of satyrs with objects originally foreign to them, such as kitharai, peltai, and sports equipment, is contemporary with the appearance of sophisticated and innovative painters in the new red-figure technique. These are precisely the painters in whose works one can first detect wit, parody, and a subtle sense of mockery. Whether the satyr biga is the invention of a poet or a vase painter is a moot point, though the evidence (perhaps by chance) comes down on the side of the vase painter. That Onesimos effectively used the biga for comic effect by juxtaposing the two scenes, however, is clear.

Since satyrs are regular companions of Dionysos on both black- and red-figure vases, it is notable that they are never shown with him in either black-figure or early red-figure depictions of the Gigantomachy. Their exclusion from the subject seems to put it in a different category from almost all other Dionysian scenes, and their eventual inclusion, first on a stamnos in Orvieto (Pl. 6A&B),⁶⁶ nearly a century after the god's first appearance in the battle, suggests that a change in the perception of the subject has taken place. On one side of the Orvieto stamnos, as on Onesimos' cup, satyrs pull a biga. Here the satyr riding in the biga is armed as a hoplite, and another similar hoplite-satyr follows blowing a trumpet. On the other side of the vase Dionysos, with the help of a small leopard, attacks a falling giant who is also armed as a hoplite. Two hoplite-satyrs follow the god, one with a leopard skin tied at his throat and a stone in his raised right hand, the other with a shield and spear. Without his tail the first satyr would be indistinguishable from a giant and is, in fact, remarkably similar to the giant fighting Apollo on the London stamnos. Clearly part of the fun of the scene is the confusion between the identities of the satyrs and the giants.

To summarize, there seem to be two developments in the early red-figure iconography of the Gigantomachy. On the one hand, specific new elements of imagery are introduced into straightforward depictions of the battle. So, for example, Dionysos dons Thracian boots, Apollo exchanges his bow for a sword, and barbaric giants who wear animal skins and throw rocks join the traditional hoplite-giants. On the other hand, scenes with satyrs which seem to be parodies of the straightforward depictions of the Gigantomachy also appear, and the satyrs are sometimes given specifically

---

⁶³ See Lissarrague (1990a).   ⁶⁴ See T. Carpenter (1986: 77–80).
⁶⁵ e.g. Florence 3897, T. Carpenter (1986: pl. 22). Also, see Seaford (1984: 5–16).
⁶⁶ Orvieto 1044, *ARV* 657.1, Vian (1951: pl. 40. 376).

Thracian attributes in their boots and peltai, which, of course, identify them with Dionysos. Onesimos emphasizes the connection between the two developments by putting a relatively straightforward scene on the inside of a cup and the parody on the outside of the same vessel. During the second quarter of the century the distinction seems to break down, and Dionysos, the most common figure in the Gigantomachy, is often part of the parody himself, a kind of mock-hero.

Elements of imagery in early red-figure depictions of Dionysos in the Gigantomachy frequently point to Thrace, and these continue to appear in scenes to the middle of the century. Dionysos' boots and satyrs' peltai have already been mentioned. The shield device of a satyr running behind the biga on the Orvieto stamnos is an ithyphallic donkey, and Ares has a shield with the same device on Onesimos' cup in London. The device is rare on Attic vases, and it is probably not by chance that it is the coin type of Mende on Pallene from about 520 on through at least until 460.[67] As mentioned earlier, Herodotus (7. 123) called Phlegra, where the Gigantomachy was said to have taken place, the old name for Pallene.[68] Thus, in early fifth-century Athens Dionysos in the Gigantomachy is cast as a Thracian with Thracian companions fighting Giants in Thrace. In other words, the emphasis is on the wild, uncivilized side of his nature, and ironically, the giants he fights are cast as noble hoplites.

It is in the Gigantomachy that the mock-heroic Dionysos first appears on red-figure vases, though there were already hints of this role in a black-figure depiction of the Return of Hephaistos. So, in the Return of Hephaistos frieze on the François vase, one of the earliest known representations of Dionysos in Greek art, the god leads Hephaistos back to Olympos to free Hera from the trick throne. The elegant warrior Ares, who tried to bring Hephaistos back to Olympos but failed, sits dejectedly on a stool, the head of his spear resting on the ground. Athena points at Ares with one hand and with the other at the outrageous procession comprising Dionysos, Hephaistos on an ithyphallic donkey, hugely ithyphallic satyrs (labelled *silenoi*), and nymphs. The irony is clear—Dionysos succeeds where Ares failed. Abbreviated versions of this story continue to be popular with vase painters throughout the sixth and fifth century.

There is, however, an important difference between depictions of Dionysos in the Return of Hephaistos and in the Gigantomachy. The Return is, from the start, a humorous subject as shown by vase painters, and Dionysos' role is that of a kind of anti-hero. The Gigantomachy, on the

---

[67] Kraay (1976: 136). It is worth noting that from the third quarter of the 6th cent. at least until 480 a satyr was part of the coin type of a Thracian mint usually associated with the tribe of Satrae, see 148–9.

[68] Also, see above, n. 5.

other hand, is a serious subject as it is shown in architectural sculpture, on black-figure vases, and surely on the peplos. The Dionysos who fights on the Parthenon metope is not different in kind from the Dionysos of the Orvieto stamnos, but the addition of satyrs to the latter radically changes its tone. It becomes a parody and its strength comes from its faithfulness to the traditional scene. For the vase painter, Dionysos can be humorous in ways he can never be for sculptors and monumental painters. He can be the ungodlike god—the mock-hero—the anti-hero—and sometimes it is difficult to tell when he is being which.

At about the same time satyrs join Dionysos in the Gigantomachy, nymphs join him in other depictions of the battle; however, satyrs and nymphs do not appear together in the Gigantomachy until the end of the century.[69] The nature of this innovation is clearly illustrated by several early vases by the Niobid Painter and his colleagues, a workshop important for any study of Dionysos in classical art.

The Altamura, Blenheim, and Niobid Painters are the names Beazley gave to the three important members of a workshop that flourished in Athens for as long as two decades starting during the second quarter of the century. The three painters include Dionysos on nearly forty of their some two hundred surviving vases,[70] and, unusually, depict episodes from the god's life. Beazley called the Altamura Painter 'the elder brother of the Niobid Painter' and noted he had sometimes thought the Blenheim Painter's work 'might be late work by the Altamura Painter himself'.[71] A recent study has placed the earliest works of the Altamura Painter in the 470s and the latest work of the Niobid Painter in the 440s.[72] The iconography as well as the style of drawing of the three painters is related. Though they rarely seem to have invented new Dionysian scenes, they often show them in their most fully developed form and as such provide a useful canon of developed Dionysian scenes from the first half of the fifth century. Eight depictions of the Gigantomachy have survived from the workshop, along with arming scenes that are sometimes said to be related to the Gigantomachy. After the middle of the century the subject is distinctly less popular, and even in the works of the Niobid Painter, there are hints that the subject has lost its sharp focus.

---

[69] One of the earliest examples is on an unpublished late archaic stamnos (from Attica), by the Tyszkiewicz Painter, in the Vlastos collection in Athens (*ARV* 291.24). I have not seen this vase but quote Beazley's description in Caskey and Beazley (1954: 71): 'On A, Dionysos, dressed in a long chiton and a skin, attacks to right, with a spear in his right hand and a vine branch in his left; the giant falls; a small panther bites the giant, and a maenad attacks him with a rock; on B, a satyr drives a satyr-biga to right.'

[70] Based on Beazley's lists in *ARV* 589–608, 1660–1, 1702 and *Para* 393–6.

[71] *ARV* 589, 617.   [72] Prange (1989: 122–3).

The treatment of Dionysos in the Gigantomachy on five vases by the Altamura and Blenheim Painters is of particular interest (Pl. 7A).[73] On all of them the groups of Dionysos and the giant are essentially the same, following a well-established tradition that has its final appearance in the Parthenon metope. The god wears Thracian boots and holds out the branch of a grape vine with his left hand, a thyrsos or a spear in his right. The giants are dressed as hoplites, and each falls in essentially the same way before the god's onslaught. The Altamura Painter has the god aided by the traditional animal or snake, but on the Ancona oinochoe, he also includes a woman to the left with a thyrsos raised to aid the god in his attack.[74] The Blenheim Painter does not include animals or snakes, but he does include female helpers. On the krater in Bologna a single woman to the right swings a thyrsos back over her head about to bring it down on the giant. On the stamnos in Boston a woman to the left balances a great rock on her shoulder while a woman to the right attacks with a thyrsos (Pl. 7B). This vase is of particular interest on account of the care the painter has taken in drawing the women and their accoutrements.

The woman with the rock on her shoulder wears a nebris over her chiton, and on her neatly dressed hair she wears an elaborate stephane decorated with protomes in-the-round of four winged horses or griffins. The other woman wears a headband of snakes over straggling locks. Stephanai similar to the one worn by the woman with the rock appear on other vases on Athena, Hera, a goddess, and Ariadne or Semele.[75] While it is clearly not the attribute of a single individual, it is only used for figures from myth. Its use here is unlikely to be the result of random choice of a decoration. The woman wearing it should be a nymph, one of the constant companions of the god, but her identity might have been more precisely understood at the time the vase was made. The inclusion of the women makes the depiction more elaborate. Dionysos fights giants with the aid of specific women, not satyrs, which seems to imply a specific narrative rather than simply the repetition of a traditional motif, and this narrative may well be part of the 'Thracian cycle' discussed in the next chapter. These are the same nymphs, his nurses, who aid him in his altercation with Lykourgos.

[73] Altamura Painter: London E 469, see above, n. 29; Ancona, see above, n. 12. Blenheim Painter: St Petersburg 765, *ARV* 598.2, Peredolska (1967: pls. 114–15); Bologna 286, *ARV* 598.3, *LIMC* III, pl. 373, Dionysos 639; Boston 00. 342, see above, n. 50. I have argued elsewhere (T. Carpenter (1993: 198–9)) that Salonica 8. 54, *ARV* 591.28, *LIMC* III, pl. 372, Dionysos 629 shows Dionysos with Lykourgos rather than in the Gigantomachy. See below p. 39.

[74] The god is aided by a panther and a maenad on the contemporary stamnos in the Vlastos collection in Athens (*ARV* 291.24). For a description see above, n. 69.

[75] Caskey and Beazley (1954: 71) for a list. Note Beazley's warning 'that these stephanai are worn by different persons, so that one can hardly attribute any special symbolic value to them'.

On two other vases by the Altamura Painter[76] women bring armour to Dionysos. In a carelessly executed scene on an oinochoe in Bologna, the god stands in the centre while a woman to the left holds a kantharos and a metal cuirass,[77] and a woman to the right holds a shield and a sword. A small panther stands beside the god. On the St Petersburg krater, Dionysos already wears the same type of cuirass, and women hold a helmet, a sword and shield, and a thyrsos (Pl. 8A). A woman just to the left of the god, at whom he looks, holds an ivy sprig and a kantharos. A woman to the far right, under the handle, looks on and serves to link the scene with the scene on the other side of the vase. There three women, one with a thyrsos and one with an ivy sprig and vine, stand with two draped men who hold spears.

These arming scenes are puzzling. On the one hand the Gigantomachy is the only narrative scene in sixth- or fifth-century sculpture or vase painting where Dionysos is shown as a warrior. On the other hand, he is almost never shown wearing armour as he fights giants,[78] or for that matter, in any other scenes.

Depictions of anonymous or named warriors arming are common on Attic vases from early in the sixth century on through the fifth, but when the bearers of the arms are all women the scene is usually the arming of Achilles. Examples of Achilles receiving his armour from Thetis and nymphs go back in Attic vase painting to before the middle of the sixth century and, in various forms, carry on into the fifth,[79] but a scene from the Niobid workshop on fragments of a krater in Bologna provides the closest parallel (Pl. 8B).[80] There the mourning Achilles sits on a stool in the centre of the scene while women approach from either side carrying armour. The woman directly in front of Achilles, who wears a stephane, must be Thetis, while the other women are Nereids. In the *Iliad* Thetis alone brings the armour to Achilles, and it has been suggested that the scenes showing Thetis and Nereids may refer to Aeschylus' *Nereids*.[81] Whatever its source, the important point here is that the Altamura Painter uses the imagery associated with Achilles to depict Dionysos in an episode for which we have no

[76] St Petersburg 638, *ARV* 591.17, *LIMC* III pl. 369, Dionysos 610; Bologna 338, *ARV* 595.65, *LIMC* III pl. 369 Dionysos 611. Related to these is Paris, Cab.Méd. 391, *ARV* 286.15, *LIMC* III pl. 369, Dionysos 609 by the Geras Painter, which may be slightly earlier. There Dionysos, in a long chiton, fastens on a linen corslet while a small ithyphallic satyr holds out toward him a helmet and thyrsos.

[77] Snodgrass (1967: 92) notes that this type of cuirass first appears on vases in the early 5th cent.

[78] On a late black-figure amphora (Paris, Cab.Méd. R 230, *LIMC* III pl. 372, Dionysos 625) the painter has put a helmet on the head of a Dionysos dressed in a long chiton. In a carelessly painted Gigantomachy on the shoulder of a later black-figure hydria recently on the London Market (Sotheby 7–8 July 1994, 327) Dionysos wears a metal cuirass and is aided in his fight by a snake and a panther.

[79] See *LIMC* I, 69–72, 122–8.   [80] Bologna 291, *ARV* 608.5, *LIMC* I pl. 10, Achilleus 511.
[81] Trendall and Webster (1971: 54, III,1,18–19).

literary source. The implication is that here again the vase painter is creating a mock-heroic scene. Again, the women with Dionysos should be the
nymphs of Nysa his nurses, associated with his birth and childhood, the
same nymphs who were chased with him into the sea by Lykourgos (*Iliad*
6. 129 f.), where he sought the comfort of Thetis. The fact that Dionysos
does not wear armour in the Gigantomachy, or in any other scene, lends
support to the idea that the arming scenes are parodies—visual jokes that
depend on a knowledge of the Achilles scenes.

Pictures on another vase by the Blenheim Painter, a krater in St
Petersburg,[82] show another aspect of this humour. On one side is a conventional depiction of Dionysos fighting a giant. On the other side a man
wearing a short chiton and an oriental headgear[83] prepares to don a linen
corslet while in front of him a woman pours from an oinochoe into a
phiale. Between them are greaves on a stand.[84] This is a traditional arming
scene, but there are exceptional details. The man's snub nose and bestial
pointed ear belong to satyrs not to warriors; though tail-less, he should
surely be understood as such. The alopekis should make him a Thracian,
and the chiton he wears and corslet he holds are similar to the ones worn
by the giant. The scene with Dionysos and the giant is unexceptional and
fits comfortably into the group of scenes that lead up to the Parthenon
metope. The scene with the satyr is a parody of a conventional arming
scene.

The Niobid Painter's one surviving depiction of the Gigantomachy is
noteworthy mainly because it is atypical. The battle fills the upper frieze of
a double register calyx krater in Ferrara.[85] A barefoot Dionysos is included
wearing an animal skin over a knee-length chiton and holding a vine in his
left hand, a thyrsos in his right. The giant he fights, however, is not in the
standard falling pose used by the Altamura and Blenheim Painters (and
others); rather, that pose has been given to the giant attacked by Athena,
and not only is his pose borrowed, but even the snake is included wrapped
around his leg. The old fashioned beard on the snake suggests that the
painter was relying on an early model for his figures and simply became
confused.[86] The Niobid Painter, who is the first to include torches in a

[82] St Petersburg 765, see above, n. 73.

[83] For a recent discussion of the difficulty identifying different types of oriental headgear, see Miller
(1991: 61–6).

[84] Beazley notes that the lower part of this side is modern, so the greaves may be a later addition.

[85] Ferrara 2891, see above, n. 14. Only fragments remain of the krater Reggio 27210 (*ARV* 602.25,
Prange (1989: pl. 50)) but these include the head and shoulders of a giant and 'a serpent held out by the
deity'—presumably Dionysos.

[86] There is only one parallel for the snake assisting Athena in the Gigantomachy: in a weak scene in
the manner of the Niobid Painter in Basle (Lu 51, see above, n. 20) the same group of Herakles, Athena,

Dionysian scene, gives two torches to a woman assisting the god on this krater. The vitality of the early red-figure scenes is gone, and one has the sense that this is simply a dutiful, if not careful, repetition of a traditional subject.[87] Wit and irony are gone.

The Gigantomachy is a subject on fewer than twenty Attic vases from the second half of the fifth century, and most of those are from the last two decades. In other words, it was no longer a common subject on vases at the time the Parthenon metopes were carved. Giants wearing only leopard skins become more common, stones and rocks are more often their weapons, and finally *c.*400 a giant fighting Dionysos is given serpent-legs.[88] Dionysos drives a biga drawn by panthers or griffins on several vases from the end of the century.[89] Iconographically these late scenes have little to do with the earlier depictions of the Gigantomachy on Attic vases or with the metopes on the Parthenon. However, there is some evidence to suggest that they may be related to the depiction of the Gigantomachy that was on the inside of the shield of Pheidias' chryselephantine statue of Athena Parthenos in the Parthenon.[90] The focus has changed and the subject itself may have taken on new meanings for Athenians. The metopes of the Parthenon made one statement by choosing old-fashioned forms for the battle; the painting on the inside of Athena's shield may have made another. That an Athenian in 430 looking at both would have understood the differences is likely; that we will never fully understand them is, alas, even more likely.

and the giant attacked by a snake has been used again, but the error has been compounded by shrinking Herakles to child-size and giving Athena a sword instead of her canonical spear. The same scene includes an Apollo wearing Thracian boots. A satyr with a spear and leopard skin shield accompanies Dionysos.

[87] The Gigantomachy is the subject of a stamped gold frieze on a mid-5th cent. silver rhyton recently found in Kuban (formerly of the Soviet Union). See *LIMC* IV, Gigantes 34*bis*. Dionysos, Hermes (twice) Hephaistos, Hera, and Zeus are shown in duels with Giants. Some details recall Attic scenes (e.g. a machaira wielded by a giant, barbarian and hoplite giants, Dionysos' lion, and, as Brian Shefton pointed out to me, Hera's temple key), but other elements show that the similarities are only superficial (e.g. nudity of all the gods, Dionysos' orientation, pose, and lack of traditional attributes, Zeus' curious thunderbolts, Hermes' central role).

[88] Berlin 3375, *LIMC* IV pl. 149, Gigantes 389.

[89] Louvre S 1677, *ARV* 1344.1, *LIMC* III pl. 375, Dionysos 660; Berlin 3375, see previous note; Würzburg 4729, *ARV* 1346, *CV* 2 pl. 40.1–6; Naples 2045, *ARV* 1338.

[90] Shefton (1982: 160), Leipen (1971: 46–50), Vian (1952: 149–60), von Salis (1940: 90–169). For an appropriately cautious review of the evidence, see Arafat (1986).

3

Thracian Narratives

ELEMENTS of Thracian dress appear during the first half of the fifth century in a distinct group of narrative scenes about Dionysos including the Gigantomachy, the Return of Hephaistos, the madness of Dionysos and the encounter with Lykourgos.[1] Before the middle of that century those Thracian elements seldom appear in other Dionysian scenes, which suggests that they should be understood as visual links connecting the episodes. Through the imagery, then, some vase painters make a clear distinction between Thracian and 'Greek' narratives about the god.

Attic dramatists seem to have made a similar distinction. Aeschylus wrote a Thracian tetralogy about Dionysos, which included the punishment of Lykourgos, as well as a Theban tetralogy, which included the death of Pentheus. Though the evidence is very fragmentary, other plays about the god also seem to have been set in Thrace or Thebes.[2] At the end of the century Euripides' curious exclusion from his *Bacchae* of any reference to Thrace suggests that, at least by then, the implications of the god's Thracian connection were quite clear to his Athenian audience (and hence inappropriate to Euripides' purposes).[3]

Evidence from literature and vases suggests that there was a well-established group of stories about Dionysos current in fifth-century Athens, but of the many accounts or allusions to individual episodes, few give more than a hint of how one episode relates to another. The first comprehensive account of Dionysos' deeds is in Apollodorus (3. 5. 1–3) from the second century AD, parts of which seem to draw on both Aeschylus' Lykourgos tetralogy and an earlier epic account by the Corinthian Eumelos.[4] There Dionysos is driven mad by Hera, roams about Egypt and Syria, is purified by Rhea at Kybela in Syria, hastens through Thrace, encounters Lykourgos, traverses Thrace and goes to Thebes, encounters Pentheus, goes to Argos,

---

[1] For a definition of these elements of Thracian dress see above pp. 18–20.

[2] Oranje (1984: 124–30). Pausanias (1. 20. 3) tells that there were paintings of the punishments of both Lykourgos and Pentheus in the oldest sanctuary of Dionysos near the theatre in Athens.

[3] See below, Ch. 7.

[4] Eumelos, *Europia* frag. 1 (*EGF*); West (1990: 26–50). For Eumelos see Bowra (1963: 145–53). Pausanias (5.19.10) attributes inscriptions on the Chest of Kypselos to Eumelos; see also (2. 1. 1).

drives Argive women mad, encounters pirates, rescues his mother from Hades and then takes her to heaven.[5]

Of the episodes he lists, Apollodorus locates only the encounter with Lykourgos in Thrace,[6] while Attic vase painters during the first half of the fifth century imply that Thrace was also the locus for the Gigantomachy, the Return of Hephaistos, and the god's mad roaming brought on by Hera. By the end of the century, however, this distinctly Thracian emphasis has faded from depictions of the god.

In Euripides' *Cyclops* (3–20) Silenos mentions as a group the god's madness sent by Hera, his participation in the Gigantomachy, and his capture by pirates. Early on Eumelos seems to have linked the Hera-induced madness with the Lykourgos story, which Homer (*Iliad* 6. 130–40) implies through the mention of nurses (*tithenai*) took place when the god was young. In fragments of Aeschylus' *Edonians* (frag. 61 *TrGF* 3) Lykourgos calls Dionysos effeminate (*gunnis*) which seems to have something to do with his beardlessness and thus his youth. This emphasis on the god's youth also appears in *Homeric Hymn to Dionysos* (VII), where the Dionysos captured by pirates is quite specifically an adolescent. Such scraps of evidence suggest, at the least, that these episodes took place when the god was young, and, in fact, there is reason to think that most Dionysian narratives are about events that happened during the god's infancy and youth.[7]

Presumably these tales about the god were part of a common tradition known in fifth-century Athens by dramatists, poets, and vase painters alike. Why, then, if everyone knew that the stories took place during the god's youth, did vase painters insist on depicting the god in these stories as a bearded adult? This is an important question to which I will return in the course of discussing the Thracian narratives and again in Chapter 6.

Diomedes' account of Lykourgos' outrages against the god in the *Iliad* (6. 130–40) is the earliest surviving narration of a story about Dionysos. Lykourgos chased down the slopes of Nysa the mad (*mainomenos*) god and his nurses who dropped their wands as they ran. A terrified Dionysos dived into the sea where Thetis comforted him. Angered by Lykourgos' audacity, Zeus blinded him. That Homer had Thrace in mind as a setting is suggested by the location of Thetis' cave between Samothrace and Imbros (24. 77–84) to which, presumably, Dionysos went after diving into the sea.[8]

---

[5] On the incomprehensible reference to India in Apollodorus' account, see Rice (1983: 100–1).

[6] Pausanias (3. 4. 3) locates Nysa in Asia.

[7] Even in Euripides' *Bacchae*, Dionysos chooses to appear as a youth when he returns to Thebes from his travels in the East.

[8] See Kirk (1990), on 6. 132–7. For other locations of Nysa, see Hesychius s.v. *Nusa kai Nuseion*. Richardson (1974: 148–9). Cf. Otto (1965: 61–4).

Aeschylus, in his lost Lykourgos tetralogy, specifically placed the event in Thrace, with Lykourgos the king of the Edonians, as did the Corinthian Eumelos in his *Europia*. Apollodorus' account, which seems to depend on both Aeschylus and Eumelos, has Lykourgos the king of the Edonians on the Strymon. He calls the companions of the god *bakchai* rather than nurses, adds satyrs to the entourage, and makes Dionysos rather than Zeus the agent of the punishment, which itself is changed.[9]

As already mentioned, an implication of the Homeric account is that the Dionysos attacked by Lykourgos was young, still surrounded by his nurses on the mountain where he was taken soon after his birth. Though the nature and cause of his madness is not made clear, it is presumably the same madness Euripides (*Cyclops* 3–4) and Apollodorus attribute to Hera.

For one mid-fifth-century Attic vase painter there was no question but that the Lykourgos episode took place in Thrace, and he indicates this with dress. On a hydria in Cracow (Pl. 9A)[10] Lykourgos wears Thracian boots and a *zeira*, a distinctive patterned Thracian cloak, as he attacks with an axe a youth on an altar, while a woman tries to run from him in terror. Dionysos stands to the right holding out a grape vine toward Lykourgos with his right hand. To the far right a nymph dances and a satyr seated on a rock plays pipes. This is certainly the mad Lykourgos mentioned in Apollodorus about to dismember his son, and the satyr and nymph represent the *bakchai* and satyrs mentioned there[11]—the nurses in Homer's version. The distraught woman between Lykourgos and his son must be his wife. The only other known depiction of the subject on Attic vases is on a hydria from the last quarter of the century where the subject is merged with elements of the death of Pentheus and no location is indicated.[12]

Depictions of the madness of Dionysos appear earlier and are from the start linked with Thrace. On a late archaic stamnos in London, the god dances a mad dance with the halves of a rent goat in either hand (Pl. 9B).[13] He has an ivy wreath on his head and a leopard skin tied at his throat over

---

[9] For Sophocles' use of the Lykourgos story in *Antigone* (956–63) see Sourvinou-Inwood (1989), particularly 147–53. Her reading of 'aulos-loving Muses' (*philauloi Mousai*) 965 as referring to Dionysos' companions is attractive. 'This metaphor presents the relationship between Dionysos and the Maenads as comparable to that between Apollo and the Muses' (149).

[10] Cracow 1225, *ARV* 1121.17, Trendall and Webster (1971: 49–50, III,1,13). Beazley (1928: 44) notes that while the vase has been extensively repainted 'in many places the old lines show through the repaint, and although small details have been lost or added, the representation is genuine in every essential'.

[11] The passage from Eumelos does not mention satyrs.

[12] Rome, Villa Giulia, *ARV* 1343(a), *LIMC* IV pl. 158, Lykourgos 12. See also Cultrera (1938). For a discussion of representations of Lykourgos, see Griffin (1983: 217–32); see also Green (1982: 237–48, esp. 242–4).

[13] London E 439, *ARV* 298, *LIMC* III pl. 312, Dionysos 151.

a chiton. On his feet he wears Thracian boots. Jane Harrison described the
figure as 'the Thracian Dionysos drunk with wine, a brutal though splendid savage'[14] and recently Bérard and Bron have called him 'the prince of
maenads and satyrs in the paroxysm of the ecstatic crisis'.[15] In fact, the
imagery links him with neither drunkenness nor ecstasy. The scene is not
an existential statement but rather a narrative account of the madness sent
by Hera. The tearing of an animal in two becomes a symbol of the ultimate
stage of this madness and is used to show the same madness inflicted by the
god on others.[16] So Plato (*Laws* 672b) has his Athenian explain that
Dionysos 'was bereft of his wits by his stepmother Hera, and that this is why
he afflicts his victims with Bacchic possession and all its frenzied dancing'.[17]

The Dionysos on the stamnos is surely connected with the depiction on
one side of a contemporary cup in London (Pl. 10A).[18] There the god again
dances wildly, again wearing Thracian boots, but this time he holds a snake
in one hand and a thyrsos in the other. A woman in front of him carries a
wineskin, a satyr behind plays pipes, and behind him a satyr and a woman
wearing a leopard skin over her chiton dance. Outcroppings of rocks to the
far right and left show that the setting is in or near a cave. On the other side
of the cup more satyrs and women dance.

Aside from this group, depictions of Dionysos dancing are rare on Attic
vases. On a few black-figure vases from the middle of the sixth century he
is shown dancing in scenes connected with the vintage,[19] but there he is the
drunken god who is different in kind from the god driven mad by Hera.
The drunken dance is in keeping with his traditional role on black-figure
vases as wine god. The mad god dancing has little to do with wine.

Though the god's altercation with Lykourgos and his Hera-induced
madness took place during his youth, depictions of him in these narratives
on red-figure vases show him in the traditional bearded form that goes back
on black-figure vases to before the middle of the sixth century. In fact,

[14] J. E. Harrison (1903: 450).   [15] Bérard, Bron, *et al.* (1989: 148).

[16] The mad Dionysos is shown dancing with the halves of a torn animal in his hands on seven Attic
vases: London E 439, see above, n. 13; London E 362, *ARV* 585.34, *LIMC* III, pl. 355, Dionysos 472;
Amsterdam 372, *ARV* 592.33, *CV* Scheurleer 1, pl. 3. 2; Private, *ARV* 605.65*bis*, see below, n. 21; Gela
N 33, *ARV* 660.73, *CV* Gela 3, pls. 34. 3–4, 37.1; Louvre G 249, *RA* 1982, 206, fig. 7; Athens, Marathon
St. inv. o. 70 (A 5349), *RA* 1982, 203, fig. 5. For a discussion of these scenes, see T. Carpenter (1993).
This is the image Euripides has in mind in his *Orestes* (1490–94) when he compares Orestes and Pylades
as they grab Hermione to thyrsos-less *bakchai* with a mountain cub.

[17] See Burkert (1993: 272).

[18] London E 75, *ARV* 406.2, *LIMC* III pl. 355, Dionysos 407. See also a late archaic stamnos by the
Syleus Painter (Copenhagen 3293, *ARV* 251.36, *CV* 3 pl. 135) where the dancing god, who wears
Thracian boots and a leopard skin, holds a kantharos and thyrsos. Cf. Madrid 11040, *ARV* 568.36, *CV*
2 pl. 15 (72).

[19] e.g. Copenhagen 5179, *ABV* 64.24, *LIMC* III pl. 329, Dionysos 298; Würzburg 265, *ABV* 151.22,
LIMC III pl. 346, Dionysos 515.

Dionysos on Attic vases is almost always bearded until the last quarter of the fifth century. Most gods and heroes are bearded on black-figure vases, but with red-figure the fashion starts to change, and by the middle of the fifth century many are beardless. Dionysos' bearded form was a particularly strong convention, probably derived from three-dimensional images connected with his role as wine god.[20]

In general, Attic painters show little concern about depicting a figure at the appropriate age for a story; rather, more interested in making important figures recognizable, they use current conventions for the same figure in all scenes. In fact, anthropomorphic figures on Attic vases are better understood as symbols than as portraits. The bearded Dionysos was instantly recognizable as the form of the god appropriate to vases, most of which were designed for the storage or consumption of wine.

In this context a depiction of the mad Dionysos by the Niobid Painter on a fragmentary hydria from the second quarter of the century is of particular interest because Dionysos is shown as a beardless youth (Pl. 10B).[21] It is nearly half a century before the beardless Dionysos appears again on Attic vases, and then the form is different in kind.[22]

On the hydria a beardless Dionysos dances by an altar with the halves of a rent fawn in either hand while a woman dances on either side of him, one with an oinochoe and kantharos, the other with a snake and thyrsos. The god wears a curious overgarment. He is a head shorter than the women. Aside from a beard or white hair, size is the only device available to vase painters of this period to indicate age—infants are simply miniature adults. The Niobid painter has consciously chosen to define the figure as the young Dionysos, and he must have had a good reason for breaking such a strong convention. His colleague, the Altamura Painter, also paints the same subject, but for him the god is bearded.[23] As I have argued elsewhere,[24] the theatre may have been the inspiration for the Niobid Painter's depiction, but the important point for this discussion is that the adolescent Dionysos shown on the vase lends support to the view that the event shown here and on the other vases, was one of the early episodes in his mythical life. It is the proverbial exception that proves the rule.

The women with the god in this scene are the nymphs, his nurses, who will later be chased with him by Lykourgos. The altar is the altar of the nymphs and serves the same purpose as the altar in Makron's two earlier

[20] See below, Ch. 6.

[21] Private, *ARV* 605.65*bis*, T. Carpenter (1993: 186, fig. 7). A companion piece from the same group is discussed below. See n. 30.

[22] For the beardless Dionysos on late 5th-cent. vases see Ch. 6.

[23] Amsterdam 372, *ARV* 592.33, see above, n. 16.   [24] T. Carpenter (1993: 203–6).

depictions of Zeus with the infant and of nymphs before the mask idol (Pls. 20 & 21) as it is on a contemporary pelike in London, where the bearded god dances by an altar holding the halves of a fawn while a woman dances and a satyr wearing a fawn skin plays pipes.[25] There a satyr seems positively repulsed by what he sees.[26] These are scenes of pathology not ecstasy; they show the disease imposed by Hera.

On a small group of vases contemporary with these, a woman, rather than the god, holds the torn animal. One of these is by the Blenheim Painter, a colleague of the Niobid Painter, on a volute krater in Newcastle (Pl. 11A & B).[27] There the god, with a kantharos and thyrsos, walks between two women, one with an oinochoe and a snake, the other with the front half of a fawn and a thyrsos. As already noted, the torn fawn stands as a symbol of the destructive side of Dionysian madness, both for the god, for his nurses, and more than half a century later for the women of Thebes in Euripides' *Bacchae*.[28] Scenes where a nymph roughly carries a fawn or a leopard, usually by the tail or by a leg, can probably be seen as less dramatic versions of this same madness.[29]

The other depiction of the beardless Dionysos from the Niobid Painter's workshop is on a fragment of a krater from Olynthos, and the two may be part of a set.[30] Only the head facing right, frontal upper body and outstretched left arm holding the thick stalk of a grape vine survive. The figure is almost a replica of the young Dionysos on the hydria. A bearded Dionysos fighting a giant is shown holding out a vine in just this way on several vases by the Altamura and Blenheim Painters,[31] and this gesture has led to the identification of the scene on this fragment as a Gigantomachy.

There is, however, another parallel for the god's pose on this fragment, on the Cracow hydria showing the madness of Lykourgos.[32] Dionysos' gesture with the grape vine in that scene, though reversed, is almost identical to his gesture on the Salonica fragment. The vine in Dionysos' hand carries

---

[25] Berlin F 2290, *ARV* 462.48, Simon and Hirmer (1981: pl. 169); Athens, Acr. 325, *ARV* 460.20, Graef and Langlotz (1933: pls. 20–2); London E 362, *ARV* 583.34, *LIMC* III pl. 355, Dionysos 472.

[26] See also Louvre G 249, see above, n. 16, where another satyr shows revulsion at what he sees.

[27] Newcastle, *ARV* 597.1. See also Syracuse 24554, *ARV* 649.42, *RA* 1983, 243.6; Cab.Méd. 357, *ARV* 987.2, Bérard, Bron, *et al.* (1989: 149, fig. 204); Athens, Acr. 717, Graef and Langlotz (1933, pl. 54); For later depictions of a similar subject, see below.

[28] See below, Ch. 7.

[29] e.g. Munich 2645, *ARV* 371.15, Boardman (1975: fig. 218); Louvre G 6, *ARV* 72.21, *CV* 10, pl. 10. 2.

[30] Salonica 8. 54, *ARV* 591.28, *LIMC* III pl. 372. Dionysos 629. Beazley attributed this fragment to the Altamura Painter. Given the rarity of the image and the remarkable similarities to the private hydria discussed above, it makes sense to think of the two works as perhaps originally parts of a set, perhaps by the same painter.

[31] e.g. Bologna 286, *ARV* 598.3, *LIMC* III pl. 373, Dionysos 639.   [32] See above, n. 10.

with it almost magical powers as a destructive weapon, both symbolic and real. Here it symbolizes the madness inflicted on Lykourgos by the god, but it can also act as a kind of trap.[33]

Evidence from vases suggests that the Return of Hephaistos should also be seen as one of Dionysos' Thracian adventures, at least in fifth-century Athens. The story, like the Gigantomachy, survives only in summary form from the second century AD, yet it is a very common subject on Attic vases from the middle of the sixth century to the end of the fifth.[34] While describing the oldest sanctuary of Dionysos in Athens, Pausanias (1. 20. 3) mentions a painting of 'Dionysos taking Hephaistos up to Heaven' and he goes on to summarize the myth:

One of the Greek legends is that Hephaistos, when he was born, was thrown down by Hera. In revenge he sent as a gift a golden chair with invisible fetters. When Hera sat down she was held fast and Hephaistos refused to listen to any other of the gods except Dionysos—in him he put the fullest trust—and after making him drunk, Dionysos brought him to heaven.

(trans. W. H. S. Jones (Loeb))

Pausanias surely has in mind the account in Book 18 of the *Iliad* (395–405) where Hephaistos tells of his great fall 'through the will of my own brazen-faced mother who wanted to hide me for being lame'. In that account, Thetis and Eurynome caught him and comforted him, and Hephaistos lived for nine years working as a smith in their cave—the same cave, presumably, in which Thetis received Dionysos (the same expression is used for both receptions).[35] In the account of Dionysos' flight into the sea attributed to Eumelos, Dionysos is also received by both Thetis and Eurynome.[36]

The association of both gods with Thetis may explain why Hephaistos put his trust in Dionysos. It was in Thetis' cave that Hephaistos made the throne for Hera, and perhaps to that cave that Dionysos had to go to find

---

[33] e.g. Paris, Cab.Méd. 573, *ARV* 417.1, *LIMC* III pl. 373, Dionysos 648, a giant is wrapped in the vine held by the god—here ivy. See also a fragmentary krater in St Petersburg (inv. 1843, *ARV* 23.5) by Phintias where Dionysos appeared in the wounding of Telephos, a story related in the *Cypria*. In Apollodorus (3.17) Telephos was wounded by Achilles when he became entangled in a vine. Pindar (*Isthmian* 8. 48) alludes to the role of the vine and a scholiast on *Iliad* 1. 59 says quite specifically that it was Dionysos who caused Telephos to trip.

[34] See Brommer (1978: 10–17, 199–205); T. Carpenter (1986: ch. 2).

[35] See Kirk (1990: n. on 6.132–7). There are two quite different accounts in the *Iliad* of Hephaistos' fall from Olympos. In the other (1. 590–4) Zeus throws him from Olympos because he tries to help his mother Hera, and he falls to Lemnos. It is obviously with the Thetis version that the story of the Return belongs. It is impossible to say whether or not Homer knew the story of the Return; however, Hephaistos' insistence (18. 404–5) that neither the gods nor mortals knew of his whereabouts would argue against it.

[36] See above, n. 4.

him. Since the cave was between Samothrace and Imbros, the journey overland to Olympos would have been through Thrace.[37]

The depiction of the Return of Hephaistos on the François Vase from the second quarter of the sixth century is both the earliest and most complete version of the story to survive on Attic vases. There, Hera on her throne and the assembled Olympians wait as Dionysos leads Hephaistos on an ithyphallic donkey toward them followed by satyrs (labelled *silenoi*) and nymphs. Later versions are always abbreviated and almost always focus on the procession. Aside from a group of fifth-century depictions where Dionysos and Hephaistos both walk, the donkey and the satyrs are the two constant elements. On a late archaic stamnos in Malibu both Dionysos and Hephaistos walk beside ithyphallic donkeys.[38]

On several black-figure vases from the end of the sixth century Hephaistos wears a Thracian *zeira*.[39] Thracian boots occasionally appear in red-figure (but never black-figure) depictions of the Return throughout the first three-quarters of the fifth century. Satyrs wear them on some early vases but not after the middle of the century;[40] Hephaistos wears them, more often after the middle of the century.[41] The Altamura Painter seems to be the first to give them to Hephaistos and the last to put them on satyrs. Dionysos wears them in the scene only rarely.[42] The original point of including Thracian boots in this scene, as in the Gigantomachy, must have been to indicate a Thracian connection.

Though the story and pictures of the Return of Hephaistos can be seen as simple, humorous entertainment, the actual images on vases suggest from the start that the nature of the connection between Dionysos and Hephaistos is complex.[43] Though the story may have been the subject of

[37] See above, n. 8.

[38] Malibu, Getty 77.AE.41, *LIMC* IV pl. 399, Hephaistos 168. On one side of an early red-figure skyphos by Epiktetos (London E 139, *ARV* 77.86, *CV* 4 pl. 28. 1) a satyr with two thyrsoi escorts two donkeys.

[39] e.g. Zurich 2467, *ABV* 285.4, *CV* 1 pl.14; Frankfurt VF ß 286, *Para* 176, *CV* 1, pls. 30. 1, 33. 6; Leipzig T 59, *CV* 2 pl. 39. 3–4; Bologna C 14, *CV* 2 pl. 21; Agrigento C 1535, *CV* 1 pl. 5. 1, 6. See *LIMC* V s.v. Hephaistos, p. 653. On Zurich ETH 8, *ABV* 274.126, *CV* 1, pl. 9.1 the figure wearing the zeira could be Dionysos?

[40] e.g. Paris, Cab.Méd. 542, *ARV* 438.133, *LIMC* IV pl. 400, Hephaistos 169b; Cairo 32378, *ARV* 590.4, Brommer (1978: pl. 81).

[41] e.g. Vienna 985, *ARV* 591.20, *LIMC* III pl. 362, Dionysos 555; Naples Stg. 701, *ARV* 591.21, Brommer (1978: pl. 3. 3); Once Roman Market, *ARV* 1051.7, *AK* 29 (1986) 12, fig. 2; Kassel T 682, *ARV* 1051.7*bis*, LIMC IV pl. 398, Hephaistos 163a; New York 56. 171. 52, *ARV* 1051.6, *CV* 4 pl. 21. 8.

[42] e.g. Once Roman Market, *ARV* 246, Brommer (1978: 14, fig. 5); Louvre G 421, *ARV* 1037.1, *CV* 4, pl. 21. 8.

[43] See Bron, Corfu-Bratschi, and Maouene (1989: 157 and n. 14) who, through different means, have arrived at a similar conclusion.

satyr plays,[44] that fact is of little or no help in interpreting the images, nor conversely should the images be used to prove the existence of satyr plays. From the start satyrs are part of the story as told on vases, as are visual links between satyrs and donkeys and Dionysos and satyrs. It is only during the first half of the fifth century that Thracian elements are added to the scene, but the Thracian connection could well have been understood as being there much earlier.

The clearest expression of the link between satyrs and donkeys is on the François Vase. In the Return frieze, Kleitias has made the bodies of the satyrs from the waist down (legs, hooves, tails) identical to the hind quarters of the donkey Hephaistos rides (Pl. 5A). Only the phalloi differ, those of the satyrs being distinctly human in form if not in size. Placing the satyrs directly behind the donkey, Kleitias has made the visual link inescapable. In fact, the satyr legs on this vase are very unusual. Attic satyrs usually have human legs and feet, and while East Greek satyrs have hooves, their legs are human.[45] In going to such pains to draw the parallel between the satyrs and the donkey, was Kleitias' intention solely bawdy humour, or was he making a narrative connection that would have been clear to his audience?

Certainly humour was part of the reason for making the donkey the mount of Hephaistos. According to Pindar, even Apollo found the lasciviousness of the donkey humorous (*Pythian* 10. 36).[46] On the François Vase the ithyphallic donkey of the Return stands in sharp contrast to the noble horses pulling the chariots of deities in the frieze above. Perhaps an equation should be set with satyrs and donkeys, that a donkey is to a horse as a satyr is to a man.[47]

Elsewhere I have suggested that the main frieze on the François Vase showing the procession of deities at the wedding of Peleus and Thetis, must depend on an earlier visual model,[48] and I suspect the same is true of the Return frieze. The fine distinctions Kleitias makes seldom appear in narratives on other black-figure vases. In fact, they recall the sophistication of the finest red-figure scenes from a century later. For example, Kleitias makes a clear but subtle distinction between Dionysos' beard and the beards of the other deities in the same scene, and at the same time, he links him through beards with the satyrs. Other imagery in his Return is different both in kind and specificity from any other surviving depictions of the subject. Though the earliest, it is the most detailed version of the story; the satyr legs are unique; the cymbals played by a nymph do not appear again on vases for over a century; the indication of Hephaistos' deformity here is rare as is the

---

[44] D. F. Sutton (1980: 70–1 and n. 228). [45] T. Carpenter (1986: 67–8, 77 n. 4).
[46] See Hoffmann (1983: 64). [47] See Lissarrague (1990b: 62). Cf. Wiesner (1969: 531–45).
[48] T. Carpenter (1986: ch. 1).

inclusion of Aphrodite and most of the other deities. It is, of course, impossible to know what that model might have been, but the fairly sudden appearance of such a fully developed form suggests that the scenes on the François Vase reflect a lost tradition of visual narratives that drew on narrative traditions (folk or poetic) for subjects. It is worth wondering whether the cymbals played by the nymph at the end of the procession in the Return (Pl. 12B) might be a reference to the purification and initiation of Dionysos by Rhea since those instruments elsewhere are almost always linked with orgiastic cults.[49]

A comparison between another of Kleitias' nymphs in the Return and a late sixth-century coin type from Thasos raises additional questions about the source of the imagery on the François Vase. The third satyr in the procession (lower body missing) carries a nymph in his arms (Pl. 12A). This is a relatively unusual pose for satyrs on Attic vases,[50] but it does have a parallel on the obverse of coins from Thasos, starting during the last quarter of the sixth century, where the satyr's human legs end in hooves in the East Greek fashion (Pl. 12C).[51] The unusual pose together with the hooves suggest that both Kleitias and the die cutter were drawing on non-Attic models, Kleitias then modifying the satyr legs to make a narrative connection.

Another coin/vase parallel relates to this point. On a fragment of a dinos or krater by Sophilos from the first quarter of the sixth century a hairy, ithyphallic satyr grabs the arm of a nymph who pulls to the right while looking back at him.[52] This was undoubtedly part of a visual narrative such as the Peleus and Thetis frieze on the dinos in London,[53] conceivably showing a Return of Hephaistos. A parallel image appears on one of the earliest coinages from the 'whole Thraco-Macedonian area' dating to the third quarter of the sixth century, perhaps produced by the tribe of the Satrae.[54] There a satyr with human legs ending in hooves grabs the arm of a nymph who looks back at him as she pulls away. Again, the model for the coin must have been non-Attic, as could the model Sophilos knew (the feet of his satyr are missing).

The Thraco-Macedonian parallels for early depictions of satyrs on Attic vases raise some intriguing questions about the source of satyrs with Dionysos in Attic iconography. Kraay wondered if 'the satyr type is

[49] For further discussion of this point see below, pp. 101–2.

[50] For another example see Boston 01.17, *ABV* 319.2., *CV* 1 pl. 54. 2.

[51] See Kraay (1976: 149–50, figs. 518–21); Svoronos (1919: pl. 10). A centaur carrying a nymph in this pose appears on the late 6th-cent. coinage of two Macedonian tribes (the Orescii and Zaielioi) see Kraay and Hirmer (1966: 375–7).

[52] Istanbul 4514, *ABV* 42.37, T. Carpenter (1986: pl. 18A).

[53] London 1971.11–1.1, *Para* 19. 16*bis*, T. Carpenter (1986: pls. 1A, 2, 3B).

[54] Kraay (1976: 148–9, figs. 514–17); Svoronos (1919: pls. 7–8).

intended as a pun on the tribe name, Satrae'.[55] Another possibility is that there was a narrative tradition that made Thrace the home of the satyrs and joined them with Dionysos in his Thracian adventures. The coins and vases would then reflect non-Attic visual representation of the stories.

To continue with this line of reasoning, the Heidelberg and Amasis Painters, who were responsible for the early development of Dionysian imagery in Athens, would then have modified the satyrs, creating the Attic type,[56] and put them with the god in non-narrative contexts where they undoubtedly represented to Athenians something that was both more and less than the satyrs in the original narrative scenes.

A caveat is in order here. In considering the development and diffusion of imagery associated with a deity, it is important to remember that narrative traditions and cultic traditions are two quite distinct forms. The narrative tradition, or as I will call it, the mythic tradition (visual or written) cannot answer questions about the source and nature of the worship of Dionysos in Athens or anywhere else. Though at some point there may well have been links between some traditional tales about Dionysos and cults of Dionysos, the links must have seemed quite remote to fifth-century Athenians. For them satyrs and the Thracian connection belonged to myth not to cult.[57]

The connection between satyrs and donkeys seems to be part of an old visual tradition where the context is usually erotic.[58] In fact, vase painters are fascinated with the sexual activity of male donkeys (and satyrs) as they are with that of no other animal. On an oinochoe from the first quarter of the sixth century an ithyphallic satyr rides a donkey in pursuit of a nymph.[59] On cups from the middle of the sixth century donkeys appear in revels with

[55] Kraay (1976: 148, n. 2). Making a similar connection, J. E. Harrison (1903: 369–71, 379) claimed that when Dionysos entered Greece from Thrace he was accompanied by the satyrs who are the Satrae.

[56] T. Carpenter (1986: 30–54).

[57] Cf. Otto (1965: 64). Henrichs (1978: 136) notes 'The satyrs of myth did not intrude into Dionysiac cult except when the mythical entourage of Dionysus was artificially revived . . .' See also Graf (1987: 100).

[58] A Thracian image also puts the donkey in a Dionysian context. From the third quarter of the 6th cent. through the first quarter of the 5th the coin type for Mende on Pallene, the wine-producing, westernmost peninsula of the Chalcidice, was an ithyphallic donkey with a crow standing on its back, sometimes with a bunch of grapes beside it. During much of the 5th cent. Dionysos reclines on the back of the donkey, and in the 4th the ithyphallic donkey and crow return (Kraay (1976: 136–7)). It is perhaps worth recalling that from Athens a similar ithyphallic donkey is the shield device for Ares on an early 5th-cent. depiction of the Gigantomachy and of a satyr in a slightly later mock-gigantomachy (Orvieto 1044, *ARV* 657.1, Vian (1951: pl. 40. 367)). A comic tale borrowed by Hyginus from Eratosthenes ties these loose elements (Gigantomachy, donkey, Dionysos) together. There (*Poetica Astronomica* 23) Dionysos, Hephaistos, and satyrs rode donkeys to fight the giants and the braying of the donkeys terrified the giants causing them to flee.

[59] Buffalo G 600, *ABV* 12.22, Boardman (1974: fig. 15).

satyrs and nymphs,[60] and on one a single ithyphallic donkey pursues a single nymph across the frieze.[61] A satyr attempting to penetrate a donkey on which Hephaistos, or later sometimes Dionysos or another satyr, rides is not an uncommon subject on black-figure vases throughout the second half of the sixth century, and variations on it carry over into red-figure as well.[62] In a generic scene on the outside of an early red-figure cup in Athens Dionysos in the centre is flanked by satyrs who are flanked by nymphs on ithyphallic donkeys which are about to be penetrated by ithyphallic satyrs.[63]

Though the donkey becomes associated with Dionysos through the Return, by the end of the sixth century it has become his regular mount on many mass-produced lekythoi and cups.[64] Whether the painters of these vases were aware that the Return was the source of their image is impossible to tell; in any case, a donkey was a reasonable mount for a crippled god and a country wine god. With red-figure comes a new interest in the connections between Dionysos, donkeys, and satyrs outside of the Return, but few if any of these refer to identifiable narratives (Pl. 13A),[65] though in some satyrs wear Thracian boots, and on occasion a Dionysos mounted on a donkey wears them himself.[66]

[60] e.g. Band cups: Munich inv. 7414, *CV* 11 pl. 19. 6–4; Munich inv. 9438, *CV* 11 pl. 27. 3–6. Cf. amphora frag. from Samos, *ABV* 151.18, Karouzou (1956: pl. 30. 3) where a donkey dances amidst satyrs.

[61] London 1958. 12–17. 1, *AK* 9 (1966) pl. 3. 4. On a cup-skyphos by Epiktetos (Naples RP 27669, *ARV* 77.85, Johns (1982: 111 fig. 92A) a naked nymph with a thyrsos reclines as an ithyphallic donkey approaches.

[62] The earliest example is Oxford 1920.107, *ABV* 89.2. On this Beazley and Payne (1929: 269) comment that this detail 'can scarcely have had an epic original and must have been invented by a painter'. See also New York 17.230.5, *Para* 78.1, *CV* 2 pl.19. 31; Munich 1525, *CV* 8 pl. 400. 2.

[63] Athens, Kanellopoulos 2572 and Rome, Vatican, Ast. 811, *Para* 329, Brouskari (1985: 67). See also Munich 2335A, *ARV* 637.34, *CV* 2 pl. 53. 1–2 where a satyr buggers a donkey. See also Munich 2469, *CV* 2 pl. 89. 4 where donkeys copulate. For a donkey mounting a horse see the early red-figure cup Heidelberg inv. 74/1, Strocka (1987: 18–19. 7).

[64] e.g. cups from the Leafless Group (*ABV* 633–49); lekythoi from the Class of Athens 581 (*ABV* 489–506). A frieze on a black-figure kyathos in the Villa Giulia from Cerveteri, Tomb 371 (*ML* 42 (1955) 867, fig. 201) from the early 5th cent. includes a jumble of imagery from both the Gigantomachy and the Return. In addition to a man on a donkey (Hephaistos?) there are: a satyr with a pelta, another with a salpinx, and another with a pelta and pointed hat; Dionysos wearing a leopard skin and a helmet and holding a thyrsos; a warrior with a Boeotian shield; a satyr in a leopard skin holding a club.

[65] e.g. Munich 2606, *ARV* 64.102, *LIMC* III pl. 341, Dionysos 384; St Petersburg 3375, *Para* 510, Peredolska (1967: pl. 71); Brussels R 253, *ARV* 64.104, *CV* 1 pl. 2. 2; Compiègne 1093, *ARV* 64.105, *CV* pl. 14. 5; Florence 81601, *ARV* 64.96, *CV* 3 pl. 74.

[66] Paris, Cab.Méd. 576, *ARV* 371.14, Bérard, Bron, *et al.* (1989: 145 fig. 202A); Amsterdam 11068, *ARV* 282.39^quater, Brijder, Drukkert, and Neeft (1986: 133, fig. 1); London E 102, *ARV* 1253.70, Lezzi-Hafter (1988: pl. 10. 15). There is another version of Dionysos' madness told by Hyginus (*Poet.Astr.* 2. 23) where, driven mad by Hera, the god is led to Dodona by two donkeys where Zeus cures him. This tale calls to mind an unusual scene on a krater from the third quarter of the 5th cent. in Bologna (244, *ARV* 531.40, *CV* 1 pl. 29. 1–3) where Dionysos and a woman wearing fawn skin and carrying a thyrsos—a nymph/nurse—walk beside two ithyphallic donkeys toward an altar.

There are well over fifty depictions of the Return of Hephaistos on surviving fifth-century red-figure vases.[67] Many repeat the conventions established by black-figure painters at the middle of the sixth century. As in black-figure, Hephaistos can, on occasion, be beardless, particularly in the decades after 450. Along with the traditional scenes a new version is introduced during the first quarter of the century in which both gods walk.[68]

As with the Gigantomachy, it is the Niobid Painter's group that provides a kind of touchstone for understanding the development of imagery in the Return on Attic vases during the first half of the century. There are three depictions of the subject by the Altamura Painter: on a volute krater in Cairo, Hephaistos rides on an ithyphallic donkey while on calyx kraters in Naples and Vienna, both gods walk and the donkey is not included (Pl. 14A & B).[69]

On one side of the Cairo krater Hermes leads a lyre-playing satyr toward a seated Hera, while on the other side Dionysos leads Hephaistos' donkey. Both Hephaistos and the satyr wear Thracian boots. This is the first inclusion of Hera in the narrative on red-figure vases, recalling the scene on the François Vase, and she appears in several more versions from the second half of the century.[70]

The other two depictions of the subject by the Altamura Painter are of particular interest because only two details keep them from being identical. On both a satyr playing a kithara precedes the two gods, and Hephaistos, wearing a chlamys, petasos, and Thracian boots, carries bellows. However, on the Vienna krater the satyr is barefoot and wears shorts that hold on an artificial phallos and tail, while on the Naples krater the satyr appears to have the conventional, ithyphallic form, and he wears Thracian boots.

The satyr shorts, together with the kithara, an instrument associated with professional musicians rather than with rural romps, suggest that the scene was inspired by a performance, or at the least that the shorts are an allusion to a performance of some sort. The absence of the shorts in the nearly identical scene points to the difficulty of ever knowing how to interpret these creatures on fifth-century vases. Vase painters were telling stories, and it is unlikely that they spent much time worrying about this problem; however, when they did include the shorts, they must have had a reason.

Douris also gives two nearly identical depictions of the Return.[71] As in

[67] See above, n. 34.

[68] For early examples see Rome, Vatican, Ast. 703, *ARV* 206.132*bis*, Brommer (1978: pl. 5. 1); Adria B 515 and B 1412, *ARV* 242.81, *CV* pl. 5. 4.

[69] Cairo 32378, *ARV* 590.4, see above, n. 40; Vienna 985, *ARV* 591.20 and Naples Stg. 701, *ARV* 591.21, see above, n. 41.

[70] See Halm-Tisserant (1986: 18–20).

[71] Paris, Cab.Méd. 542, *ARV* 438.133, see above n. 40; Paris, Cab.Méd. 539, *ARV* 438.134, *LIMC* IV pl. 400, Hephaistos 169a.

two of the Altamura Painter's scenes, all the figures walk and the satyr leading the procession wears Thracian boots in one scene and not in the other.
So too, the booted satyr appears in one of the Kleophrades Painter's versions of the subject, but not in the other.[72] Clearly the boots were appropriate but not necessary elements of imagery. The implication is that people
knew of the Thracian dimension of the story; on vases before the middle of
the century the Thracian link also included Dionysos and his companions,
satyrs and nymphs.

Depictions of the Return of Hephaistos on vases after the middle of the
fifth century are often staid in comparison with the raucous scenes from the
first half of the century. Compare, for example, the Kleophrades Painter's
lively procession on the krater at Harvard with the scene by the Kleophon
Painter on the skyphos in Toledo (Pl. 15A & B).[73] The outrageously aroused
satyrs on the earlier piece have scraggly curls and overgrown beards, wear
cat-skins and play pipes and lyre and kithara and carry an enormous krater,
amphora, and wine skin. On the later vase they have been replaced by one
modest, young (though balding) satyr who plays pipes as he leads the deco-
rous procession. The wild-eyed, impish Dionysos of the earlier piece, who
rushes along dressed in a panther skin over a short chiton has been replaced
by a stately, almost lugubrious figure dressed in a himation over a long chiton, who raises his kantharos in a dignified toast to Hephaistos. In short, the
ribald humour, and with it the life, has gone out of the scene.[74]

The Kleophon Painter's depiction from the third quarter of the century
comes at the end of a series of Returns attributed to the Group of
Polygnotos, which starts around the middle of the century. On these
Hephaistos rides a donkey which becomes less and less sexually aroused the
later it is in the series. The god wears a short, decorated, sleeveless shift
often referred to as an *exomis* or an *ependytes*. He is accompanied by well-
behaved satyrs who often play pipes or lyres and are never ithyphallic.
Sometimes he is bearded, sometimes not.[75] On about half of them he wears
Thracian boots. A dignified Dionysos wearing a himation over a long
chiton often precedes him. The Kleophon Painter's example is unusual only
in that it includes Hera on her throne.

---

[72] Louvre G 162, *ARV* 186.47, *LIMC* IV pl. 391, Hephaistos 117; Harvard 1960. 236, *ARV* 185.31,
T. Carpenter (1991: 26 fig. 13).

[73] Harvard 1960.236, *ARV* 185.31, see previous note; Toledo 82. 88, *CV* 2 pls. 84–7.

[74] Exceptions are scenes where the drunken gods walk, clinging to each other (e.g. Naples 2412,
ARV 1114.1, *LIMC* IV pl. 400, Hephaistos 170c) and a scene on a chous by the Eretria Painter (New
York 08.258.22, *ARV* 1249.12, *LIMC* III pl. 364, Dionysos 565) where the two drunken gods ride
together on the same donkey. Dionysos wears a short chiton and boots.

[75] Compare New York 56.171.52, *ARV* 1051.6, see above n. 41 with Munich 2384, *ARV* 1057.98,
LIMC IV pl. 398, Hephaistos 164a.

The Thracian boots worn by the god in some of these later scenes may have a less specific meaning than they did in the earlier ones. A comparison with horsemen on the frieze of the Parthenon, some of whom wear similar boots, is instructive. There, elements of Thracian dress including the *alopekis* and boots seem to have become fashionable dress for aristocratic Athenian horsemen, and the adoption of this dress seems to go back to the beginning of the century.[76] To put the same boots on the crippled smith-god who rides a hugely ithyphallic donkey might have been intended in the early scenes to heighten the mock-heroic character of an essentially comic episode. As the scene becomes more dignified and controlled during the latter part of the century, the contrast is less obvious, and the similarities between the later Hephaistos and the Parthenon horsemen might be seen as the reflection of an attempt to dignify a traditional scene in monumental art, such as the painting of the Return Pausanias (1. 20. 3) saw in the temple of Dionysos within the god's precinct by the theatre in Athens. It is not surprising that the scene all but disappears from Attic vases during the last quarter of the century. A dignified Return of Hephaistos in the vase painter's tradition is, quite simply, an oxymoron.[77]

Finally, one more Dionysian scene with distinctly Thracian connotations should be mentioned even though its meaning and implications remain something of a puzzle. In a frieze on a late archaic psykter by Douris ten satyrs cavort about various wine vessels, oblivious to an eleventh dressed as Hermes who strides through their midst (Pl 16A).[78] The Hermes-satyr carries a kerykeion and has a petasos, both regular attributes of the god, Hermes, but in place of a chlamys he wears a Thracian *zeira* and in place of winged boots, he wears Thracian *embades*.[79]

Two of the cavorting satyrs are ithyphallic; the rest are infibulated.[80] Only the Hermes satyr has the tidy genitals appropriate to gods and heroes. The activities of the satyrs are focused on wine. Two have kantharoi, the high-handled cup usually associated with Dionysos and seldom used (on vases) by mortals. Two more satyrs dance on either side of a kantharos set on the ground. Two satyrs pour wine from oinochoai—as if pouring

[76] e.g. W IV, Brommer (1977: pl. 13) for *alopekis* and *embades*. Compare the youth on horseback with Hephaistos on the Kleophon Painter's skyphos. See above, Ch. 2, n. 15.

[77] A unique depiction of the Return on a krater from the last quarter of the century is attributed to Polion (Ferrara 3033, *ARV* 1171.1, Alfieri (1979: 80–2, figs. 182–5)). There, in a scene with multiple groundlines, time and space have been compressed. Hera sits to the far left while to the right a small satyr helps Hephaistos up from a couch he shares with Dionysos. A satyr with torch and tongs indicates the procession while here and there satyrs and nymphs converse. For possible connections with wall painting see (Robertson 1992: 246).

[78] London E 768, *ARV* 446.262, Buitron-Oliver (1995: pls. 54–5 and frontispiece).

[79] Cf. London 1900.7–27.4, *ARV* 643.117, *LIMC* V, pl. 217, Hermes 197.

[80] On infibulation, Lissarrague (1990b: 59–61).

libations—but rather than phialai the receptacles into which they pour are a kantharos balanced on the erect phallos of a reclining satyr[81] and the open mouth of another reclining satyr into which yet another satyr also pours wine from a wine-skin.

It has long been assumed that this scene is connected with a satyr play, but this assumption is neither necessary nor helpful.[82] The vase itself is a wine cooler, designed to be placed inside a krater. In other words, it has no other possible function than to cool wine, presumably for symposia. The purpose of the scene in that context must be to entertain, and the vivid imagery must make the story it tells easily accessible. The central figure is the Hermes-satyr whose dress is an explicitly Thracian version of that god's usual dress. Hermes, however, never wears Thracian clothing on Attic vases, so the Thracian character of the dress must be a key to the meaning.[83] Why, then, might Douris have used a satyr to allude to both Hermes and Thrace?

Hermes appears with satyrs, usually accompanied by goats, on some late black-figure vases,[84] and on a few other black-figure vases contemporary with those satyrs wear articles of clothing associated with Hermes. So, on a late black-figure oinochoe in Florida a satyr wearing a petasos, chiton, and winged boots, holds a drinking horn as he reclines on the back of a goat led by another satyr playing pipes (Pl. 17A).[85] This seems to echo a scene by the Berlin Painter on a contemporary red-figure stamnos in Paris where Hermes, wearing a petasos, chiton with chlamys, and winged boots, holds a kantharos and kerykeion as he reclines on the back of a ram between two satyrs, one playing pipes and the other carrying a krater and wineskin (Pl. 17B).[86] It is unlikely that the similarities between the scenes are purely coincidental, though it is not possible to know the nature of the model to which either refers. Both seem to be humorously idiosyncratic allusions to the symposion, but this makes it unlikely that the black-figure scene with the satyr represents a parody of the red-figure scene with the god, since the latter seems to be a kind of parody itself.

[81] For a satyr performing a similar feat, see Boston 01. 8024, *ARV* 173.9, Hartwig (1893: pl .5).

[82] Brommer (1937: 47. 91); Buschor (1943: 100). Cf. Bérard, Bron, *et al.* (1989: 126–8).

[83] On an unpublished Etruscan red-figure cup in Basle the Hermes who receives the infant Dionysos from Zeus wears a zeira and perhaps an alopekis.

[84] e.g. Bologna C44, *ABL* 250. 35, *CV* 2 pl. 42. 1–3; Chicago, Univ. 1967.115.68, *ABV* 396.23, *AJA* 47 (1943) 394, fig. 9; Oxford 563, *ABV* 396.21, *CV* 2 pl. 8. 7. One of the most memorable depictions of Hermes is on the name vase of the Berlin Painter (Berlin F 2160, *ARV* 196.1; Arias, Hirmer, and Shefton 1962: pls. 150–3) where he walks with a satyr.

[85] Sarasota 1600. G5, *ABV* 527.17, Shapiro (1981: 51).

[86] Louvre G 185 *ARV* 207.142, *LIMC* V pl. 222, Hermes 257. On the other side Dionysos reclines on the back of a goat.

The earliest extant references to satyrs and silenoi in Greek literature link them with Hermes and new evidence has recently been published leading to the conclusion that Hermes was named as father of the satyrs in the post-Hesiodic *Catalogue of Women*, a connection repeated by Nonnos (14. 105–19) in the fifth century AD.[87] I suspect Athenians might have understood these Hermes-satyrs (and perhaps some other satyrs as well) as sons of Hermes, who, by imitating their father, humorously express a dimension of the god himself. A satyr wearing a petasos and a himation over a chiton as he stands in front of a herm on an early classic krater in Geneva, would also seem to reflect this process (Pl. 13B). Hermes is never ithyphallic, satyrs usually are; here the herm is and the Hermes-satyr is not.[88]

Dionysos is, of course, the deity with whom satyrs are usually associated, and the Thracian dress on the Hermes-satyr on Douris psykter points toward his Thracian episodes. Hermes himself is involved in only one of those, transporting the infant Dionysos to the nymphs of Nysa, a depiction that appears on many red-figure vases.[89] It is possible that the scene contains an allusion to that event. In fact, we can probably go no further than this in deciphering what levels of meaning symposiasts might have brought to the scene. That it would have been understood as belonging to the larger group of depictions of Dionysos' Thracian adventures seems likely.

From the evidence on vases it can be argued that there was current in fifth-century Athens a group of stories about the young Dionysos with specifically Thracian implications, which is not, of course, to say that the stories were new—only the emphasis in vase painting. The god's madness and his encounter with Lykourgos were included as were his participation in the Return of Hephaistos and the Gigantomachy. During the second half of the century the distinctly Thracian emphasis fades, but some images, such as the boots, continue to appear, having taken on lives of their own, and it is entirely possible that vase painters and sculptors at the end of the century were not aware of the meaning carried by the images at the beginning.

[87] For a discussion of the evidence see T. Carpenter (1986: 78–9). Henrichs (1987: 117 n. 42) adds: 'In P.Oxy. 1038 = Soph.fr.dub. 1130. 7 Radt (from a satyr play) the satyrs of the chorus introduce themselves as "sons of nymphs" (paides nymphon) and "ministers of Bakchos".'

[88] Geneva HR 85, *LIMC* V pl. 211, Hermes 130*bis*. See also two early classic lekythoi Karlsruhe 85.1, *ARV* 685.164, Berard, Bron, *et al.* (1989: 61, fig. 86); London E 585, *ARV* 685.162, *LIMC* V, pl. 206, Hermes 95c where silhouettes of satyrs on pinakes hang beside herms.

[89] See *LIMC* V s.v. Hermes 365–80. See also Ch. 4. Seaford (1984: 94) notes with reference to Euripides' *Cyclops* that 'the satyrs and the nymphs are all associated, in both literature and art, with *kourotrophia* in general and the nurture of Dionysos in particular'.

4

Dionysian Women

In most depictions of Dionysos *mainomenos* and in many depictions of the Return of Hephaistos, women accompany the god. In the preceding pages I have used the term 'nymph' rather than the more common 'maenad' when discussing these women, and this distinction is more than a matter of conventions. The term 'maenad', which on the most basic level simply means 'madwoman', is used in fifth-century literature principally for mortals.[1] The term 'nymph', on the other hand, implies a divine or semi-divine status.[2] I believe that during the first half of the fifth century Athenians would probably have understood most of the women with the god on vases to be nymphs connected with him directly or indirectly through narratives about his infancy and youth.[3] Though this narrative connection is less clear during the second half of the century, and the women are often assigned symbolic names, there is still no reason to think of them as mortals.

As I have discussed elsewhere, the groups of women in early Attic Dionysian scenes are companions of the satyrs more than they are companions of the god, which is in keeping with the few surviving references to satyrs in early literature.[4] Satyrs and nymphs first appear together with the god in the Return of Hephaistos frieze on the François Vase, and it is possible that satyrs and nymphs entered Attic imagery though depictions (and accounts) of that myth.

The Amasis Painter, the mid-sixth-century vase painter who was in large part responsible for defining early canons of Dionysian imagery, understood

---

[1] Wilamowitz-Moellendorff (1932: 60 and n. 3) was convinced that the word used in *Iliad* 22. 460 meant 'mad woman' and nothing more. See Richardson (1974: 281) on l. 386. The term does not appear on vases before the middle of the 5th cent., see below, n. 61.

Henrichs (1987: 100) defines maenads as 'ritual nymphs' or nymphs as 'proto-maenads who have not yet acquired the ritual identity that constitutes the hallmark of the true maenad in myth as well as in actual cult'. For him (following Edwards (1960)) the 'distinguishing marks of the maenad . . . are her ritual dress and paraphernalia'.

For what might be called expansive readings of the term, see recently Schlesier (1993); Seaford (1993).

[2] *Homeric Hymn to Aphrodite* (V), 259–60 'they rank neither with mortals nor with immortals: long indeed do they live, eating heavenly food and treading the lovely dance among the immortals and with them the Sileni and the sharp-eyed slayer of Argus mate in depths of pleasant caves' (trans. H. Evelyn-White, Loeb). See also *Theogony* 130 and *Iliad* 24. 616.

[3] Hedreen (1994) has independently come to a similar conclusion via a different route.

[4] T. Carpenter (1986: 76–97).

the underlying narrative connection between Dionysos and nymphs as he shows on an amphora in Paris from the third quarter of the sixth century where two women, arms over each other's shoulders, carry a hare and a deer as they rush toward the god (Pl. 18A).[5] This is the earliest depiction of women alone with Dionysos, and unlike the earlier scenes with nymphs and satyrs, there is nothing lighthearted or humorous about it. They have been transformed into maddened companions of the god required by narratives, similar to those who appear on early red-figure vases as, for example, those who accompany the god's chariot on cup by Oltos in Tarquinia. (Pl. 18B).[6] As I suggested in the previous chapter, animals torn apart or roughly carried by the god or by his female companions come to be a symptom—an iconographic signal—of Dionysian madness.

In the earliest reference to Dionysos in extant literature (*Iliad* 6.132) the god is accompanied by his nurses (*tithenai*) on Mount Nysa when Lykourgos chases him into the sea.[7] Eumelos, in his account of the story,[8] also seems to have called them nurses (*tithenai*), and at the end of the fifth century Sophocles uses the same word to describe the god's companions in *Oedipus at Colonus* (680)[9]. On the other hand, the companions of the god in Aeschylus' *Bassarai* were Thracian women (the chorus) and in Euripides' *Bacchae* they are Lydian women (again the chorus). The nature of the god's companions when they are the chorus of a tragedy seems to be a special case, and it may have been the enormous popularity of Euripides' play that led later authors to use the terms *bakchai* or maenads for all groups of women who accompanied the god or satyrs.[10] Thus Apollodorus, in his account of the Lykourgos story (3. 5. 1), refers to the women as *bakchai*.[11]

Detailed accounts of the infancy of Dionysos are late. According to Apollodorus' summary (3. 4. 3) Zeus snatched the six-month foetus from the dead Semele and, after sewing it into his thigh, gave birth to the child at the proper time. He then gave the child to Hermes who gave him to Ino and Athamas, a sister of Semele and her husband, a Boeotian king, who were subsequently driven mad by Hera. Hermes then brought the child to the nymphs of Nysa who reared him. One of the most explicit statements of the connection between these nymphs of Nysa and the women who

---

[5] Paris, Cab.Méd. 222, *ABV* 152.25, Carpenter (1986: 90 and pl. 17). For the Amasis Painter's role in the development of early Dionysian imagery, ibid. 30–54.

[6] Tarquinia RC 6848, *ARV* 60.66, Arias, Hirmer, and Shefton (1962: pl. 100).

[7] For the use of this word in Homer and its possible maenadic implications there see Seaford (1993: 116 n. 3).

[8] See above, Ch. 3.

[9] A similar role for nymphs is mentioned in Euripides' *Cyclops* 4, but the word used is *trophos*.

[10] See Villanueva-Puig (1980: 52–9); Kirk (1970: 4–6).

[11] For a discussion of the Lykourgos episode, see above, Ch. 3.

accompany the adult god is in a *Homeric Hymn to Dionysos* (XXVI). There they are said to have received the child from Zeus, and after having raised him, joined him in his wanderings. A passage in Sophocles *Oedipus at Colonus* is hardly less clear: 'Where he holds each night his revels wild, with the nymphs who fostered the lusty child' (678–80).[12]

The infancy of Dionysos does not become a subject on Attic vases until the first quarter of the fifth century when scenes usually said to show the delivery of the child to the nymphs of Nysa first appear. Variations on this theme continue to appear on through to the end of the century, though most are clustered around the middle.[13] Two of the earliest depictions, both in Ferrara, are on vases by one of the 'standard bearers' of classical Dionysian imagery, the Altamura Painter.[14]

On one side of a volute krater a king with a sceptre, presumably Zeus, hands a child who holds a kantharos and an ivy sprig to a woman (Pl. 19A).[15] The central group is flanked by two more women, one with a small leopard, the other with stylized flowers. Though there is no indication of setting,[16] the scene must show Zeus delivering the infant Dionysos to the nymphs of Nysa as in the *Homeric Hymn*. One of the women has an attribute, a leopard, which is associated with Dionysos and his companions in many other scenes as well.

The imagery of this scene is connected with that on a bell krater by the same painter (Pl. 19B).[17] There a naked child holding a kantharos and vine branch stands on the lap of a bearded man seated on a chair. A woman with stylized flowers stands behind him, a woman holding a small himation stands in front. The seated man wears a wreath of pointed leaves (laurel?) and holds a thyrsos. The child wears an ivy wreath.

These figures have frequently been mis-identified as Dionysos and Oinopion, but they are almost certainly intended to be Zeus and the infant Dionysos.[18] Only the thyrsos raises doubt. The child has the attributes appropriate to the young Dionysos; the women are sisters of the women in the other scene by the Altamura Painter discussed above. The seated man wears the same wreath Zeus wears on that other vase.[19] If there were still any doubt, a scene on a pelike by the Nausikaa Painter, a Mannerist who

---

[12] Kamerbeek (1984: 106 on l. 680): '*amphipolon* with dative "accompany". The nymphs, who nurtured him, are his companions'.

[13] See Arafat (1990: 47–50, 187–8); Brommer (1980: 16–19); Loeb (1979: 39–56, 286–300).

[14] For a discussion of Dionysos and the Niobid Painter and his colleagues, see above, Ch. 2, pp. 30–4.

[15] Ferrara 2737, *ARV* 589.3, *LIMC* III pl. 380, Dionysos 702.   [16] Cf. Arafat (1990: 49).

[17] Ferrara 2738, *ARV* 593.41, LIMC III pl. 381, Dionysos 705.

[18] Properly identified as Zeus with the infant Dionysos in its first publication (*NSc* 1925, 166). The mis-identification started with Fuhrmann (1950/1: 118–20) and is followed by Beazley *ARV* 593.41.

[19] For Dionysos wearing a wreath with pointed leaves (myrtle?) see Robertson (1986: 81–2).

drew heavily on imagery from the Altamura Painter, should dispel it.[20]
There the child with kantharos and vine stands on the lap of a seated man
who holds a sceptre, while a woman holding a wreath stands in front of
them. The simple explanation for the ivy leaves rather than a finial at the
top of the seated man's staff (thyrsos rather than sceptre) on the Ferrara bell
krater is that the painter 'nodded' while drawing his Zeus.[21] This is one of
the few occasions when such an assertion can be made with confidence.

The complex pictures on fragments of a cup by Makron from the
Acropolis in Athens are slightly earlier than these (Pl. 20A).[22] The scene is
unique. On one side Hermes leads a procession of deities toward an altar in
front of a rock-face where two women make a sacrifice; one holds an
oinochoe, the other a kanoun. Zeus follows Hermes holding the infant
Dionysos who wears an ivy wreath and holds a branch of a vine with clus-
ters of grapes hanging from it. He is followed by Poseidon and Athena.
Much of the other side is missing, but it seems to have included a continu-
ation of the procession with several women. Only Amphitrite can be even
tentatively identified, by the fish she carries. The woman in front of her carries a sceptre, and there are three more women to the far left, one with a
leafy branch from a grape vine(?).[23] Again, *Homeric Hymn to Dionysos*
(XXVI) is pertinent: The lovely-haired nymphs nurtured him and from his

lordly father took him to their bosoms to cuddle and nurse in the dells of Nysa. He
grew up by his father's will inside a sweet-smelling cave as one of the immortals

(3–6; trans. H. Evelyn-White (Loeb))

On an amphora contemporary with Makron's cup Dionysos and a woman
clearly labelled *nynphaia* both pour libations, and on a fragment of a cup
contemporary with both of these, a woman pursued by a satyr is labelled
nymphe.[24]

The major variations in the other depictions of the delivery of the infant
to his custodians include: the substitution of Hermes,[25] or in one case a
satyr, for Zeus, and later the inclusion of Papposilenos as the recipient.
Some of the scenes may represent different stages in the same narration, but

[20] London, Christie's 12 July 1977, 125; *Ede Pottery from Athens* V, 1979, 22. For the Nausikaa
Painter, see Mannack (forthcoming).

[21] Cf. Simon and Hirmer (1981: 133).

[22] Athens, Acr. 325, *ARV* 460.20, Graef and Langlotz (1933: pls. 20–2); Pease (1935: 232–4);
Karouzou (1983: 57–64).

[23] By comparison with a procession on a cup by the Sosias Painter in Berlin (F 2278, *ARV* 21, Simon
and Hirmer (1981: pl. 118) the three women to the left might be identified as Horai. One of the women
on the Berlin vase carries a similar branch.

[24] London E 350, *ARV* 256.2, *LIMC* III pl. 405, Dionysos 860; Basle, Cahn HC 432, Kossatz-
Deissmann (1991: 143, fig. 6).

[25] For Hermes' role, see Zanker (1965: 77–80).

it also seems clear that there was no one canonical version of the god's childhood. That the infancy of Dionysos was the subject of plays is undisputed, but the content of those plays can only be guessed at on the basis of very slight evidence.[26] There is no good reason to look to the lost plays for the source of the imagery on the majority of the vases; the argument too quickly becomes circular.

Three depictions of the young Dionysos from the second quarter of the fifth century are linked by the inclusion of architectural elements that raise special problems. On a hydria by the Syleus Painter a named Zeus with a sceptre hands the child Dionysos, also named, to a woman who sits on a stool in front of an Ionic column (Pl. 22A).[27] Behind her stands a woman with a sceptre who faces away but looks back. The child and the seated woman hold ivy sprigs, and the standing woman wears an ivy wreath. On a slightly later stamnos in the Louvre a similar male with a sceptre stands facing a woman who already holds the child. [28] To the left of them is an Ionic column supporting an architrave, and a woman holding a thyrsos and phiale sits within. On the third vase, a hydria in a private collection, Hermes with the infant faces a woman (Pl. 22B).[29] A Doric column stands between them, and another, behind the woman, stands between her and a seated figure who holds a phiale and a sceptre. A table with two kantharoi and a cake on it is in front of one of the columns.

The architectural members obviously indicate grand buildings, probably in each case a palace rather than a temple. On the Louvre stamnos the architrave supported by the Ionic column has regulae, a feature normally associated with the Doric order, suggesting that the painter far from having a particular building in mind, is not even concerned with the distinctions between the orders. The buildings in themselves make it unlikely that we should call the women nymphs, who by definition live in the wild. Apollodorus' account of the role of king Athamas and Ino provides a logical alternative. Inscriptions on a second-century 'Homeric bowl' show, at the least, that Dionysos and Athamas both figured in Sophocles' lost play *Athamas* (A), making it clear that the role of Athamas and Ino in the infancy of Dionysos was current in fifth-century Athens.[30]

---

[26] Sophocles' *Dionysiskos*, frags. 171–3 (*TrGF* 4). For a recent discussion, D. F. Sutton (1980: 39–41).

[27] Paris, Cab.Méd. 440, *ARV* 252.51, *LIMC* III pl. 380, Dionysos 701.

[28] Louvre G 188, *ARV* 508.1, *LIMC* III pl. 380, Dionysos 703.

[29] Athens, Kryou, *AK* 25 (1982) pl. 8. I see no reason to interpret the seated figure as male. Cf. Oakley (1982: 44–7). In *LIMC* II s.v. Athamas, Schwanzar mistakenly refers to an inscription identifying Ino.

[30] Fuhrmann (1950/1: 104 figs.1–2). Pipili (1991: 143–7) has argued that a scene on the late archaic Amyklai Throne showed Athamas and Ino receiving Dionysos.

The scene on the hydria by Hermonax has recently been said to show Hermes delivering the infant Dionysos to Athamas and Ino, which is a plausible interpretation.[31] However, the fragmentary seated figure holding a phiale and sceptre to the left of 'Ino' recalls the seated woman with a phiale and thyrsos in the same position on the Louvre vase and the woman with a sceptre on the Syleus vase. If that figure is a woman, then all three pictures would tell the same story. Zeus could replace Hermes without changing the story, but the woman with the sceptre/phiale is essential. In all three she is quite distinctive. On the Syleus vase she holds a sceptre and faces away from the action while looking back at it. Without the ivy wreath she would be Hera, the nemesis of young Dionysos and the source of the madness that strikes Ino and eventually Dionysos. On the Louvre stamnos the woman sits statue-like within the building with her phiale and thyrsos, and on Hermonax's hydria she sits with a phiale and sceptre. If these scenes reflect a version of a story current in Athens, the woman should have been instantly identifiable. If the woman receiving the child is Ino, it is possible that the other woman represents Hera and the madness she will bring, which is, of course, the point of the story. On roughly contemporary vases discussed below, the women flanking Hermes with the infant are labelled *mainas* (mad (woman)) and *methuse* (drunken (woman)).[32]

Most depictions of the infant Dionysos, of which there are about twenty, are clustered around the middle of the fifth century.[33] Four are from the workshop of the Villa Giulia Painter, and three of those are by the name painter himself. These scenes are of particular interest here because of the special attention the workshop pays to Dionysian scenes in general and because of inscriptions that appear on three of the four.[34]

The scene by the Villa Giulia Painter on a bell krater in London (Pl. 23A) is nearly identical to a scene on a calyx krater in Moscow by the same painter.[35] On both a named Hermes holding the named infant sits on a rock between two women. On the London vase the woman in front of Hermes is *mainas* (mad (woman)). Much of the woman behind him is missing, but the letters *..thus* remain beside her.[36] On the Moscow vase the woman in front of Hermes is not labelled, but the woman behind him is *methose* (a variant of *methuse*—drunken (woman)). A woman in a Dionysian procession on a krater in New York from the same workshop is labelled *methuse*,[37]

---

[31] Oakley (1982: 44–7).   [32] See below, n. 35.   [33] See above, n. 13.

[34] All three of the Villa Giulia Painter's depictions of the subject were found in graves at Nola in central Italy.

[35] London E 492, *ARV* 619.16, *LIMC* V pl. 229, Hermes 365a; Moscow II 1b 732, *ARV* 618.4, Sidorova *et al.* (1985: 85–7. 45).

[36] For the inscriptions see H. Immerwahr (1990: 103).

[37] New York 07.286.85, *ARV* 632.3, Richter and Hall (1936: pls. 109–10).

and it is possible that this was the name of the woman behind Hermes on the London vase as well. On the reverse of the New York vase *mainas* and *methuse* both appear as labels for women with thyrsoi.

Ironically, the women in these scenes are notable for the dignity of their demeanor. On the London vase *Mainas*, who holds a thyrsos with her right hand, rests her left hand on her hip and stands in a relaxed pose with much of her weight on her right foot. *Methuse* stands in a not dissimilar pose. Clearly the names are not descriptive, as none of the women in either scene shows any signs of being either mad or drunk. Rather, the vase painter has attached to traditional depictions of the nymphs, terms that refer to the effect the god can have on others. The terms have nothing to do with the figures depicted; without the labels there is nothing about them that would allow a viewer then or now to guess the terms.

These are early examples from a sizable group of companions of Dionysos on vases from the second half of the fifth century who are given appropriately Dionysian labels. Given the subject here the women obviously cannot be seen as mortals, nor is there reason to see later examples as mortals either.

On a hydria by the Villa Giulia Painter in New York a satyr carries a child to a woman who sits on a rock, wearing a nebris and holding a thyrsos (Pl. 23B).[38] Another woman stands behind the satyr. The child here is distinctly older; the Villa Giulia Painter is capable of making this distinction, which would suggest that the scene represents a story/stage in the god's growth different from that on the two kraters. The women should be nymphs, but little more can be said about the story aside from noting that the satyr is not Papposilenos. Satyrs are regular companions of nymphs, and their presence in depictions of the infant god need not be explained by a 'lost satyr play', as it often is.

On a pelike in Palermo by the Chicago Painter, a close follower of the Villa Giulia Painter, all of the figures are named (Pl. 24A).[39] A standing Hermes hands the infant Dionysos to a woman labelled *ariagne* (a variant on Ariadne). W. F. Otto has argued strenuously that this last inscription is not an error, but rather that Ariadne is 'maiden and nurse, or mother, at one and the same time'.[40] However, there is probably a simpler explanation for her appearance. On a pelike in Syracuse by the Villa Giulia Painter, a young male, similar to the London Hermes with the infant (petasos, chlamys, boots) faces a woman almost identical to the Chicago Painter's Ariagne, while another woman moves to the right (Pl. 24B).[41] The male here is

[38] New York x. 313. 1, *ARV* 623.69, *LIMC* III pl. 379, Dionysos 691.
[39] Palermo 1109, *ARV* 630.24, Zanker (1965: pl. 4).   [40] Otto (1965: 183).
[41] Syracuse 22177, *ARV* 622.48, *LIMC* III pl. 729, Ariadne 50.

named Theseus, the women Aithra and Ariadne. The similarity between the woman facing Theseus in Syracuse and the woman facing Hermes in Palermo is striking. The name Ariagne on the Palermo vase is most likely a simple error in naming similar figures. Ariadne would, of course, make more sense if the male were Theseus.

That the women in the Villa Giulia Painter's depictions of the young Dionysos are nymphs seems clear, as does the fact that some of them have been given the names of Dionysian characteristics. Similar figures appear in other scenes by the Villa Giulia Painter where it would also seem appropriate to call them nymphs. So, on a calyx krater in Karlsruhe a woman labelled *mainas* walks in a procession led by a white-haired satyr playing pipes and labelled Marsyas (Pl. 25A).[42] A balding boy satyr with a torch, labelled *posthon* (small penis)[43] walks in front of her while a satyr labelled *soteles* with a kantharos and thyrsos walks behind. Mainas also carries a kantharos and thyrsos; she wears a chiton and fillet over a wreath. The woman here should surely be seen as a nymph rather than as a mortal.

The nature of many other women on vases by the Villa Giulia Painter is less clear. Groups of women wearing chitons or himatia over chitons appear on many of his kraters and stamnoi. Only the objects the women carry distinguish them one from the other.[44] A skyphos and pipes are two of the more common attributes. Processions of these women appear on both sides of a stamnos in St Petersburg.[45] There one woman plays pipes, another plays a lyre, while others carry skyphoi and thyrsoi. The thyrsoi must define them as followers of Dionysos, presumably nymphs, but with reference to scenes by the same painter said to represent mortal women celebrating a festival of Dionysos, these women have also been identified as 'maenads'. Scenes by the same painter on a stamnos in Oxford show the complexity of the issue.

On one side of the Oxford vase a woman sits on a rock facing right; a woman behind her holding pipes moves to the left, while a woman in front of her holds up a skyphos (Pl. 26A).[46] The skyphos, a wine cup, and the pipes would seem to link them with the Dionysian women on the St Petersburg stamnos; however, on the other side of the Oxford vase Apollo with a lyre stands between two of these women, both holding pipes (Pl. 26B). Surely these women are Muses, who rank with the nymphs in their

---

[42] Karlsruhe 208, *ARV* 618.3, *CV* I, pl. 19.

[43] Henderson (1975: 40, 109) who suggests that by the time of Aristophanes, at least, the word had developed a more or less innocuous tone and might be translated 'wee-wee'.

[44] There is no consistency in the treatment of the women's hair. Some wear wreaths, some fillets, some sakkoi, some nothing.

[45] St Petersburg 806 (St.1714), *ARV* 620.32, Peredolska (1967: pls.122. 3–4, 123).

[46] Oxford 524, *ARV* 620.30, *CV* I pl. 28. 3–4.

semi-divine status.[47] If these women are Muses, and if the women with the
infant Dionysos on the kraters in London and Moscow are nymphs, then it
would seem to follow that the women on the St Petersburg stamnos are
nymphs as well.

The Villa Giulia Painter's most controversial scenes are on a series of
stamnoi where women are shown at an idol of Dionysos which consists of
a mask attached to a column with a cloak hanging down from it. These are
part of a larger group with similar scenes, conventionally called 'Lenaia
vases', which has received much attention from scholars since the discovery of the first of them at the end of the eighteenth century. Discussions
usually start from the assumption that these are mortal women participating
in an Attic festival. These scenes are discussed in the next chapter; however,
for our purposes here the important point is that the women in these scenes
are no different from the nymphs with the infant Dionysos, the Muses, or
the other nymphs in the painter's Dionysian scenes in St Petersburg,
Karlsruhe and New York.

In fact, on the last of the 'Lenaia Vases', a stamnos by the Dinos Painter
from the last quarter of the century, four of the women are given labels
which illustrate well the way 'names' are used in Dionysian scenes on Attic
vases during the second half of the century (Pl. 25B).[48] *Dione* holds a
skyphos and ladle, *Mainas* and *Choreia* beat tympana and *Thaleia* holds a
thyrsos and torch.

Of the four names, Dione and Thaleia can refer to specific figures from
myth, but this is of little help here. Hesiod mentions Dione twice in
Theogony, once (17) in a list of deities and once (353) as a sea nymph, daugh-
ter of Okeanos and Tethys.[49] Homer makes her the mother of Aphrodite
(*Iliad* 5. 370), but in classical times she is known primarily as the consort of
Zeus *Naios* at Dodona.[50] A fragment from Euripides makes her the mother
of Dionysos, but on a lost amphora from the end of the fifth century, Dione
was named together with Thyone, the other name for Semele.[51] On that
vase, in the presence of Dionysos and a satyr labelled *simos*, she held a phiale.
In none of the scenes does she have any special attributes or characteristics.

[47] Cf. Schwerin 1261, *ARV* 618.6, *CV* pls. 35–7. For a literary connection between nymphs and
Muses, see above, Ch. 3 n. 9.

[48] Naples 2419, *ARV* 1151.2, Arias, Hirmer, and Shefton (1962: pls. 206–7). See Heydemann (1880);
Fränkel (1912); Webster (1972: 68–73); Kossatz-Deissmann (1991).

[49] Tethys is named as one of the women dancing with satyrs on a contemporary cup, Warsaw
142458, *ARV* 1253.58, Lezzi-Hafter (1988: pls. 57, 58E, F).

[50] *LIMC* III s.v. Dione. West (1966: 156, 266); Kirk (1990: 99); Parke (1967: 69–70).

[51] Frag.177, *TrGF* 2. Lost, *ARV* 1316.2, Welcker (1851: III, pl.13. On a much-repainted vase by the
Dinos Painter (Louvre G 488, *ARV* 1154.27, *CV* 5 pl. 33. 1–3, 5) a woman with cymbals is said to be
Semele while a woman in front of her seems to be labelled Thyone. I have not seen this vase. See also
Ruvo 1093, *ARV* 1184.1, Sichtermann (1966: pls. 12, 17 K10).

In the *Theogony* (77) Thaleia is once one of nine Muses and once (909) one of three Charites, but her name means rich or plentiful, particularly applied to banquets, so it can also be associative.[52] She appears as a Muse with Melpomene, Kleio, and Euterpe in the wedding frieze of the François Vase and on a few red-figure vases from the second half of the fifth century.[53] On two red-figure cups by Oltos from the end of the sixth century, however, she appears in distinctly Dionysian scenes.[54] On one side of both cups an ithyphallic donkey stands between a satyr and a woman. On the Brussels cup the satyr *simaios* (flat-nosed) restrains the donkey while the woman Thaleia, who wears a short chiton, strikes it with a 'proto-thyrsos'. On the Compiègne cup, the satyr *eraton* (beloved) plays pipes, and the woman, in a long chiton, is *euope* (fair-eyes) who holds the donkey's tail as she strikes it with a stick. On this cup, however, *thalia* (a variant form of Thaleia) is one of three women with krotala on the other side; the other two are *chione* (snow white) and *rodo* (rose red). On a krater in Providence[55] from the last quarter of the fifth century, Thalia is one of two women (the other is *eudia* (fair weather)) who dance wildly between the satyrs *komos* and *oinos* (wine) to the music of *pothos* (longing). Here Thalia holds a thyrsos with her right hand, has a fawn skin draped over her left arm, and throws back her head as she dances. In these scenes she is simply part of the entourage of Dionysos, as on the Dinos Painter's stamnos where she holds a thyrsos and torch. Thalia also sometimes appears in Aphrodite's entourage on late fifth-century vases.[56] The label *choreia* above the woman who follows her there, beating a tympanon, simply means choral dance and music.[57]

As already noted, the Villa Giulia Painter and his colleague, the Methyse Painter use *Mainas* as a name for nymphs. It appears on a few later vases as well. On a krater in Warsaw from the third quarter of the Century *maina* holds a thyrsos as she reaches down to pet a fawn (Pl. 27A).[58] Beside her Dionysos watches a satyr, *onopion* (= *oinopion*—wine drinker) fill a krater with wine and a woman with a thyrsos, *polynika* (many victories) listens to

---

[52] I avoid the term 'personification' in discussing these labels because, as I attempt to demonstrate in what follows, I think that little thought is given to which names are included; rather, they are scattered about as vaguely appropriate names for companions of Dionysos.

[53] e.g. Paris, PP 308, *ARV* 1040.22, *CV* pl. 17. 4–8; Athens, *Deltion* 18 (1963) 2, pl. 34C; London E 805, *ARV* 1080.6.

[54] Brussels R 253, *ARV* 64.104, *CV* 1 pl. 2. 2; Compiègne 1093, *ARV* 64.105, *CV* pl. 14. 1–2, 5. Bruhn (1943: 65, 66) also found her name on a fragment with a nymph from the Campana collection (Rome, Villa Giulia, *ARV* 59.60); however, I have not been able to examine the fragments and cannot read the inscription on the photographs in the Beazley Archive.

[55] Providence 23. 324, *ARV* 1188.1, *CV* pl. 23.   [56] Burn (1987: 32–3).

[57] See Euripides, *Phoenician Women* 1265, Aristophanes, *Frogs* 336.

[58] Warsaw 142355, *ARV* 1045.6, *CV* Goluchow pl. 24.

the satyr *mimas* (?) playing pipes.[59] On a krater in Athens from the end of
the fifth century[60] *Mainas* stands with a thyrsos and tympanon at the foot of
Dionysos' kline while *ioleia* (violet), with a tray of fruit, stands at the head.
As with the other women, there is nothing distinctive about those with the
name *Mainas*; rather, it appears to be one of several given to women who
accompany the god.[61]

The Dinos Painter seems to have chosen the labels for the women from
a fairly large group of nouns and adjectives associated with Dionysos and to
have sprinkled them into his scenes without a great deal of care on whom
they landed. He could as well have chosen other names from the list and
not have changed the meaning of the scenes. While later authors tended to
make tidy distinctions between different types of nymphs, it is not at all
clear that these distinctions were common in fifth-century Athens. Semi-
divine women accompanied various deities on occasion, and their names at
times seem to have been interchangeable. So, for example, *choro* appears on
different vases as the name of a nymph with Dionysos, a Nereid, and a
Muse;[62] as already noted, Thaleia can be a Muse, a nymph, and one of the
Charites.

In any case, there is no reason to see any of the women to whom the
labels are attached as mortals, and, in fact, it is probably true that aside from
Ariadne, Semele and her sisters, mortal women do not appear in Dionysian
scenes on Attic vases before the end of the fifth century.

The two mortal women with whom Dionysos is explicitly associated in
early literature are his mother, Semele, and his sometime lover, Ariadne. A
named Semele first appears with him on a black-figure cup from the mid-
sixth century, but a named Ariadne is not shown with him on an Attic vase
until the second quarter of the fifth century, and there is no compelling
reason to see her as the woman with Dionysos on any Attic vases before the
last quarter of the sixth.[63]

---

[59] For the various uses of this puzzling name (names of a centaur, a giant, a man and a satyr) see *LIMC*
V s.v. Mimas I–III.   [60] Athens 12594, *LIMC* V, pl. 465, Ioleia 1.

[61] The earliest occurrences of the inscription *mainas* on Attic vases are from the mid-5th cent. by the
Villa Giulia Painter, who with his colleague the Methyse Painter, is responsible for three of the seven
known examples, see Kossatz-Deissmann (1991: 183–4). A fragment of a cup from the first quarter of
the 5th cent., once in the Castle Ashby collections (*ARV* 371.16, *CV* pl. 41. 1) was said by Furtwängler
(*Archäologische Zeitung* 1881, 302–3) to have the inscription *mai . . .* on it. Beazley (1929: 20) corrected
Furtwängler, noting that the drawing in Hartwig (1893: pl. 33. 2) was correct, showing lamda and a
blob. Boardman and Robertson in the *CV*, p. 25, repeat this correction. None the less, the fragment
continues to appear in lists of occurrences of *Mainas* on Attic vases, e.g. *LIMC* V s.v.Mainas.

[62] Once Berlin F 2471, *ARV* 1247.1, Lezzi-Hafter (1988: pls. 144–5); Munich 2619A, *ARV* 146.2,
LIMC III, pl. 220, Choro I, 1; Athens III Ephoreia, *LIMC* III, pl. 221, Choro III, 1.

[63] See T. Carpenter (1986: 21–5) where I have argued that the woman facing the god in some early
scenes is Aphrodite.

By all accounts Semele was killed before Dionysos was born, yet she appears named with the bearded god on three Attic black-figure vases from the second half of the sixth century, and she is named as one of his companions on a red-figure amphora from the second quarter of the fifth century and on several late red-figure vases.[64] The story of her death is an old one, so for her to appear on these vases the fact, if not an account, of her rescue from the underworld must have been known in Athens by the mid-fifth century.

The earliest surviving accounts of Dionysos' recovery of his mother date from the second century AD.[65] Pausanias gives two sites for the god's descent—the Alcyonian Lake at Lerna (2. 27. 5) and Troezen (2. 31. 2). Clement of Alexandria (*Protrepticus* 2. 32–4) tells an etiological story about figwood phalloi in which Dionysos pays an obscene price to a Prosymnus at Lerna to find the way to the underworld. There is no reason to think that this tale was known 600 years earlier in fifth-century Athens. If it had been, given its obscene character, it is hard to believe that Aristophanes would not have made some use of it in *Frogs* when an effeminate Dionysos is seeking instructions from Herakles on how to reach the underworld. In fact, Dionysos' need for a guide to the underworld in *Frogs* is puzzling since he had made the journey once before, and part of its humour may lie in its obvious untruth.

Some scenes that have been said to refer to the rescue of Semele show Dionysos in a chariot.[66] On a black-figure hydria in Berlin a woman named both Semele and Thyone stands beside a chariot Dionysos mounts; a goat stands in front of it.[67] Late sources explicitly state that Thyone was the name given to Semele after her return from the underworld,[68] though Pindar uses it once (*Pythian* 3. 99) with reference to her original encounter with Zeus. While his usual mount is a donkey, Dionysos is occasionally shown in or mounting a chariot from soon after the middle of the sixth century as on a fragment of an amphora by the Amasis Painter,[69] though it is never clear where he is going or where he has been. Chariots are appropriate vehicles

[64] Naples Stg. 172, *ABV* 203.1, *CV* 1 pls. 21–2; Florence 3790, *ABV* 260.30, *CV* 5 pls. 26.1–2, 28.1–2; Berlin 1904, *ABV* 364.54, Gerhard (1843: pls. 4–5). For red-figure, New York, White/Levy Collection, Bothmer (1990: no. 121), assigned to the Copenhagen Painter.

[65] e.g. Diodorus 4. 25. 4, Apollodorus 3. 5. 3. However Pindar, *Olympian* 2. 25 already placed her on Olympos.

[66] Kerenyi (1976: 161 n. 88 and fig.47); Arafat (1990: 45 n. 51).

[67] Berlin F 1904, *ABV* 364.54, see above, n. 64. Cf. Hearst 5589, Raubitschek (1969: 29–33. 7) where a woman (Semele ?) rides in a chariot beside which Dionysos stands and in front of which is a goat.

[68] See above, n. 65. See also Otto (1965: 71 and n. 31).

[69] Palermo, *ABV* 151.19, Karouzou (1956: pl. 42. 1). For Dionysos in chariots, see T. Carpenter (1986: 110).

for many deities, as on the François Vase, but they are also used for transport between realms. So, Herakles rides in a chariot to Olympos, and Hades uses a chariot to take Persephone to the underworld.

On the outside of an early red-figure cup in Tarquinia by Oltos, Dionysos mounts a chariot beside which a satyr plays a kithara (Pl. 18B).[70] Behind the chariot is a nymph labelled *kali[s]* with a small lion balanced on her shoulder and outstretched right arm, and behind her a satyr plays pipes. In front of the horses a nymph dangles a doe by a rear leg, and above her arm is a bearded snake suspended in front of the horses' heads. The lion recalls contemporary depictions of Dionysos in the Gigantomachy; the fawn recalls the god's madness. The name *Kalis* appears only one other time on vases, on a black-figure cup in Naples where Semele also appears.[71] The position of the bearded snake suspended in front of the chariot is unusual. From the mid-sixth century on through the first quarter of the fifth, snakes—often bearded—are sometimes carried (or worn) by women in Dionysian scenes, and snakes sometimes aid the god himself in his battle with the giants,[72] but apart from these scenes the occurrence of such snakes is limited primarily to funerary scenes where they have chthonic implications.[73] While these links may make plausible the suggestion that scenes of Dionysos and a chariot, with or without a woman, refer to his trip to the underworld to recover Semele, without further evidence, particularly inscriptions, it remains a suggestion. Against it is the fact that Semele's role in myth was to conceive Dionysos, and outside of that she has little place in the narrative tradition.[74] When she accompanies the god on vases she is little more than a visual epithet, and while there is substantial epigraphical evidence for her role in cult, this is not reflected in fifth-century imagery.[75]

Two different stories about the connection between Dionysos and Ariadne were known in fifth-century Athens. In the older (*Odyssey* 11. 324–5) Dionysos had Artemis kill Ariadne when she ran off with Theseus

---

[70] Tarquinia RC 6848, *ARV* 60.66, see Ferrari-Pinney (1988: 23–9. 3). For the inscriptions see *Monumenti inediti publicati dall'Instituto di Corrispondenza Archeologica* 10 pls. 23–4. In Arias, Hirmer, and Shefton (1962: 322) the inscription by the first women is given as *theos* rather than *thero* and the word *kalis* is given as *kalos* and is applied to the satyr. In Simon and Hirmer (1981: 95) the first inscription is also given as *theos*. Ferrari-Pinney (1988: 25) gives the inscriptions by the women as *thero, kal[e]* and *kali[s]*.

[71] Naples Stg.172, *ABV* 203.1. See above, n. 64.

[72] For bearded snakes see Guralnick (1974); also T. Carpenter (1986: 71 ff.). For chthonic implications in a depiction of Dionysos reclining see T. Carpenter (1995: 148–52).

[73] e.g. Paris, Cab.Méd. 355, *ABV* 346.8, Boardman (1974: fig. 220); Boston 63.473, *Para* 164.31*bis*, Carpenter (1991: fig. 316).

[74] There is one Attic depiction of the birth of Dionysos from Semele, Berkeley 8. 3316, *ARV* 1343.1, *CV* pls. 47–50.

[75] Otto (1965: 67–9). See also Henrichs (1990: 263 and n. 31).

to the island of Dia. Nothing more is known about this version,[76] but it must be the one to which Phaedra refers in Euripides' *Hippolytos* (339),[77] and Polygnotos' inclusion of Ariadne in the underworld in his fifth-century painting in the lesche of the Knidians at Delphi (Pausanias 10. 29. 3) also implies it. The other version, which first appears in what may be a later addition to Hesiod's *Theogony* (947–9)[78] calls Ariadne the wife of Dionysos, made immortal by Zeus, and later authors tell how Dionysos rescued the abandoned Ariadne on Naxos and subsequently married her.[79] So, two incompatible versions of the story seem to have been current at one time; in one Dionysos has Ariadne killed presumably because she abandons him; in the other Dionysos rescues Ariadne when Theseus abandons her.

The union between Dionysos and Ariadne depends upon her abandonment by Theseus. Evidence from vases and architectural sculpture shows that during the last quarter of the sixth century new Theseus stories began to appear in some quantity as he was rejuvenated or reinvented perhaps to become the hero of the new democracy in Athens. A late sixth-century date has been posited for a *Theseid* mentioned by Aristotle (*Poetics* 1451[a]) to provide the literary version of the painted scenes.[80] The appearance on black-figure vases during the last quarter of the sixth century of scenes best explained by the marriage of Dionysos and Ariadne suggests that this event may have been part of the revised interest in Theseus. Prior to these there are no confirmed depictions of Ariadne with Dionysos in Greek art.[81]

The earliest of these marriage scenes is on a black-figure amphora in Cambridge.[82] There the god holds a phiale while the woman, naked to the waist, who reclines beside him, reaches up to touch her wreath. Another phiale sits on the table beside the kline along with strips of meat, and under it a dog chews a bone. A small male stands by the table with an oinochoe, and at either end of the kline satyrs and nymphs cavort. On the other side of the vase a procession of satyrs moves to the right. One plays pipes, one carries a column krater and an oinochoe, and one carries a wineskin.

The scenes on a contemporary amphora in a New York collection clarify the meaning of the scenes on the Cambridge amphora.[83] There a man and a woman who is naked to the waist recline on a kline. Beside the kline is a table with food on it and at either end is a naked man, one holding out a wreath, the other dancing. On the other side a woman playing pipes leads a procession of three naked men who carry wine skins and a volute krater.

[76] Heubeck and Hoekstra (1989: ii. 97 on 324–5).   [77] Barrett (1964: 222–3 on l. 339).

[78] West (1966: 398).

[79] Apollodorus, *Epitome* 1. 8. For bibliography see Frazer's n. 2 p.136 (Loeb edn. vol. ii).

[80] See recently, Shapiro (1989: 144).   [81] Cf. Hedreen (1992: 31–66).

[82] Cambridge 48, *ABV* 259.17, *CV* 1 pl.10.

[83] New York, White/Levy Collection, Bothmer (1990: 140–1, no. 107).

Both vases tell the same story, one on the level of myth, the other on the level of mortal life. The scenes are most likely connected with a marriage celebration and here, unusually, the specific has borrowed from the generic.[84] The new scene with Dionysos and a woman reclining together on a kline is relatively common on black-figure vases during the last decades of the sixth century and the first decades of the fifth, particularly on hastily painted lekythoi, though in most the woman is fully clothed. It does not appear on red-figure vases.

A scene on a contemporary amphora in Boston should be considered in this context.[85] There Dionysos and a woman standing side by side face right while satyrs and nymphs cavort on either side of them. To the far right is the end of a kline. The atmosphere of the scene is highly erotic and the kline must be for Dionysos and the woman—satyrs and nymphs have no use for such furniture.[86]

The woman in these scenes should be Ariadne. She obviously cannot be Semele or Aphrodite or one of Dionysos' nurses, or a passing nymph he happened to fancy. The only other woman with whom Dionysos was said to be intimately associated was the Basilinna, the wife of the archon Basileus in Athens, who each year, perhaps during the festival of the Anthesteria, was 'married' to Dionysos, whatever that means, in or near the Agora. This possibility deserves some comment since it would require an explicit mixing on vases of the realms of Dionysian myth and Attic life and cult.

No ancient source tells of the nature of the union between the Basilinna and Dionysos,[87] but several red-figure vases, which date to half a century or more after the black-figure scenes, have been said to show elements of that sacred marriage.[88] Of a mid-fifth-century scene on a red-figure krater where Dionysos approaches a named Ariadne who reclines on a mattress, Simon has written that 'the picture shows an etiological myth closely connected with the sacred wedding of the Anthesteria'.[89] Burkert agrees that

---

[84] For a discussion of the antecedents of these scenes see T. Carpenter (1995). As noted there, the scene with the reclining couple on the New York vase is closely connected with an amphora by Lydos in Florence (70995, *ABV* 110.32, *LIMC* III pl. 388, Dionysos 756), where all of the figures are mortals.

[85] Boston 76.40, *Para* 144.1, *CV* I pl. 39.

[86] The immodesty of the scene on the Cambridge vase (and the implications of the scene on the Boston vase) is noteworthy. It has no parallels with any other deities in archaic art, and there is irony in this. Of the deities depicted in archaic art, Dionysos is the least sexual. Though he is often surrounded by promiscuous sexuality, he always appears fully clothed and disinterested—even in 5th cent. scenes he is only rarely shown naked. Also, in both literature and art he is singularly lacking in lovers. See Kaempf-Dimitriadou (1979); Jameson (1993).

[87] Pickard–Cambridge (1988: 11–12) for evidence and commentary. See also Hamilton (1992: 53–6).

[88] e.g. Simon (1963: 6–22).

[89] Tübingen 5439, *ARV* 1057.97, *CV* 4 pl.18; Simon (1983: 97); also (1963: 12); Avagianou (1991: 177–97).

in such scenes Ariadne and the Basilinna are interchangeable.[90] These conclusions are troubling in the way they require the merging of mythic and cultic traditions in an image that decorates the outside of a wine-mixing bowl. Given the little we know about the union between Dionysos and the Basilinna, it strikes me as unsafe to take this leap, particularly when the scenes with Ariadne can be more simply seen as part of a new Dionysian narrative on Attic vases that becomes increasingly popular toward the end of the century.

Contemporary with the first appearances of the scenes of Dionysos and Ariadne reclining together are black-figure depictions of the god reclining in the presence of an unnamed woman, and variations on these also appear on later red-figure vases. The earliest is a black-figure amphora in Boston where a woman dressed in a chiton and himation sits on the edge of a kline by the knees of the reclining Dionysos and offers him a flower.[91] A grape vine in which a satyr climbs grows up to the right of the kline and at the foot are two satyrs, one playing pipes, and a nymph with krotala. Here, too, the woman should be Ariadne; a named Ariadne in a similar pose on a recently published red-figure psykter-krater from the second quarter of the fifth century helps to confirm this identification (Pl. 27B).[92] The same pose is used for another named Ariadne sitting by the reclining Dionysos on a cup from the third quarter of the century in London.[93]

The romantic link between Dionysos and Ariadne, so popular in later centuries, starts with depictions of his rescue of her on Naxos. During the second quarter of the fifth century Attic vase painters showed a version of the Ariadne story in which Theseus abandons Ariadne at Athena's bidding and Dionysos rescues her.[94] The version is clearest on a hydria in Berlin where Athena waves Theseus off to the left while Dionysos leads Ariadne off to the right.[95] On an oinochoe by the Niobid Painter in Paris the meaning is unmistakable when Dionysos pursues Ariadne between Eros and Aphrodite.[96] On a hydria in London from the middle of the fifth century he leads her toward a pillow on the ground while a satyr plays pipes to the left and Aphrodite and Eros observe to the right.[97] On a contemporary fragment of a krater in Tübingen he stands in front of a mattress on which Ariadne reclines while Eros holds a phiale above her head.[98]

[90] Burkert (1983: 233). [91] Boston 01. 8052, *ABV* 242.35, CV 1 pl. 24.
[92] New York 1986.11.12, Christie's 16 July 1986, 141.
[93] London E 82, *ARV* 1269.3, see T. Carpenter (1995: 146–8, figs. 1–3).
[94] See Webster (1966: 21–31); *LIMC* III s.v. Ariadne I, L.
[95] Berlin F 2179, *ARV* 252.52, Kaempf-Dimitriadou (1979: pl. 22.1–2).
[96] Paris, Cab.Méd. 460, *ARV* 606.83, *LIMC* II pl. 133, Aphrodite 1357.
[97] London E 184, *ARV* 1113.4, *LIMC* II pl. 133, Aphrodite 1358.
[98] Tübingen 5439, *ARV* 1057.97. See above, n. 89.

Vivid imagery in the description of a mime of Dionysos and Ariadne at the end of Xenophon's *Symposion* (9. 2–7) should be mentioned here since the symposion described seems to have taken place in 421, though the essay was not written until *c*.380.[99] The pantomime is directed by the Syracusan dance-master who places an elegant chair (*thronos*) in the centre of the room and announces that Ariadne will enter the room (*thalamos*) set aside for her and Dionysos, that she will be joined by Dionysos who will come to her flushed with wine from a banquet with the gods, and that the two will disport themselves together. Ariadne then enters dressed as a bride and sits on the throne. Soon thereafter, announced by the sound of pipes, the young Dionysos enters, sits on her lap and embraces her. After some fondling they rise, kiss and caress each other again, and head off for their bridal couch.

The scene is romantic. It plays on emotions and titillates—to the extent that the married banqueters rush home to their wives and the bachelors swear that they will get wives! Certainly there are no parallels for this tone in any Attic depictions of Dionysos and Ariadne before the end of the fifth century. Though Eros sometimes appears in depictions of the rescue, he is more a statement of fact than of feeling. Even the half-naked Ariadne reclining with the god on the late sixth-century amphora in Cambridge provokes no emotions. Without the white paint that identifies her as a woman she would simply be another male symposiast.

The eroticism of Xenophon's description does find parallels in an entirely new group of Dionysian scenes which start to appear at the beginning of the fourth century, where a young, naked Dionysos sits or walks with Ariadne; often they have their arms around each other.[100] Two of the figures on the bronze krater found at Derveni *c*.330(?) provide a useful parallel to Xenophon's account; a naked young Dionysos sits with a leg resting on the lap of Ariadne who sits modestly next to him holding her veil away from her face.[101] Clearly the impulse that provoked these depictions is significantly different from the one that led to the fifth century scenes. The early stages of a trend toward romanticism appear in scenes on vases during the latter part of the fifth century, but the god remains relatively undemonstrative until the fourth. The union with Ariadne is a distinct episode in fifth-century imagery that has little or nothing to do with other episodes in the god's mythical life—in art or in literature. The focus on this episode by fourth-century painters is an expression of changing tastes and of a diminishing of the god's vitality in mainstream Attic culture. A discussion of this change belongs more appropriately in a study of fourth-century Attic and South Italian imagery.

[99] On the date see Anderson (1974: 66 n. 1).   [100] For examples see Metzger (1951: 110–54).

[101] Salonica, *LIMC* III pl. 386, Dionysos 755.

To conclude this discussion, it is perhaps worth reiterating the point that aside from Semele and Ariadne, the female companions of Dionysos on fifth century Attic vases are never mortals—never Greek women gone wild—nor is there reason to look to ritual to explain the scenes, poses, or attributes. Rather, when in groups or with satyrs they are nymphs who early in the century allude to narratives of the god's infancy and youth, but later, as their energy dissipates, come to represent, in some vague way, various Dionysian traits. Semele, who in the sixth and early fifth century can be the god's companion, particularly at official gatherings like the wedding of Peleus and Thetis,[102] appears less frequently as the century progresses, while Ariadne, who probably does not appear with the god before the late sixth century becomes linked with him in narrative scenes during the fifth, which during the fourth century take on a romantically erotic tone.

[102] e.g. at the wedding of Peleus and Thetis, Florence 3790, *ABV* 260.30, see above, n. 64; New York, White/Levy, see above, n. 64.

5

Worship?

WHERE in the previous chapter I suggested that the female companions of Dionysos on Attic vases would have been understood by Athenians as nymphs rather than as maenads, here I turn to some scenes said to show mortals (presumably Athenians) participating in worship of Dionysos, scenes which raise important questions about the value vase paintings can have as evidence for Attic worship of any sort. I start with a depiction of orgiastic worship on a krater in Ferrara, then turn to the so-called 'Lenaia vases', which seem quite clearly to be connected with some sort of worship of the god, and conclude with some observations on vase paintings often cited as evidence for Athenians' familiarity with ecstatic cult practices connected with Dionysos. The central question here is, on the basis of these images can we draw any firm conclusions about the nature of worship of Dionysos in fifth-century Athens?

From the outset it is important to remember that Attic vase painters relied heavily on conventions and that in what follows we are looking at the works of artisans who use visual images as a means of expression, but who more often than not looked to other visual images rather than to life to find their models. It is all too easy in the enthusiasm of the moment to forget this and to try to read scenes on vases as if they were photographic snapshots, an urge to be resisted.[1] It is also important to remember the nature of the objects on which the images appear.

The krater in Ferrara, found during excavations of a rich tomb in Valle Trebba at Spina in 1923, is attributed to the group of Polygnotos and dates to the third quarter of the fifth century (Pls. 28–9).[2] On it there are two related scenes in a frieze around the body of the vase. On one side, facing right, a bearded male and a female sit on thrones on a platform between columns in front of which is an altar with wood piled on it. The woman sits to the man's left. He wears a fillet and wreath in which two snakes are entwined; she wears a diadem or crown. They both hold sceptres and phialai from which liquid spills. A procession of three figures approaches

---

[1] For recent comments on this problem see Boardman (1990a).

[2] Ferrara 2897, *ARV* 1052.25, *LIMC* III pl. 406, Dionysos 869. For the most complete illustrations of the vase, see Aurigemma (1960: i, pls. 20–30).

them. A white-haired figure with a veiled liknon on his/her head is followed by a woman playing pipes who is followed by another beating a tympanon. Behind the building housing the seated figures a professional pipes-player (*aulete*), defined by his long ornamented chiton and *phorbeia*, faces to the left as he plays his pipes.[3] In front of him a woman and a girl dance wildly.[4] Both hold small snakes in their hands, and the older one has a snaky fillet similar to the one worn by the seated male.

The two scenes on the vase are defined by the orientation of the figures; the difference is one of focus indicating that the two should not be read as one continuous narrative but, perhaps, that they should be seen as two perspectives on the same subject. Under each handle a figure facing away from the building might be said to mark the division between the two scenes. On side B a woman playing pipes stands near the centre while a youth, five women, two girls, and a boy dance near her. Several of the dancers carry snakes and wear snaky fillets. One woman beats a tympanon and a boy clangs small cymbals. The scenes seem to depict mortals worshipping at a temple, and the term 'ecstatic' is probably appropriate to describe the nature of that worship. On one side the focus is on preparations for a sacrifice, on the other it is on wild dancing before or after the event.

Since the discovery of the vase the seated figures have been given many names.[5] Beazley, originally described the scenes as 'Dionysos and Ariadne in their temple with worshippers',[6] but later he wrote, 'God (Sabazios?) and goddess (Cybele?) with priestess and votaries dancing to the flute' citing Erika Simon with the comment 'her identification of the deities seems to me probable and preferable to my own (Dionysos and Semele or Ariadne)'.[7] Recently Gasparri, in *LIMC*, has listed the vase under the heading ' Assimilazioni' referring to the figures as 'Dionysos-Sabazio' and 'Kybele'.[8] Vermaseren, following Patitucci, also calls them 'Cybele' and 'Dionysus-Sabazius'.[9] For our purposes the important issue is whether or not those scenes show some aspect of the worship of Dionysos. More precisely phrased, the question is: did the vase painter intend the subject to be understood by his contemporaries in Athens as specifically related to Dionysos?

Every element of imagery in the scenes appears on other Attic red-figure

[3] In what follows I use 'pipes' to refer to double *auloi*, the reed-instruments which occur frequently in Dionysian scenes.

[4] The girl is half the size of the woman. This has nothing to do with an attempt to create a sense of depth; rather it indicates her age or possibly her status. My use of the terms boy and girl are based on the size of the figures on side B as well. For a similar use of size, see above, p. 39.

[5] For a summary of the various identifications see Naumann (1983: 172). Cf. Loucas (1992).

[6] *ARV*[1] 696.23.

[7] *ARV* 1052.25, Simon (1953: 79–87).

[8] *LIMC* II 496 no. 869.

[9] Vermaseren (1977–89: iv. 213); Patitucci (1962: 146–64).

vases but never in these combinations. The vase painter, then, was using conventional imagery to create a new scene, and we are probably safe in assuming that he knew the conventional contexts as well. Thus an attempt to interpret the scene should start with an examination of the various elements of imagery in their traditional contexts before trying to understand them in this new configuration.

The seated female wears a crown or diadem which is of a type worn by many goddesses on Greek vases and probably has no specific meaning. Likewise, her dress, comprised of a chiton and himation, is unexceptional. The sceptre is usually an attribute of Hera, particularly when the goddess is seated, but it can also be carried by other goddesses such as Persephone, Demeter, and Aphrodite.[10] The lion is her one distinctive attribute and, posed as it is, standing on her outstretched arm, it has parallels on one red-figure vase with a depiction of Hera in the Judgement of Paris[11] and in many depictions of nymphs associated with Dionysos, at least one by a painter from the same group.[12] The phiale which she has in her right hand is held, at one time or another, by almost every deity, male or female, who appears on Attic vases.[13]

The seated male wears a chiton and himation, dress worn by all of the senior male deities (and some of the junior ones) at one time or another. He holds a sceptre with his left hand—properly an attribute of Zeus, Hades, or mortal kings—and a phiale. His hair is long with curls hanging down over his shoulders. After the middle of the fifth century most bearded deities on vases have short hair or hair tied in a bun, with the exception of Dionysos for whom long curls such as these are characteristic.[14] However, this is not a rule; there are many depictions from this period of Hades, Zeus, and Poseidon with similar curls.[15] The seated male's only unusual attribute is his fillet with two snakes entwined about it, which is similar to the headgear

[10] London 95.10–31.1, *ARV* 583.1, *CV* 3 pl. 4. 1 (Persephone); Trachones, Geroulanos *ARV* 1154.38bis, *LIMC* IV pl. 212, Hades 29 (Demeter); Paris, Cab.Méd. 460, *ARV* 606.83, *LIMC* II pl. 133, Aphrodite 1357 (Aphrodite).

[11] Berlin F 2536, *ARV* 1287.1, *CV* 3 pl. 118. 1. For other depictions of Hera with a lion see Bologna 283, *ARV* 1151.1, *CV* 4 pls. 68. 3–5, 69, and Christie's (London) 28 April 1993, 36–7. 14 (a lekythos attributed there to the Brygos Painter). See also Lévêque (1949: 125–32).

[12] London E 462, *ARV* 1057.103 *Anz* 1977, 214, fig. 19. See also, Tarquinia RC 6848, *ARV* 60.66, Arias, Hirmer, and Shefton (1962: pl. 100); London E 510, *ARV* 307.8, Boardman (1975: fig. 207); Basle Lu 45, *Para* 352; Warsaw 142326, *CV* Goluchow pl. 13. 1. Dionysos himself can carry a lion this way, e.g. Ferrara 2892, *ARV* 1041.6, *LIMC* III pl. 375, Dionysos 656. See also Ancona 3125, *ARV* 595.66, *LIMC* IV pl. 149, Gigantes 377; Munich 8766, *ARV* 198.21bis, *Münchener Jahrbuch der bildenden Kunst* 31 (1980) 6–9.

[13] See Simon (1953); Patton (1990: 326).

[14] For examples by related painters: Harvard 60.343, *ARV* 1042.2, *CV* Robinson 2, pl. 46, 47.1; Copenhagen ABc 1021, *ARV* 1035.2, *CV* 4 pl. 146.

[15] e.g. Zeus: Naples 2041, *ARV* 1122.1, Kaempf–Dimitriadou (1979: pl. 16. 3–4); Poseidon and Hades: London E 82, *ARV* 1269.3, T. Carpenter (1995, 147, fig. 2).

worn by some of the worshippers. The snaky fillet is discussed in more detail below; suffice it to say here that there are no black- or red-figure depictions of Dionysos (or of any other god) with snakes in his hair.

The professional musician standing behind the seated figures is a well-established iconographic type and seems curiously out of place here. He wears a carefully defined mouthpiece strap (*phorbeia*) and theatrical chiton, and his wreath—laurel?—is different from those of all the other figures on the vase. Such figures are often shown on vases performing alone (on a *bema*), or accompanying athletes or actors.[16] They do not appear in depictions of sacrifice.[17]

A word should also be said about the setting. The two deities sit between Doric columns on a raised platform with an altar on the ground in front of it. The columns and platform most likely represent a temple with an altar properly placed in front of it.[18] It has recently been suggested that since the seated figures on the Ferrara vase are larger than the worshippers, they must be cult statues and the platform must be a statue base.[19] This conclusion strikes me as unlikely; the seated deities in the Panathenaic frieze on the Parthenon are larger than mortals, though they are certainly not intended to represent statues there,[20] but the important point here is that the suggestion does not clarify anything about the meaning of the scene. Worshippers making offerings to cult statues of gods are, of course, making offerings to gods.

Turning to the worshippers, the women and girls wear unexceptional chitons and have curls hanging down to or over their shoulders. The youth and the boy both have short hair and wear decorated smocks, much like the *exomis* often worn by Hephaistos in depictions of his Return by related painters.[21] The youth wears his over a chiton, as does a woman dancing beside him, while for the boy it appears to be the sole garment. Here the garment can probably be understood as a type of 'fancy dress' with a foreign flavour.[22] The objects carried by the worshippers include a *liknon*, tympana, cymbals, and snakes.

[16] e.g. London E 288, *ARV* 423.119, *CV* 5 pl. 47. 3 (performing alone); Basle Kä 425, *ARV* 430.31, Buitron-Oliver (1995: pl. 36, with athletes); Boston 03. 788, *ARV* 571.75, Boardman (1975, fig. 325, satyr play). For comments on *auletai* see Beazley (1955: 308–15); Taplin (1993: 69).

[17] A youth playing pipes is sometimes included in scenes of sacrifice (e.g. Boston 92. 25, *ARV* 1149.9, Bérard, Bron, *et al.* (1989: fig. 82)) but he wears neither *phorbeia* nor theatrical chiton; these seem to be reserved for performance.

[18] Cf., Ferrara T 6 C VP, *ARV* 1033, *Numismatica e antichità classiche. Quaderni ticinessi* 15 (1986) 59, fig. 13; Ferrara T 416 B VP, *ARV* 1144.21, *BABesch* 45 (1970) 64–5, figs.27–8 by related painters.

[19] Bérard, Bron, *et al.* (1989: 26).

[20] The liquid poured from the phialai of the seated figures on the vase also goes against seeing them as statues.

[21] e.g. Munich 2384, *ARV* 1057.98, *LIMC* IV pl. 398, Hephaistos 164a.

[22] For other uses of such an *ependytes* see Miller (1989: 329). See also T. Carpenter (1993).

The *liknon* or winnowing shovel with fruit and a phallos in it, often covered, is associated with Dionysian mysteries in Hellenistic and Roman times. However, as Nilsson has noted, 'in the classical age the liknon was not sacred in itself but like other profane implements sometimes occurred in sacral use.'[23] On the Ferrara krater there is clearly no phallos beneath the cover, and the *liknon* should probably be seen simply as a basket of offerings which may well (but need not) imply the presence of initiates of some sort.[24]

Two of the women have tympana. One, who is part of the procession led by the liknon-bearer, holds hers at chest height with her left hand and taps it with the fingers of her right. The other woman, on side B, who wears a snaky fillet, holds hers up in front of her face and beats it with the open palm of her right hand as she dances. The tympanon first appears on Attic vases around the middle of the century, not long before this vase was painted, and until the last quarter it is limited almost exclusively to Dionysian scenes.[25] The two earliest examples of it are probably those in two scenes connected with the madness of Dionysos by the Agrigento and Achilles Painters.[26] Soon thereafter it appears in depictions of the Return of Hephaistos in the Group of Polygnotos.[27]

Cymbals rarely appear on Attic vases before the last quarter of the fifth century. The first occurrence is in the Return of Hephaistos frieze on the François Vase *c.*570, where a nymph plays them (Pl. 12B).[28] That is, in fact, the only occurrence of cymbals on Attic vases before the mid-fifth century when they appear in a Return of Hephaistos and on the Ferrara krater, both from the group of Polygnotos.[29]

Snakes were common attributes of female companions of Dionysos during the early part of the fifth century, but they had not been regular elements in Dionysian scenes for nearly two decades when this vase was painted. In the meantime the role of snake handler was taken up by Furies. A winged Fury with a snake in her hair and snakes in her hands on a white-

---

[23] Nilsson (1957: 21–30).   [24] For various uses of the liknon see Bérard (1976: 101–14).

[25] By the end of the century it is often carried by Eros as well, e.g. New York 24.97.35, *LIMC* III pl. 648, Eros 692.

[26] Bologna 258, *ARV* 575.22, *CV* I pl. 50. 2–3; Paris, Cab.Méd. 357, *ARV* 987.2, Bérard, Bron, *et al.* (1989: 149, fig. 204). The fawn (torn in two on the Paris vase) probably connects these scenes with the madness of Dionysos. See above, Ch. 2 and T. Carpenter (1993).

[27] e.g. Berkeley 8. 983, *ARV* 1052.24, Anderson and West (1982: 65 no. 53); Naples, Capodimonte, *ARV* 1058.117. Also, by the Kleophon Painter, Ferrara 44894, *ARV* 1143.1, Alfieri (1979: 76–8, figs.174–7); Munich 2361, *ARV* 1145.36, *LIMC* IV pl. 401, Hephaistos 172c.

[28] Florence 4209, *ABV* 76.1. For an example of such instruments, see Wegner (1963: ii. 4, 61. 33). Cf. Bérard, Bron, *et al.* (1989: 29) where they are called castanets.

[29] Naples, Capodimonte, see above, n. 27. For other rare exceptions, Louvre G 488, *ARV* 1154.27, *CV* 5 pl. 33.1–3, 5 and Sotheby's (New York) 8–9 February 1985, 335.

ground lekythos in Basle from the second quarter of the fifth century is one of the earliest (Pl. 30A).[30] The similarity between her snaky crown and that of the mad woman on the Brygos Painter's cup in Munich[31] is striking, and it seems that vase painters transferred the image from Dionysian nymphs to the Furies. They continue to wear them on Attic vases from the second half of the fifth century and on South Italian vases from the fourth century.[32] There is a noteworthy distinction to be made between the snakes here and the snakes on earlier vases. In the earlier scenes there is always an under-current of violence—the women brandish the snakes, often as weapons with which they defend themselves from satyrs, and the snakes themselves are often fearful, bearded creatures. On the Ferrara vase the snakes are more worm-like, and the bearers do not seem to know quite what to do with them. It is as if the painter had been told that snakes were part of orgiastic worship and having no idea what people did with them, he turned to depic-tions of the Furies as an iconographic model and borrowed them back.

There are Dionysian parallels on other vases for much of the imagery on the Ferrara krater, yet there are no parallels that allow the seated male to be identified as Dionysos. Quite simply, he lacks any of the basic attributes used by vase painters to signal that a bearded male is Dionysos (kantharos, ivy wreath, and thyrsos), and he has an attribute in the snaky fillet that is never given to that god. A scene on a krater at Harvard by another painter from the group of Polygnotos illustrates this point (Pl. 30B).[33] There a 'standard' fifth-century Dionysos wearing an ivy wreath and holding a kan-tharos and an ivy stalk stands between a seated satyr playing pipes and a dancing nymph beating a tympanon. What is exceptional about this scene is that the dancing nymph wears a snaky fillet and is almost identical to dancers on the Ferrara krater. The hair, beard, and dress of Dionysos are, in fact, very close to those of the seated figure in Ferrara—only the attributes are different. For the painter the female figure with the snaky fillet and tym-panon could be Dionysian, but the seated male on the Ferrara vase could not be Dionysos.

Some women on the Ferrara krater dance in poses reminiscent of those of dancers in Dionysian scenes on contemporary vases,[34] and as already noted, the tympanon and cymbals are almost exclusively reserved for those scenes at this time. Yet males accompany the women here, while (aside

---

[30] Basle Lu 60, *LIMC* 3 pl. 595, Erinys 1. Of the snakes she holds, one is bearded at the other is not. Cf. Baltimore 48. 2019, *ARV* 774.1, Wehgartner (1983: pls. VI, 44, 46. 2–3).

[31] Munich 2645, *ARV* 371.15, Boardman (1975: fig. 218).

[32] See *LIMC* III s.v. Erinys. For the possible influence of Aeschylus' *Oresteia* on imagery see Prag (1985: 48–9).

[33] Harvard 1960. 343, see above, n. 14.

[34] Lawler (1927: 69–112).

from satyrs) males never accompany the dancing women (nymphs) in other Dionysian scenes.[35]

An identification of the seated woman on the basis of parallel images is even more problematic since it depends either on the lion or on the identity of her companion. The lion on vases can belong to Hera or to a nymph, but neither of these seems a likely identification. As we have seen, the identity of the male remains unclear.

Given the conventional nature of their craft, vase painters depend upon attributes to make clear the identity of many of their figures. By the mid-fifth century the attributes for most prominent male members of the Olympian family were well established, so it seems likely that by giving the seated male an unusual attribute the vase painter was signalling that the god was not to be seen as part of that traditional group. By using well-established iconographic devices in new combinations, he created something new.

Of course, other vase paintings were not his only sources of imagery. Monumental paintings, textiles, and various types of sculpture, most of which have been lost, could also have served as sources. Some surviving representations of Kybele, the name often given to the Phrygian Mother, Meter, in Greek literature connect her with the seated female on the Ferrara vase.[36] Depictions of Kybele in reliefs and terra cottas appear in Greece as early as the sixth century. Usually she sits on a throne, sometimes in a naiskos, holding a phiale, sometimes a tympanon. A lion often sits in her lap or beside her on the ground.[37] During the second half of the fifth century a statue of Meter by Pheidias or his pupil Agorakritos was placed in the Metroon in the Athenian Agora.[38] Arrian's description, which is supported by archaeological evidence, has the goddess seated on a throne holding a tympanon and accompanied by a lion.[39] Thus, there is evidence to suggest that the vase painter could well have known of a visual connection between Meter, the lion, and the tympanon. To date, however, Meter has not been recognized on any other Attic vases.[40]

If the vase-painter intended the seated female to be recognized as Kybele, who did he intend the seated male to be? Certainly not the boy Attis who,

[35] Metzger (1951: 148–53). Of course, this is not to say that males did not participate in Dionysian mysteries. See Burkert (1985: 290–3); Henrichs (1982: 147).

[36] See Burkert (1985: 177–9); Graf (1984: i. 117–20).

[37] Vermaseren (1977–89: esp. ii. 359, 362; vii. 89). See Roller (1991: 135–6).

[38] Pliny 36. 17; Pausanias 1. 3. 5; Arrian, *Periplus ponti Euxini* 9.

[39] See Naumann (1983: 159–69).

[40] The danger of assuming that a woman with a lion must be Kybele is highlighted by the long-accepted misidentification of the woman driving the lion-chariot on the north frieze of the Siphnian Treasury at Delphi as Kybele, while a recent study of inscriptions has shown that she is Themis. See Brinkmann (1985: 77–130, esp. 101).

in any case, has never been identified on Attic vases. Comparative visual evidence here has taken us as far as it can, and we must cautiously turn to textual evidence to proceed any further.

Versnel has recently shown that there is documentation for the introduction of relatively few new deities in Athens during the fifth century, and of the few only Adonis and Sabazios are male.[41] The scene on the Ferrara vase obviously has nothing to do with the wailing worshippers of Adonis. On the other hand, as already noted, some scholars have identified the seated male as Sabazios though there is little basis for that identification.

The earliest Greek reference to Sabazios is in Aristophanes' *Wasps* (8–10), produced in 422, where his effects are compared to a 'korybantic frenzy'. Elsewhere Aristophanes points clearly to his Phrygian origin, associates the music of pipes with his worship, and makes a comparison between the noise of women worshipping Adonis and Sabazios.[42] A century later Theophrastus (*Characters* 16. 4, 27. 8) implies a connection between Sabazios and snakes and shows that his was a cult into which one was initiated. The only other possible reference to Sabazios before the end of the fourth century is in a speech by Demosthenes (*De corona* 259–69) in which he accuses Aeschines of having participated in mystic initiations that involved, among other things, the handling of snakes, and this initiation has been connected with Sabazios through the ecstatic cry 'Euoi Saboi'. As Lane has recently noted[43] the first explicit connection between this cry 'Saboi' and Sabazios is from three centuries later in a passage from Strabo (10. 3. 18). There are no confirmed representations of Sabazios in all of Greek art before the Roman period, and it seems likely that if he did appear there would be some indication in his dress of his Phrygian origin.[44] There is little reason to see a connection between Dionysos and Sabazios in fifth-century cult; 'it is only in literary sources, usually hostile ones, that Sabazios is identified with Dionysos.'[45] There is no archaeological evidence supporting the identification.[46]

To summarize, there are good reasons to think that the vase painter did not want us to see the seated male as Dionysos, and there are no good reasons to think he wanted us to seem him as Sabazios. There is no iconographic evidence of any sort to support any other identification of him. There is iconographic evidence on vases to support an identification of the

---

[41] Versnel (1990: 102–23). [42] *Birds* 873; *Horae* frag. 566; *Lysistrata* 387–9.

[43] Lane (1989: iii. 3).

[44] So the Thracian Bendis, whose cult was officially installed in Piraeus in 429, is depicted on an Attic cup (Tübingen s/10 1347, *CV* 5, pl. 21) named, as a kind of Thracian Artemis wearing a nebris, alopekis and Thracian boots. See *LIMC* III s.v. Bendis.

[45] Johnson (1984: 1586).

[46] Lane (1989: iii. 14). Cf. a recent resurrection of Sabazios in Burn (1991: 123 and n. 54).

female as Hera or as a Dionysian nymph, but neither of these makes any
sense in the context. There is visual evidence outside of vase painting to
support her identification as Kybele, but if she were Kybele, it would be
hard to come up with a name for the male. The only argument favouring
Sabazios as her companion would be their common origin in Phrygia. In
short, the vase painter has given us insufficient data to name the deities. I
would argue that there was also insufficient data for fifth-century Athenians
to name them and that the omission was intentional. On the other hand,
the vase painter has used many images that have distinctly Dionysian connotations, and I would argue that this too was intentional.

It is easy to forget that the scenes that interest us here are decorations on
the outside of a large terra cotta vessel that was designed to hold wine and
was found with many other drinking vessels in a tomb associated with a
Greek-Etruscan emporium on the north-east coast of Italy.[47] It is not a
photograph nor is it a religious text. There is little reason to think that the
vase painter was concerned with the faithful reproduction of details of a
particular cult or that he expected his scene to be carefully studied. Rather,
I suspect, he expected that key images would quickly reveal meaning.

The professional musician (*aulete*) may be one of those keys. He, of all
the figures on the vase, seems out of place. His dress unmistakably defines
him as a professional, but it is not clear why he is there. His back is turned
to the sacrificial procession, so it is unlikely that he is connected with that,
and with women playing pipes (one in the procession on A; the other
amidst the dancers on B) he seems a bit superfluous.[48] Might the painter
have included him as a signal that the context for the scene is a performance, not real-life, much as a similar professional musician on a hydria in
Boston confirms that the satyrs with pieces of furniture there are to be
understood in the context of a satyr play (Pl. 16B)?[49]

As types of reference one might think of the performance of a
dithyramb—Pindar's description of Olympian revels in the presence of the
Great Mother (frag. 70b)[50] comes to mind—or of a tragedy such as
Aeschylus' *Edonians* (frag. 57 *TrGF*1) where he describes the holy rites of
Kotys, of which pipes and tympana are a part, or of a comedy such as
Eupolis (frags. 76 ff. *PCG*) that featured the same cult. The use of the cult
of Kotys by Aeschylus and Eupolis is of particular interest because that
cult was probably never admitted into Athens; thus, neither playwright had
to be concerned with the accuracy of his description.[51] The descriptions

---

[47] For the tomb context, see Aurigemma (1960: i. 37–62).

[48] For illustrations of the use of the pipes in cult scenes, see Nordquist (1992: 143–68).

[49] Boston 03. 788, *ARV* 571.75, Boardman (1975: fig. 325).

[50] Van der Weiden (1991: 52–85).   [51] Versnel (1990: 113).

only had to confirm popular beliefs about what went on in such strange cults.

Whether or not the scenes on the Ferrara krater are an allusion to a performance, I believe they are best understood as depictions of worship from a generic ecstatic cult. The hints of Dionysian imagery, which, it should be remembered, refer to myth, not daily life, set the tone. Kybele is the subject only as she is reflected in Dionysian imagery. Part of the effect of the scene probably came from its confirmation of popular prejudices, and one wonders if those prejudices are the source of the snakes, which had to be borrowed from the Furies.[52] A comparison between the scenes and Demosthenes' description of an initiation into a mystery cult a century later is useful here in part because of the similar details. The event had taken place many years before, and Demosthenes was obviously not striving for accuracy in his account but was trying to embarrass Aeschines and sway the Athenian jury. An accomplished orator, he knew which images would impress his audience and which prejudices to play upon. He probably also knew that not many members of the jury knew much about ecstatic worship. So, I would argue, the vase painter here chose his subject for its value as entertainment and chose his images for their dramatic effect. If the krater was ever used in a symposion, one can only assume that the response of the symposiasts to the scenes was not one of thoughtful introspection or holy awe.

This reading of the scene is plausible and perhaps 'true'. Based as it is on iconographic parallels from other Attic vases, it is on a sounder footing than is a reading that starts with an assumption that the scenes represent a specific cult practice and then proceeds through the scraps of surviving textual evidence in search of a match. However, the iconography of Attic vases exists within a kind of closed circle, so a comparative reading by itself must inevitably create a loop and come back on itself. The critical task is to break out of that loop by finding a way to link the rich, closed world of iconography that we know quite well with life and thought in fifth-century Athens. As I have argued before, it is an undertaking that requires the cooperation of scholars from the various disciplines that make up classical studies and, as such, it has not yet been accomplished. Suffice it to say for the moment that as documentation for religious activity in fifth-century Athens, these scenes are to be treated with utmost caution.

Scenes on a group of red-figure vases, mostly stamnoi, with women at a mask-idol of Dionysos have usually been interpreted as depictions of

---

[52] As Bremmer (1984: 268) has pointed out 'we do not have a single literary report outside of the *Bacchae* that [women] handled snakes in the maenadic ritual'.

mortal worship. The vases, conventionally called 'Lenaia vases', have received much attention from scholars since the discovery of the first of them at the end of the eighteenth century; strenuous attempts have been made to identify the festival represented or, more recently, to interpret the religious significance of the images.[53]

A stamnos in Boston is typical of most of these vases (Pl. 31).[54] On one side two women, who wear himatia over chitons, flank a table on which two stamnoi stand on either side of a stack of cakes or bread. Behind the table is a column to which a bearded mask is attached. A chiton and himation hang down from the mask while ivy sprigs stick out above it. The women are dignified figures—sisters of the nymphs on kraters by the same painter in London and Moscow.[55] Both hold skyphoi, and the one to the left dips into a stamnos with a ladle.

The series of stamnoi, most dating to around the middle of the century, start with the Villa Giulia Painter, who puts women at the mask-idol on ten vases, and it continues with his follower, the Chicago Painter.[56] The Villa Giulia Painter also paints stamnoi with similar women without the mask-idol but with the table and others without either the mask-idol or the table. The Chicago Painter puts women at the mask-idol on only one of his stamnoi but puts similar women on at least eight others, sometimes at a table, sometimes not.

The mask-idol first appears on a group of black-figure vases, mostly lekythoi from a small group of workshops, at the beginning of the fifth century. Women move about the idol. Sometimes satyrs or ithyphallic donkeys join the women, and on one lekythos a woman grabs and twists the head of a fawn.[57] This gesture recalls the Hera-induced madness discussed earlier as does a dancing woman holding a deer on the earliest red-figure depiction of the mask-idol, on a cup by Makron (Pl. 21).[58] Details on the black-figure vase and on Makron's cup allude to myth, and the women should be seen as nymphs. Nymphs at the mask-idol are no less appropriate than satyrs at a herm, of which there are many red-figure examples.[59]

On the last of the 'Lenaia' vases, a stamnos in Naples by the Dinos Painter from the last quarter of the century, the mask-idol, the table with the stam-

[53] Frontisi-Ducroux (1991) has undertaken a thorough review of the scholarship. See also, Pickard-Cambridge (1988: 30–4). For discussions of the scenes see also Durand and Frontisi-Ducroux (1982: 81–108) and Bérard, Bron, *et al.* (1989: 151–65). See above, Ch. 4.

[54] Boston 90. 155, *ARV* 621. 34, *RA* 1982, 84, 89–91 figs. 1, 4–6.   [55] See above, Ch. 4 n. 35.

[56] For the painters see *ARV* 618–31; Robertson (1992: 169–73). For a catalogue of 'Lenaia vases' see Frontisi-Ducroux (1991: 233–53).

[57] Eleusis 2409, *ABV* 504.18, Frontisi-Ducroux (1991: fig. 74).

[58] Berlin F 2290, *ARV* 462.48, Simon and Hirmer (1981: pl. 169).

[59] e.g. Dresden ZV 2535, *ARV* 531.29, *LIMC* III pl. 314, Dionysos 161; Copenhagen 598, *ARV* 873.30, *CV* pl. 158.9.

nos on it, and the women are all in place, but there some of the women wear nebrides, one beats a tympanon, two swing torches as they dance, and some of the women are named (Pl. 25B).[60] On the other side is a procession of similar women. The woman on the front of the vase who holds a skyphos and ladle to the left of the mask idol is *Dione*. The woman with a tympanon to the right of it is *Mainas*. On the other side a woman with a thyrsos and torch is *Thaleia* and the woman with the tympanon behind her is *Choreia*. The poses of the women in this scene connect them with the nymphs on Makron's cups, while the names connect them with nymphs on vases by the Villa Giulia Painter in London, Moscow, Karlsruhe, and New York.

The women on both the earliest and the latest vases with the distinctive mask-idol on them are nymphs, not mortals. A woman holding a satyr child on a mid-century stamnos by the Phiale Painter should also be a nymph (Pl. 32A), as should a woman playing pipes as a satyr offers a kantharos to a mask idol on an unattributed stamnos of the same date (Pl. 32B).[61] It is entirely reasonable to conclude that the women on the other 'Lenaia vases' should also be understood as nymphs.

The vase shape to which the name 'stamnos' has been given by modern scholars seems to have originated in Etruria, and thus it is perhaps not a coincidence that most Attic stamnoi have been found in Italy, including most of the 'Lenaia' stamnoi, none of which has been found in Greece.[62] Also, the only depictions of the stamnos shape on Greek vases are precisely on these stamnoi, where it is shown that it could be used in place of a krater for mixing wine. There are few Attic stamnoi later than the Dinos Painter's, though the shape continued to be made in Italy. There is reason to see the Attic stamnos as primarily an export commodity; however, as Frontisi-Ducroux has rightly noted, it would be unwise to conclude that the iconography was composed on demand.[63] On the other hand, it would be equally unwise to conclude that the scenes were careful records of female behaviour at an Attic festival.

I suggest that the 'Lenaia' stamnoi, probably produced as export commodities, were decorated with unspecific Dionysian scenes composed of stock Dionysian elements. The women are the nymphs we have seen in

[60] Naples 2419, *ARV* 1151.2, Arias, Hirmer, and Shefton (1962, pls. 206–7). For a more detailed discussion of this vase see above, Ch. 4, pp. 60–2.

[61] Warsaw 142465, *ARV* 1019.82. Oakley (1990 pls. 62A–B and p. 36) for a discussion of the scene. Socrates, in Xenophon's *Symposion* (5.7) refers to Naiads as the mothers of Silenoi. See also *Homeric Hymn* V, 262–3; Hesiod frag. 123 (Merkelbach–West) and above, Ch. 3. Louvre G 532, Froutisi–Ducroux figs. 85–6.

[62] For the stamnos, see Philippaki (1967); Isler-Kerényi (1977); Getty Museum (1980).

[63] Frontisi-Ducroux (1991: 69–70).

other scenes, and, as I argue in the next chapter, the mask-idol is simply a traditional rustic form that any Athenian would have recognized, and as such it is no more unusual or significant than the thyrsos or pipes or kantharos carried by some of the women. In fact, the only unique element is the stamnos on the tables, and vases of that shape seem to have their reference outside of the loop in Etruria, which seems to have had the principal market for the vessels. As with the Ferrara krater, we must exercise extreme caution if we intend to use the 'Lenaia vases' as documentation for any specific aspect of religious life in fifth-century Attica.

E. R. Dodds, in a much-quoted study of maenadism, wrote of 'certain resemblances in points of detail between orgiastic religion of the *Bacchae* and orgiastic religion elsewhere, which are worth noticing because they tend to establish that the "maenad" is a real, not a conventional figure'.[64] One of these points is what he calls 'the carriage of the head in Dionysiac ecstasy'. He notes that we see 'this back-flung head and upturned throat in ancient works of art', implying that this pose is an expression of the to and fro tossing of the head mentioned by Euripides (e.g. 150, 930). Though the specific visual evidence he cites is from much later gems and reliefs, he notes that Lawler 'finds a strong "backward bend" of the head in 28 figures of maenads on vases'.[65]

In the half century since Dodds wrote that essay, the idea that depictions of 'maenads' with their heads thrown back on Attic vases express the painters' awareness of ecstatic behavior in Dionysian cult has become something of a truism.[66] However, an analysis of the early scenes where this pose first appears suggests that those vase painters may have had something else in mind.

The Kleophrades Painter is one of the early painters to use the pose, on a pointed amphora in Munich (Pl. 33A).[67] On one side of this vase Dionysos moves vigorously to the right between two nymphs who use their thyrsoi to fend off amorous satyrs. On the other side a satyr playing pipes moves to the right between two nymphs with thyrsoi, one who moves off to the left, the other to the right in front of him. The nymph to the right is shown with her head thrown back and her mouth open in precisely the pose often said to represent an ecstatic state.

---

[64] Dodds (1951: 273). This essay was originally published as 'Maenadism in the Bacchae', in *HSCP* 33 (1940) 155–76.

[65] Ibid. 280 n. 25. See Lawler (1927: 101–2). Also Dodds (1960: 184–5, n. on 862–5).

[66] e.g. Arias, Hirmer, and Shefton (1962: 330); McNally (1978: 121); Houser (1978: 38 n. 11); Henrichs (1987: 105); Schöne (1987: 146–50).

[67] Munich 2344, *ARV* 182.6, Arias, Hirmer, and Shefton (1962: figs. 122–4, pls. xxx–xxxi).

That pose, however, can have another meaning. It is the one adopted by red-figure painters early in the fifth century to show that a figure is singing, and during the first quarter of the century it is a convention often used in symposion scenes.[68] Perhaps the most useful comparison for the woman on the Kleophrades Painter's amphora is a kitharode on a contemporary amphora in New York by the Berlin Painter (Pl. 33B).[69] The angle of the head and the open mouth of the youth here are the same as the nymph's. Given the satyr playing pipes behind her, it makes sense to conclude that she too is singing, and the same can be said for many of the nymphs shown in the pose on vases from the first half of the century.

A cup by the Brygos Painter in Paris is instructive here (Pl. 34A & B).[70] On the inside Dionysos, with his head thrown back and his mouth, open plays a lyre as satyrs with krotala dance on either side of him. There are two scenes on the outside of the cup; in both a satyr is shown playing a lyre and singing in precisely the same pose as the god on the inside. On one side a satyr wearing Thracian boots and a leopard skin follows the god who walks beside a donkey and is preceded by a satyr with a wineskin who holds a leopard by the tail. A nymph with a thyrsos and a snake follows the procession. On the other side the singing satyr is preceded by a nymph, her head thrown back like his, and followed by a satyr pestering a nymph and a satyr in Thracian boots who plays pipes while another nymph dances. The scene has virtually all of the elements associated with the Thracian narratives discussed above.[71] Like most Dionysian processions going back to the François Vase, it is a noisy affair, but in addition to the sound of pipes, lyre, and krotala, there is singing here. The back-flung head is introduced on Attic vases to indicate song, not ecstasy.

Another element of imagery often said to show the 'intense emotions released by ecstatic cult' is the 'rapturous expression' or the eyes that 'stare wildly' of some 'maenads' on fifth-century Attic vases.[72] The dancing nymph on the white ground interior of a cup by the Brygos Painter in Munich is often cited as a prime example, as are the nymphs on the pointed amphora by the Kleophrades Painter.[73]

Expressions are precisely what do *not* appear on the faces of figures on Attic vases, particularly during the first half of the fifth century. A mouth

[68] See Lissarrague (1990c: 123–39).

[69] New York 56.171.38, *ARV* 197.3, Boardman (1975: fig. 152. 2). See also, Louvre G 122, *ARV* 428.10, Buitron-Oliver (1995: pl. 13); once Küsnacht, Hirschmann, Buitron-Oliver (1995: pl. 2. 4).

[70] Paris, Cab.Méd. 576, *ARV* 371.14, Boardman (1975, fig. 255 (I)) and Bérard, Bron, *et al.* (1989: 142, fig. 202 (A, B)).

[71] See above, Ch. 3.   [72] e.g. Henrichs (1987: 105); Otto (1965: 94).

[73] Munich 2645, see above, n. 31; for the pointed amphora see above, n. 67.

might be opened slightly to show strain or pain,[74] but almost all faces are idealized profiles that express nothing. The first quarter of the fifth century is also the time when vase painters slowly learn how to depict a profile eye, rather than a frontal eye, in a profile face, and the intermediate stages can seem quite odd. Taken by themselves and viewed from a modern perspective, the faces and eyes of figures on red-figure vases might be seen as meaningful, but viewed within the context of developing style they clearly are not. Far from being an innovation, the style of the Brygos Painter's white ground nymph is quite traditional, even mannered. Martin Robertson writes of her that the figure shows the 'sterile conventionality into which Greek art might have lapsed if great spirits had not dared to break with the archaic tradition'.[75] All this leads to the conclusion that depictions of dancing or singing nymphs on red-figure vases are not reliable evidence for ecstatic cult practices or maenadic ritual in Athens during the first half of the fifth century.

That being said, Henrichs is surely right in his comment that 'regardless of the extent to which the Attic vase-painter preserved authentic details of cultic maenadism, they created once and for all the image of the ideal or archetypal maenad.'[76] During the second half of the fifth century the pose with 'back-flung head' continues to be used for Dionysian nymphs, but it is less often used for other singers. Whether vase painters toward the end of the century, like the Eretria Painter, continued to understand the convention as a representation of singing or not is unclear.[77] When the Meidias Painter gives the pose to women dancing in the presence of Aphrodite and Eros where cymbals and a tympanon provide the only music, it is unlikely that we are to think of the women as singing.[78] The poses are repeated in the maenad reliefs said to be copies of Attic works by Kallimachos from the end of the fifth century, and these women can have nothing to do with song.[79] In other words, in post-Euripidean Athens the women with 'back-flung heads' may well have come to represent maenads in an ecstatic state.[80]

---

[74] e.g. Louvre G 103, *ARV* 14.2, Boardman (1975: fig. 23, Antaios); Berlin F 2278, *ARV* 21.1, Boardman (1975: fig. 50.1, Patroklos). Rare examples of a frontal face may serve the same purpose; see Korshak (1987).

[75] Robertson (1992: 109).   [76] Henrichs (1987: 105).

[77] e.g. Berlin F 2532, ARV 1253.57, Lezzi-Hafter (1988: pl. 26. 7).

[78] Louvre MNB 2110, *ARV* 1314.14, Walter (1985: 75, fig. 71).   [79] See Fuchs (1993: 521–4).

[80] Picon (1993: 96) notes that 'it seems as if statues of maenads did not appear in Greek art until the fourth century'.

6

Beards

MOST of the surviving narratives about Dionysos (written or visual) tell of
events that took place during his childhood or youth, but prior to the middle of the fifth century the Dionysos who appeared in Greek art was almost
always a bearded adult, even when he was shown in episodes that must have
taken place during his youth.[1] Then, in the 430s Pheidias put a beardless
Dionysos in the east pediment of the Parthenon and probably in the east
frieze. By the last quarter of the century this beardless Dionysos appeared
on pots by the Dinos Painter, and almost immediately the new form
became the dominant one on vases.[2] In sculpture the two forms continued
to appear side by side on into Roman times.[3]

The reclining nude male in the east pediment of the Parthenon (Figure
D) is most often identified as Dionysos, though he has also been given a
variety of other names (Pl. 35A).[4] Since the identification is still disputed by
some[5] and since it is of considerable importance for this discussion, a re-
examination of the evidence is in order. Arguments for the identity of the
figures in the pediment are of two types: iconographic/archaeological and
literary/historical. The iconographic arguments depend on attributes and
parallels in surviving imagery; the literary historical arguments use myth, literary connections and cult practices to determine who *should* be present,
and who *should* be near whom at the Birth of Athena.

The iconographic evidence for an identification of Figure D is of two
kinds: attribute and pose. The nude figure sits on a cloak thrown over the
skin of a feline on a rock. In fifth century Attic iconography Dionysos and
Herakles are the two figures usually associated with cat-skins—Dionysos

---

[1] For two early exceptions see above Ch. 3 nn. 21 and 30 and T. Carpenter (1993).

[2] See below, n. 77. A similar change can be traced in the coinage of Sicilian Naxos. See Cahn (1944);
Kraay (1976: 206, 217, 225).

[3] Pochmarski (1974).

[4] For chronologically arranged tables showing the various identifications see Michaelis (1871: 165);
Brommer (1963: 181); Palagia (1993: 61). Identifications (aside from Dionysos) include: Aietes, Apollo,
Ares, Herakles, Hermes, Iacchos, Kekrops, Kephalos, Mt Olympos, Orion, Pan, and Theseus. Of 64
works cited in the three lists, Dionysos is named as figure D in 35.

[5] e.g. R. Carpenter (1962: 265–8, Ares); E. Harrison (1967: 27–58, Herakles); Jeppesen (1984:
267–77, Herakles or Orion). Cf. Pochmarski (1984: 278–80, Dionysos).

with a leopard's and Herakles with a lion's. The sculptor has not included the animal's head here, so it is not clear which kind this is. In early publications of the Parthenon sculpture Visconti called figure D 'Hercule' and compared him to the figure of Herakles seated on a lion skin on a coin from Croton *c*.360. On that coin the lion's head is clearly shown making the identity of the figure certain.[6] More often than not, the head is included in depictions of Herakles' lion skin in classical vase paintings and sculpture, and this is not surprising since it was the skin of a specific lion (Nemean) and a regular attribute. The same is not true for Dionysos. When leopard skins are included in Dionysian scenes on classical vases, the head is often omitted. The name vase of the Dinos Painter in Berlin with a figure of Dionysos very similar to Figure D is a case in point (Pl. 35B).[7] The leopard skin on which the satyr sits is distinguished by its spots, not by its head. For Dionysos the skin is a secondary attribute. Also, it would have been barely visible from the ground some fifteen metres below and was surely not intended by the sculptor to be a major device for the identification of the figure.[8]

Arguing that the figure is Herakles, Harrison writes: 'if our recognition of the person depended on which kind of cat it was, the artists would have shown the head, but he expects us to know, by the time we see the big feline paw sticking out from under the folded mantle.'[9] Ironically, the observation supports an identification of Dionysos. Had the sculptor intended Herakles, he would have included a head, but since he meant Dionysos, for whom the skin is a secondary attribute, he only included the paws, which might well have been painted. Other attributes, then, would have served to identify him.

Rhys Carpenter called attention to a groove at the back of the figure's head and argued it indicated that a metal helmet had been fitted.[10] This seems unlikely, if only because there is little room for it.[11] Smith, in a British Museum *Catalogue of Sculpture* wrote that the 'headdress is in the form of the krobylos', and Olga Palagia has recently explained the groove as remains of 'somewhat old-fashioned braids bound across the nape of the neck'.[12]

---

[6] For references to early descriptions see Smith (1892: 107). For the coin, Kraay and Hirmer (1966: pl. 94. 270R).

[7] Berlin F 2401, *ARV* 1152.3, *BCH* 108 (1984) 153, fig. 28.

[8] Carrey did not indicate it in his drawing. See Bowie and Thimme (1971).

[9] E. Harrison (1967: 44).   [10] R. Carpenter (1962: 268).

[11] See the photograph of a cast of the figure in place, Brommer (1979: pl. 138).

[12] Smith (1892: i. 107); Palagia (1993: 19). The Dinos Painter's Dionysos in Berlin (see above, n. 7) wears a headband; Palagia (1993: 31 n. 19) dismisses that possibility for Figure D; 'The braids are rather perfunctory but can hardly be explained as a headband in this low position.'

Both hands are missing from the statue:

The right arm is bent, but, as the hand is wanting, we can only form conjectures as to what its action may have been. It probably held a spear, or some other long object, the end of which may have attached to the left ankle at the place where a dowel hole is still visible. According to some writers, the hole served for the attachment of the laced work of a sandal in bronze.[13]

If the figure held a thyrsos, that would, of course, have served to identify him as Dionysos. Harrison would have the figure hold a club with his left hand, its lower end resting on the cornice, and wave at rising Helios with his right. The only possible iconographic parallel for this gesture is on a group of black-figure vases from the end of the sixth century where Herakles sits on a rock and waves to Helios whose chariot rises from the sea.[14]

While the absence of a head on the cat-skin may increase the probability that Figure D is not Herakles, the missing attributes make any identification tentative at best. Pose, however, is more useful here. As already noted, the Dinos Painter used the same pose a decade later for Dionysos on his name vase in Berlin, one of the earliest vase depictions of the god as a beardless youth.[15] A century after the Parthenon was dedicated the sculptor of the frieze on the choregic monument for Lysikrates in Athens (335/4) (Pl. 36A)[16] used the same pose for his Dionysos. There the nude god sits on his cloak on a rock. He holds a cup in his left hand and strokes the head of an affectionate leopard with his right. At the least, one can conclude that the sculptor of that frieze thought Figure D was Dionysos; given the proximity in space and time, the similarities cannot be accidental.[17] The reclining Herakles appears in Greek sculpture toward the end of the fourth century, and then he is almost always bearded.[18]

The pose of Figure D is different from the poses of other pedimental reclining figures both here (e.g. west pediment A and W) and elsewhere

---

[13] Smith (1892: i. 107). Palagia (1993: 19) has recently suggested that the hole in the ankle 'may well have served for the fastening of an anklet' such as the one worn by Dionysos riding a panther on a late 4th-cent. pebble mosaic from Pella.

[14] E. Harrison (1967: 44–5 and n. 141); see also Jeppeson (1984: 436, nn. 48 and 49, pl. 24.1). See Taranto 7029, *ABV* 518.21, *LIMC* V pl. 91, Herakles 2546.

[15] See above, n. 7. Also, see Ruvo 1093, *ARV* 1184.1, *LIMC* III pl. 339, Dionysos 372.

[16] The frieze itself is still in place on the monument but has been badly damaged by weather, pollution and vandalism. However, Elgin had casts taken of it (one copy is in the Ashmolean Museum Cast Gallery) and drawings (incomplete) from the casts are published in Hawkins (1842: pls. 22–6). See now Ehrhardt (1993).

[17] Robertson (1975: 78 n. 14) warns that the borrowing of such a form does not necessarily imply the borrowing of the content as well.

[18] *LIMC* IV s.v. Herakles I, C, 4 (1088–65).

(e.g. Temple of Zeus at Olympia). It is the pose of a symposiast reclining on his left elbow, and the essence of the pose can be traced in vase painting back to the beginning of the sixth century, and ultimately to an Assyrian model.[19] Symposiasts usually wear cloaks over the lower body as on the Dinos Painter's name vase, but the pose is the same. The sculptor's decision to leave Figure D nude is not iconographically significant. John Boardman has pointed out that the symposion form was 'deemed inappropriate for Olympians . . . it was only exceptional demi-gods and heroes like Dionysos, Hermes and Herakles who might be shown reclining'.[20] In fact, only Dionysos and Herakles appear regularly as solitary symposiasts, and of these it is Dionysos, as wine god, who is a principal deity of the symposion.[21]

Harrison writes that 'if we had the figure (D) alone outside the context of the pediment no one would think first of calling him Dionysos'.[22] In fact, if we had determined that he represented a hero or a god, we could *only* have concluded that he was Dionysos or Herakles, and given the several parallels in vase painting and sculpture for Dionysos, and given the use of the cat-skin as a secondary rather than a primary attribute, probability comes down on the side of Dionysos. To this is added one further point for the iconographic/archaeological argument. Dionysos regularly appears in depictions of the birth of Athena on Attic vases while Herakles does not. That subject is a common one on black-figure vases where it appears before the middle of the sixth century, and it continues in red-figure until the second quarter of the fifth.[23] From the start Dionysos is sometimes included as one of the attendant deities, and he appears on one of the latest red-figure examples as well.[24]

Herakles does appear in one certain depiction of the birth of Athena on a black-figure amphora from the middle of the sixth century assigned by Beazley to Group E, a group which includes several depictions of that subject.[25] Brommer suggests that Herakles' presence here is probably a result of the painter confusing the scene with another similar one, the introduction of Herakles on Olympos.[26] On another vase, roughly contemporary with this one, Herakles appears in a scene that may represent a moment

---

[19] See Dentzer (1982: 51–68).   [20] Boardman (1990*b*: 124).

[21] Achilles also reclines on a solitary kline, but on Attic vases only in depictions of the Ransom of Hektor. For a unique example of a divine symposion, see London E 82, *ARV* 1269.2, T. Carpenter 1995: figs. 1–3).

[22] E. Harrison (1967: 44).

[23] *LIMC* II s.v. Athena with bibliography; Arafat (1990: 32–9).

[24] For black-figure examples see Palagia (1993: 32 n. 30). On London E 410, *ARV* 494, one of the latest red-figure examples, it is worth noting that Dionysos is the only god to look away from the central event.

[25] London B 147, *ABV* 135.44, *LIMC* II pl. 256, Apollo 819c.   [26] Brommer (1961: 74).

prior to the birth.[27] A man with a sceptre sits on a stool between two women (Eileithyiai?) while Hermes and Apollo, Herakles, and Ares observe. The drawing is rough. There is reason to believe that the inclusion of Herakles in both of these scenes may be simple errors made by careless painters who mixed conventions from different scenes. Dionysos regularly appears in depictions of the birth of Athena, early and late; Herakles appears in it twice in the mid-sixth century. Again, the weight of the evidence inclines toward an identification of Figure D as Dionysos rather than Herakles.

The literary/historical arguments for the identities of various figures in the east pediment tend to be complex, in part, at least, because of the lack of firm identifications for so many of the figures. However, most scholars have accepted identifications of Kore and Demeter for Figures E and F,[28] and these have been used to support the identification of Figure D as Dionysos because of his connection with the Eleusinian mysteries and as Herakles because of his connection with the same.[29]

Rhys Carpenter argued that Figure D cannot be Dionysos because he 'was not one of the older gods (he is scarcely even mentioned in Homer, and never as an Olympian) so that he should not have been present at Athena's birth'.[30] This is clearly wrong; undisputed evidence now shows that Dionysos was one of the ancient gods of Greece,[31] and the evidence from vase paintings shows that in the sixth and fifth centuries in Athens he was thought to have been present at the birth of Athena. Brommer argues that Herakles should not be present at the birth since Athena herself was instrumental in his apotheosis.[32] Harrison counters this with the observation that Pheidias included Herakles among the gods observing the birth of Aphrodite on the base of the statue of Zeus at Olympia for which Pausanias (5. 11. 8) is our only source.[33] Noting the inappropriateness of Herakles' presence at the birth of Aphrodite, Robertson writes: 'it seems a particular feature of these bases for cult statues that an event is taken as ostensible subject but treated undramatically as the centrepiece of an assembly of immortals who take no part in the action.'[34] It seems unlikely that the same could be said for the choice of figures in the east pediment of the Parthenon.

Attributes and pose make the identification of Figure D as either Dionysos or Herakles all but certain. Parallels for the pose of the figure on

---

[27] Florence 3804, Gerhard (1840: pl. 5. 2).

[28] See charts in Michaelis (1871: 165); Brommer (1963: 181); Palagia (1993: 60).

[29] E. Harrison (1967: 43–4); Lloyd-Jones (1970: 181).   [30] R. Carpenter (1962: 267).

[31] On the antiquity of Dionysos see Burkert (1985: 162). See now Hallager, Vlasakis, and Hallager (1992: esp. 76–81) for an offering tablet with Dionysos' name found in a Late Minoan 3 B context.

[32] Brommer (1963: 149).   [33] E. Harrison (1967: 45).

[34] Robertson (1975: 318).

vases and in sculpture, and for the participants in the subject on vases, make an identification of Dionysos much more likely. Literary/historical arguments are of little help here. On the basis of present evidence it is far more probable that Figure D was intended as Dionysos than as Herakles.

A brief digression on method is in order here. Jeppeson has recently written of his proposed restoration of the east pediment 'most mythological features derive from traditions that are at least as early as Hesiodos or Homer. It [the pedimental sculpture] could, however, hardly have been fully understood unless it were based on a detailed Epic account of the episode familiar to most observers living in or visiting ancient Athens.'[35] The assumption underlying this statement is that the visual arts are best understood as dependent on and illustrative of literary arts, which reflects what one scholar has recently called 'the imperialism of philology in classical studies'.[36] Thus, when literary sources for new imagery are missing, they have to be invented. This approach ignores the very different conventions used by poets, playwrights, painters, and sculptors and denies the possibility that artisans created visual narratives based on popular story-telling traditions rather than on literary forms.

Given the proliferation of mythological narratives in Athens of the fifth century on vases, in wall paintings, in architectural sculpture, on woven fabrics, and in metal work, it is probably safe to assume that the average Athenian was as familiar with some visual narratives as he was with literary versions. It follows that he would have known how certain gods usually appeared in the various visual forms and that he would have been able to 'read' new narratives through his knowledge of the forms (attributes and pose) and regular companions. Just as a playwright might modify a myth for his own purposes, so a sculptor or painter might introduce a new perspective on a deity. Whether Pheidias was the first to portray the beardless Dionysos or whether he borrowed the form from other sculpture or painting now lost remains unanswerable. At the least, the prominence of his depictions helped to popularize the new image.

Dionysos may also have appeared as a beardless youth in the east frieze of the Parthenon.[37] He is usually identified as Figure 25 (BaDok2,04) (Pl. 37A). Naked to the waist (and beardless, if Carrey's drawings are to be believed),[38] he sits on a stool facing right, but, turning to look left, he rests

[35] Jeppeson (1984: 276).   [36] Buxton (1994: 69–70).

[37] For the east frieze see now Jenkins (1994: 76–82).

[38] Bowie and Thimme (1971: pl. 26). Leake (1841: 549 n. 3) writes of figure 25: 'Enough of the head . . . remains to distinguish that it was bearded.' But the frieze was already in London when he saw it and presumably little changed from the way it is now. Robertson (1979: 77 n. 6) writes with reference to Carrey's drawings: 'Beard or no beard is a point on which one cannot always be sure which the draughtsman meant; and where one can he seems sometimes to have got it wrong.'

his right arm on the shoulders of Hermes, who sits behind him. His left arm
is raised and held a shaft of some sort added in another material. He wears
sandals (part of one survives) and his stool has a cushion. The figure to the
left of him (24) who has a petasos and chlamys on his lap and wears boots is
certainly Hermes. His hand is pierced, presumably to hold a kerykeion. The
figure to the right (26), who is a woman, holds a torch and is probably
Demeter. 'Dionysos' between them, would also have been identified by
attributes: the staff he held and perhaps a wreath. His stool facing in the
opposite direction from those around him might also have served as a clue.
If the figure is Dionysos, the staff would have been part of a thyrsos, though
there is little room for its head. His wreath would have been of ivy. Like
figure D in the east pediment, he is the odd man out in facing the opposite
direction from his companions.

That some of the twelve seated figures in the east frieze are deities is certain, and there is no reason to doubt that the others are as well.[39] Three of
the figures, Hermes (Figure 24), Athena (36), and Aphrodite (41), can be
identified by their attributes; a fourth woman who holds a torch (26) must
be Demeter, Hekate, or Persephone. The bearded man in front of Athena
leaning on a stick (37) should be the crippled Hephaistos. The veiled
woman (29) attended by a winged woman should be Hera, by comparison
with other scenes,[40] and the man behind her (30) should then be Zeus. The
other five figures are identified primarily through a process of elimination.
Artemis and Apollo should be there, so they must be the young man and
woman next to Aphrodite (39, 40). Poseidon should be there too, so he
must be the remaining bearded figure (38) between Hephaistos and Apollo.
That leaves two men, both probably beardless according to Carrey's drawing. The figure clasping his knee (27) to the right of Demeter has been
identified as Ares on the basis of both his pose, which recalls later depictions
of him,[41] and the remains of what has been called the shaft of his spear on
which he rests his left ankle.[42] This process of elimination also leads to the
conclusion that Figure 25 is Dionysos. His inclusion in the east pediment
and in the east metopes strengthens the supposition that he should be here.

Robertson has argued, primarily on the basis of Harrison's identification
of Figure D in the east pediment as Herakles, that Figure 25 in the east frieze
might also be Herakles rather than Dionysos.[43] In response, John Boardman

---

[39] For discussions of the gods in the east frieze: Michaelis (1871: 261–5) with a chart of earlier identifications. Smith (1892: 152–62); Robertson and Frantz (1975); Brommer (1977); Robertson (1979);
Boardman (1984: 213).

[40] Arafat (1990: 90–9).

[41] e.g. Rome, Museo Nazionale 8602, (Ares Ludovisi) *LIMC* II pl. 360, Ares 24.

[42] Robertson (1979: 76 n. 4).   [43] Robertson (1979: 75–8).

has noted that we would expect Dionysos to be present and that 'the cushion and sandals go uneasily with Herakles'.[44]

Robertson also comments that the young Dionysos 'is generally rather a slight figure' and concludes that in the east frieze the forms 'like those of D in the east gable, are massive and powerful; and this, in a youthful figure, is in both cases a slight argument in favor of Herakles'.[45] In fact, the early depictions of the beardless Dionysos on vases, particularly those by the Dinos Painter, are not slight figures, but are as robust and muscular as Figure D from the pediment and Figure 25 from the frieze (Pls. 36B & 37B).[46]

The lack of extant fifth-century depictions of Dionysos in architectural sculpture before the Parthenon makes it impossible to know whether there was a sculptural tradition for representing him as a young god. The fact that he is also bearded on those artifacts other than vases that have survived from before the last quarter of the century, such as coins and terracotta reliefs,[47] argues against early representations of the beardless Dionysos in any form, but the evidence is too scarce and scattered to be conclusive. It is only by chance that Figure D retained its head, the only one in the pediment to do so. In any case, the change in representations of the god on vases came after the Parthenon sculptures were put in place, and the new form for the god on them seems to have been influenced by Figure D.

The change in representations of Dionysos from bearded to beardless on vases is particularly noteworthy because on them he maintained his archaic bearded form long after other figures who were bearded in archaic art had become clean shaven—e.g. Herakles, Hermes, Paris, and Theseus—and for at least a decade after the creation of the Parthenon sculpture. On vases there are two important dimensions to the change. First, it required the breaking of an old and very tenacious convention, and second, it heralded the introduction of new Dionysian scenes, which reflect tendencies in other vase paintings and other media. The impulse that led to the change, then, need not be connected with the source of the new imagery; a discussion of the change should start with an examination of why the bearded form was originally chosen by vase painters and why it was so resistant to change.

From the earliest depiction of Dionysos in Greek art, on an Attic black-

---

[44] Boardman (1984: 213).   [45] Robertson (1979: 77).

[46] e.g. Vienna 1024, *ARV* 1152.8, *CV* 3 pl. 105. 1–4; London E 503, *ARV* 1159, *LIMC* III pl. 64, Bakche 2 where even Dionysos' pose is quite similar to Figure 25 of the East frieze. See Queyrel (1984). E. Harrison (1967: 44) notes that the 'powerful physique' of figure D is not characteristic of Dionysos. Burrow (1817: 188) looking at the same body wrote 'the muscles are, it is true, in celestial repose; but they have evidently never received the extension caused by incessant labors' and thus he concludes that the figure cannot be the 'Theban Hercules' but 'another Hercules far more ancient than the son of Alcmene'.

[47] e.g. *LIMC* III s.v. Dionysos 76–9, 177, 402, 538.

figure dinos in London,[48] his beard is used to single him out from other gods. There, in a procession of deities on their way to celebrate the wedding of Peleus and Thetis, his large scraggly beard is similar to the one worn by the centaur Chiron and unlike the neatly trimmed beards of Zeus, Poseidon, Ares, and Hermes. Not much later in the Return of Hephaistos frieze on the François Vase it is only Dionysos' long scraggly beard that distinguishes him physically from the other gods in the scene, and it is clear that Kleitias has gone to some pains to make this distinction.[49] The moustaches and beards on the other gods do not join or overlap as they do on Dionysos; rather, his beard is similar to those of the satyrs in the same frieze. In the Peleus and Thetis frieze on the same vase, Kleitias gives Dionysos a frontal, mask-like face with an enormous beard reaching down to the middle of his chest (Pl. 38A).[50]

Both Sophilos and Kleitias chose to use the unkempt beard as a characteristic for Dionysos and both made distinct parallels between his beard and those of half-human creatures of the countryside rather than with those of other gods. Centaurs and satyrs live in the wilds, not in cities, and the implication seems to be that this Dionysos too belongs to the uncivilized world rather than to the city or to Olympos. Kleitias went a step further in his Peleus and Thetis frieze in giving Dionysos the staring frontal face (and running pose) usually reserved for gorgons.

The unkempt beard continues to be a characteristic of Dionysos on later vases after canons were established by the Heidelberg and Amasis Painters in the mid-sixth century, but the depictions by Sophilos and Kleitias are of particular importance here because, being at the beginning, those painters had to look elsewhere—outside of vase painting—to find the Dionysos to include in their scenes. For both, in their Peleus and Thetis friezes, Dionysos is the humble, barefoot bringer-of-wine and little more. Whatever the models were for this figure, they obviously no longer exist, but I suggest there is enough evidence to conclude that they were probably traditional rustic masks of the god made of perishable materials.[51]

As mentioned earlier, there is indisputable evidence from vases that a mask of Dionysos attached to a pillar of some sort was an image familiar to

---

[48] London 1971. 11–1.1, *Para* 19.16*bis*, T. Carpenter (1986: pls. 1A, 2, 3B).

[49] Florence 4209, *ABV* 76.1, T. Carpenter (1986: pl. 4A).

[50] In addition to the François Vase there is only one other black-figure depiction of Dionysos with a frontal face, Boulogne 559, Bérard, Bron, *et al.* (1989: 152, fig. 208), where, between eyes, he sits on a throne and holds grape vines with either hand. This seems to be connected with a later group of mask-vases discussed below. For a catalogue of frontal face figures on archaic vases see Korshak (1987).

[51] For example, Athenaeus (3. 78c) tells of a type of wooden mask (*prosopon*) of Dionysos made by the Naxians: of vine-wood for *Bakcheos* and of fig-wood for *Melichiou*.

Athenians by the end of the sixth century.[52] This image would have made no sense unless it represented an actual form familiar to Athenians, a point reinforced by the fact that the earliest depictions are often careless drawings on black-figure lekythoi, some of which are all but unintelligible without reference to other vases, or for Athenians, to the masks themselves. They are almost a kind of shorthand.

From the start the column to which the mask is attached usually has a capital of some sort, and sometimes a base; in other words, it is man-made, not a tree, though there is never any indication that it is part of a building. Sometimes, however, ivy winds up around it.[53] On the lekythoi the mask is sometimes double and sometimes has a cloak hanging down below it. Human figures in those scenes are usually as tall or taller than the column. Vessels associated with wine are not depicted on the lekythoi.

The image of the mask attached to a column is more clearly defined on the series of red-figure vases already discussed in Chapter 5, most of which date to the decades around the middle of the fifth century. Many of the red-figure depictions are on stamnoi where the mask is usually frontal and almost always has some sort of cloak hanging down below it (Pls. 25B & 31). Vessels associated with wine (skyphoi, kantharoi, stamnoi, or kraters—but never cups) are almost always included in the red-figure scenes.

On a chous from the last quarter of the fifth century a mask lies in a *liknon* on a table between two women who hold a kantharos and a tray of grapes.[54] The mask is of the same type as the one attached to a column on a contemporary stamnos, which is the last in the red-figure series, but the context is very different.[55] Many unsuccessful attempts have been made to connect the scenes in which the mask-idol appears with specific festivals of Dionysos;[56] however, the one solid conclusion that can be drawn from the images is that they provide very strong evidence for the existence of masks of Dionysos in Attica during the fifth century. Some of the masks are associated with wine, but there is no hint that any of them have anything to do with the theatre, where, of course, masks of a different sort were commonly seen in fifth-century Athens.

[52] See above, Ch. 5.

[53] e.g. Brussels A 1311, *ABV* 488.3, Frontisi-Ducroux (1991: 135, fig. 63). For a red-figure example, Louvre G 532, ibid. 147, fig. 85.

[54] Athens, Vlastos, *ARV* 1249.14, Lezzi-Hafter (1988: pls. 137, 138D).

[55] A krater and kantharos have replaced the stamnos and skyphos. The tray of fruit including bunches of grapes is new, and requires, if we were to take the scene as a depiction of actual cult practices (Nilsson (1957: 29)) that the rite take place in late summer, thus excluding the Anthesteria and the Lenaia. Rather, the woman with the tray should be understood as a sister of Dione and Opora who hold similar trays on the Dinos Painter's krater, Vienna 1024, see above, n. 46.

[56] For a summary of the various interpretations of the scenes see Frontisi-Ducroux (1991: 17–63).

The lekythoi provide the most convincing evidence for the actual existence of columns with masks of Dionysos attached to them. As noted, the
scenes on some are so carelessly drawn that it would be almost impossible
for us to make sense of them without other, better drawn examples with
which to compare them.[57] This would seem to imply that for the purchaser
of the vase, the image was a familiar one, needing only the barest of shorthand indications to be recognizable on a vase. The figures on the lekythoi
in addition to the mask are mostly women. Similar women appear without
the mask on other lekythoi from the same group.[58] Sometimes satyrs appear
with the women and the mask-column.[59] On one lekythos women riding
ithyphallic donkeys approach it (Pl. 39A).[60] Women on donkeys—an image
that is derived from depictions of the Return of Hephaistos—appear on
many vases from the same group, always in a Dionysian context.[61] All of
the women with the mask-column can best be understood as nymphs,[62] the
traditional companions of Dionysos, and the scenes themselves are of
the mix-and-match generic type. They all include appropriately Dionysian
elements, but there is no necessary narrative connection between the elements. The nymphs, the satyrs, and the ithyphallic donkeys all appear on
earlier vases—it is only the mask-column that is new to vases, and it stands
to reason that its model must have been from some other medium.

The disembodied frontal face of Dionysos, or sometimes of a satyr, does
appear on some earlier vases. On a lekythos in Munich by the Marathon
Painter, who also paints mask-columns, women dance on either side of a
huge frontal face of a satyr from whose mouth a bunch of grapes hangs.[63]
On a contemporary lekythos by the Gela Painter a huge frontal face of
Dionysos is flanked by the god himself walking beside an ithyphallic donkey and a dancing woman.[64] Clearly the face here, presumably a mask, is
again simply one of several Dionysian images, as are the god, the donkey,
and the nymphs.

These huge frontal faces are similar to masks that appear on a group of
somewhat earlier vases (last quarter of the sixth century) mostly cups and
amphorae. A frontal face of Dionysos appears between two eyes on the
cups.[65] On the amphorae a face of Dionysos or occasionally of a satyr

[57] e.g. Corinth 295–10 (T2846), ibid. fig. 54; Naples 127946, ibid. fig. 70.
[58] e.g. Brussels A2193, *ABL* 244.67, *CV* 2 pl. 21. 26.; Bologna P 1195, *ABL* 244.66, *CV* 2 pl. 40. 4.
See also *ABV* 553.395–9.
[59] e.g. Louvre MNB 2039, *ABL* 247.10, Frontisi-Ducroux (1991: fig. 48); also a skyphos, Athens
498, *ABL* 251.44, ibid. fig. 97.
[60] Athens, Agora P 24472, *Para* 228, ibid. fig. 72.
[61] e.g. *ABV* 549.296–305; 550.307–9.   [62] See above, Ch. 4.
[63] Munich 1874, *ABV* 487. Cf. New York 75.2.21, *ABL* 222.27, Frontisi-Ducroux (1991: fig. 51).
[64] Athens 11749, *ABL* 208.55, ibid. fig. 101.
[65] See Bell (1978: 1–15); Ferrari-Pinney (1986: 5–20); Frontisi-Ducroux (1991: 177–88, 253–55).

appears between eyes or the mask of Dionysos appears by itself.[66] On a red-figure kantharos in Malibu from the second quarter of the fifth century masks of Dionysos and of a satyr are attached to the sides of the vase (Pl. 39B).[67]

The disembodied frontal face is uncommon in archaic and classical Greek art. In fact, aside from those of Dionysos and satyrs, only that of the Gorgon appears regularly on Greek vases, but there is an important difference. Where the terrible face of the Gorgon turns men to stone, the faces of Dionysos and satyrs as they appear on vases are essentially comic though their function may be, in part, apotropaic. While the word 'mask' might be used for the disembodied frontal faces of the Gorgon, Dionysos, and satyrs, none is shown as a mask that is worn. In other words, none is used to disguise anything. None allows an individual to take on the identity of an other.

The frontal masks of Dionysos on the cups and amphorae recall the frontal faced Dionysos in the Peleus and Thetis frieze on the François Vase.[68] In fact, the position of the god's head in front of the amphora he carries on his shoulder seems to be echoed on an amphora in Tarquinia even to the detail of the cluster of grapes hanging down from the vine, which could hint at a mask hung on the outside of wine container on some occasions.[69]

Though vases provide the major evidence for masks of Dionysos in sixth- and fifth-century Athens, three pieces of sculpture should also be noted. A larger than life-size marble face of Dionysos from Ikaria, on the Attica/Boeotia border, was long thought to be a marble mask.[70] Though a recent study has shown the face to be part of a seated figure found at the same time, probably the earliest surviving cult image of Dionysos, the mask-like character of the face is noteworthy.[71] In addition, two smaller than life-size marble masks of Dionysos from the first half of the fifth century have been found in Athens, one on the Acropolis and one in the

---

[66] *ABV* 275.1–9; Burow (1989: 33–4); Frontisi-Ducroux (1991: 178–88, 253–55).

[67] Malibu, Getty 88 AE 150, attributed to the Foundry Painter.

[68] Jeanmaire (1951: 6).

[69] Tarquinia RC 1804, *ABV* 275.5, Burow (1989: pl. 137).

[70] Athens 3072–4, 3897. Wrede (1928: 67) first published it as a mask.

[71] Romano (1982: 398–409). This seated figure, or one like it, is probably reflected in the frontal depictions of the seated god on Boulogne 559, see above, n. 50. See also the silhouette figure painted on an altar in front of the mask idol of the god on a cup by Makron, Berlin F 2290, *ARV* 462.48, Simon and Hirmer (1981: pl. 169). See also the colossal, unfinished draped figure of a standing male still in a quarry on Naxos (*BSA* 37 (1936–7) pls. 2–5). This is probably Dionysos and dates to the first half of the 6th cent. according to Kokkorou-Alewras (1975: 24, 94–5, K20).

Agora, both of which are more likely to have been votives rather than cult images (Pl. 38B).[72]

On the evidence of vases, it is clear that the disembodied face was a well known form associated with Dionysos by the last quarter of the sixth century; however, it is unlikely that this image was invented by vase painters. Explicit evidence from the end of the sixth century shows that by then the mask was well known in a plastic form; the implication is that the plastic form had been in existence for some time and could thus have been the model for the masks on cups and amphorae and even for the frontal face of Dionysos in the Peleus and Thetis frieze on the François Vase.

Just how and where these masks were originally used is unclear, but the fact that masks of the god and of satyrs seem to be interchangeable on some vases suggests that they were not originally cult images. That at least one of their uses was apotropaic makes more sense. So, on some eye cups a gorgoneion appears in the tondo while on the ouside there is a mask of Dionysos between eyes.[73] The two masks together with the eyes provide three apotropaic images—though their inclusion there may be more for design and humour than for actual effect.[74] The bearded mask with human ears affixed to a potter's kiln on a black-figure hydria in Munich from the end of the sixth century must have an apotropaic function—as do the relief satyr masks as devices on shields.[75] Siebert's recent comment on the development of the 'herm' may well apply in part to the mask of Dionysos on vases: 'L'innovation . . . fut d'inventer une formule plastique qui transformait un fetiche de la religion populaire en œuvre d'art . . .'[76] It was most likely from the realm of 'popular religion' that vase painters borrowed not only the mask but also their image for Dionysos, the wine god, and the unkempt beard was an essential part of this. While the form seems to have been adopted for cult images as well, it had little impact on poets and dramatists.

The tenacity of the bearded image on vases is explained at least in part by its origin in popular religion. The vase painter's Dionysos was the rustic god

[72] Athens, Acr. 1324, Payne and Young (1936: pl. 103. 3–4). Brouskari (1974: 82, fig. 160) calls it Severe Style and suggests it is one of the earliest examples of archaizing. Athens, Agora S 2485, Shear (1973: 402–4, pl. 74D). For a series of Boeotian terracotta masks of Dionysos, mainly from the 5th cent., see Frontisi-Ducroux (1991: 257–63). For a mid-4th-cent. marble mask of Dionysos in Musée Rodin in Paris see Frel (1967).

[73] e.g. Providence 63.48, *Para* 95.4*bis*, *ClassAnt* 10 (1977) pl. 8. The gorgoneion can also appear between eyes as on Louvre C 10346, Frontisi-Ducroux (1991: 185, fig. 112).

[74] On the crossover between 'comic' and 'apotropaic' see Faraone (1992: 38, 55–7, and 121–2).

[75] Munich 1717, *ABV* 362.36, Beazley (1986 pl. 87. 1). See Eisman (1978: 394–9) for speculation on connections between herms, Dionysos and kilns. For an ithyphallic demon on a kiln on a Corinthian pinax (Berlin F 683, 757, 822, 829), see discussion in Pernice (1898: 75–80).

[76] Siebert, *LIMC* V s.v. Hermes (p. 376). See also Goldman (1942: 67).

of the countryside, first and foremost the bringer-of-wine, as he appears on
Sophilos' and Kleitias' early depictions of him. That most of the vases on
which he appears were connected with the drinking of wine reinforced the
connection with the rustic form.

In the fifth century when red-figure vase painters expanded their reper-
toire of Dionysian stories, they continued to use the old, bearded form,
which shows the power of the traditional image since many of the events
depicted had to take place during the god's youth. That the Niobid
Painter's depiction of the young god as an adolescent failed to inspire copies
further emphasizes the strength of the old tradition. It was not until the last
quarter of the century that the tradition seems to have weakened enough to
allow the beardless Dionysos to appear.

He first appears in his new form on vases in works by the Dinos Painter
who also used the old bearded form on at least two of his vases and was the
last to paint a 'Lenaia' stamnos.[77] According to Beazley, he was a pupil of
the Kleophon Painter, who was 'a younger member of the Polygnotan
Group'.[78] Polygnotos, the leading artist of that group and teacher of the
Kleophon Painter, 'came from the school of the Niobid Painter',[79] whose
workshop is a principal source of our Dionysian imagery during the first
half of the fifth century. The Dinos Painter is, then, at the end of an un-
broken sequence of 'mainstream' vase painters who took a special interest
in Dionysian subjects, starting during the second quarter of the century
with the Altamura Painter, the Niobid Painter's 'elder brother', and continuing on to near the end of the century.

On stylistic grounds the Dinos Painter is dated to the last quarter of the
century, which is allowed by the archaeological evidence for those few
vases that do come from controlled excavations.[80] This gives us the approx-
imate time for the change on vases. The new Dionysian scenes on the
Dinos Painter's vases, both in subject and imagery, are in keeping with a
developing tendency in other Attic vase paintings, and some are certainly
influenced by imagery from other media as well. The scene on the dinos in
Berlin, the painter's name vase, illustrates some important elements of the
new form (Pl. 35B).[81] There a beardless Dionysos, naked to the waist,

[77] *ARV* 1151–55, 1685; *Para* 457. See Robertson (1992: 242–7). For the beardless Dionysos: *ARV*
1151.1; 1152.3, 4, 5, 8; 1154.26, 29; 1155.43*bis*. Bearded: Naples 938, *ARV* 1154.30, photo in the
Beazley Archive. On one side the god in a chiton and himation, holding a thyrsos and kantharos, walks
in a procession led by a satyr with a thyrsos; then a woman beating a tympanon; behind the god walks
a woman with torches. On one side of Bologna 283, see below, n. 82, the Dionysos in the Return of
Hephaistos was probably bearded.

[78] *ARV* 1143, 1151.   [79] *ARV* 1027.

[80] e.g. Corbett (1949: 343. 146); Sparkes and Talcott (1970: 582, P8:2 and Q8:1).

[81] Berlin F 2402, see above, n. 7. According to Furtwängler (1883–7: on pls. 56–7) the vase was found
in an Athenian tomb near Lykabettos.

reclines on a kline of sorts (a satyr sitting on the foot of the couch rests his feet on a rock). Dionysos' hair is short except for two curls that hang down behind his ears and over his collar bone. He wears an elaborate fillet over a wreath and holds a thyrsos with his right hand. A satyr playing a lyre sits on a panther skin at the foot of the kline which is flanked by two couples, each comprising a woman and a white haired satyr who wears a fawn skin and leans on a crooked staff. The woman at the head holds a tray with a bunch of grapes and two cakes on it. The woman at the foot holds a thyrsos and a kantharos. A procession of three younger satyrs and two women approaches moving to the left. One satyr holds a thyrsos, one plays pipes and a third, wearing a fawn skin, dances as he beats a tympanon. Both women carry thyrsoi, and one also carries a torch. Two pointed amphorae stand on the ground, one resting against an outcropping of rock.

The pose and muscular torso of this reclining figure are remarkably similar to those of the reclining Dionysos from the east pediment of the Parthenon, which was probably its model (Pl. 35A). There is nothing soft or effeminate about this Dionysos—he is simply young. In other words, there is no obvious connection between the physical appearance of this figure and the effeminate Dionysos in Aeschylus' *Edonians* or Euripides' *Bacchae*. The Dinos Painter has chosen an athletic form for the beardless god. Only later, with other painters, does the beardless figure degenerate into the soft effeminate form so common in fourth-century painting and sculpture.

The Dinos Painter knows several quite different personae for Dionysos. Coming from a tradition of vase painters who often depicted the god, he knows well the old forms. As already noted, he paints the last of the 'Lenaia' stamnoi, where a bearded mask is affixed to a pillar (Plate 25B). He also paints one of the last depictions of the Return of Hephaistos, on a krater in Bologna where, for the most part, he uses traditional Polygnotan imagery.[82] The centre of the scene is missing, but Hephaistos on his donkey and Hera on her throne have survived and show that the closest parallel is probably that by the Kleophon Painter on a skyphos in Toledo (Plate 15B).[83] Only the lion beside Hera's throne and the use of multiple groundlines with figures set up and down the surface of the vase are unusual. Another traditional scene by the Dinos Painter appears on a krater in Naples.[84] There the bearded Dionysos in chiton and himation with a thyrsos and kantharos walks in a procession, preceded by a satyr with a thyrsos and a woman with

[82] Bologna 283, *ARV* 1151.1, *CV* 4 pls. 68. 3–5, 69, 70. 9.

[83] Toledo 82.88, *CV* 2 pls. 84–7. Compare the figures of Hera and even the throne. For the throne see also Ferrara 2897, *ARV* 1052.25, *LIMC* III pl. 406, Dionysos 869, from the Group of Polygnotos.

[84] Naples 938, see above, n. 77.

a tympanon and followed by a woman with torches. Both the torches and the tympanon had begun to appear in Dionysian scenes by the middle of the fifth century.

Few of the scenes in which the beardless Dionysos appears refer to recognizable narratives. On the dinos in Berlin the god simply reclines amongst his companions who entertain him and serve him. Though one satyr beats a tympanon as he dances, the overall tone is peaceful—even blissful. This gentle tone is repeated and made even more explicit on a krater in Vienna (Pl. 36B).[85] There a beardless Dionysos of athletic build, reminiscent of Figure D from the east pediment of the Parthenon, naked except for a cloak across his lap, sits holding a thyrsos and a kantharos. Women, labelled *Dione*[86] and *opora* (fruit) approach the god with trays of fruit; *himeros* (desire) stands by the god's head with a fillet, a nameless satyr sits on a (headless) leopard skin playing a lyre, and the satyr *komos* wearing a nebris and holding a thyrsos stands to the right. Seated above to the left and right are the women *eirene* (peace) with a drinking horn and torch and *oinanthe* (grape-bloom) who is about to be attacked by an unnamed satyr from the other side. To the far left, above the handle, is the satyr *hedyoinos* (sweet wine). Beside Dionysos is a table or bema with fruit (?) on it, and below that is a leopard. Various ground-lines drawn in white and a bush suggest that the setting is out of doors and rural. Though the god holds a kantharos, there are no kraters, oinochoai, or wine skins—the emphasis is on fruit. The names of the figures all contribute to an overall sense of calm and stand in sharp contrast to the general character of the names on earlier vases.[87]

The inclusion of *eirene* (Peace) as a label for one of Dionysos' companions is particularly interesting here. The label only appears on one other Attic vase, which is contemporary with this, there too in a Dionysian context.[88] The name on the Dinos Painter's vase has nothing to do with the specific figure any more than *mainas* or *methuse* did on earlier vases.[89] Rather, it helps to set the tone for the scene. It also brings to mind a passage from Euripides' *Bacchae* (417–23) that almost could have been written as a commentary on the Vienna scene:

[85] Vienna 1024, see above, n. 46.   [86] See discussion above, Ch. 4.

[87] See above, Ch. 4. One puzzling inscription by the Dinos Painter appears on a krater, Naples 2369, *ARV* 1154.29, *LIMC* VI pl. 44, Komos 18. There a nymph with a thyrsos is named *choiros* which means piglet and is slang for female genitalia (see Henderson (1975: 131. 10)). The other figures in the scene are *Komos*, *Simos*, and Dionysos. One can only wonder if the inclusion of the seemingly innocuous *Choiros* was a joke on the ignorant foreigners to whom the vase would be sold—it was found at S. Agata de'Goti near Naples.

[88] Once Paris, *ARV* 1316.3. For discussion, see E. Simon in *LIMC* III s.v. Eirene, 11 and 12. See also the late 5th-cent. round altar from Brauron where a named Eirene follows a bearded Dionysos also named, *LIMC* III pl. 542, Eirene 10 and Vikelas and Fuchs (1985).

[89] See above, Ch. 4.

The deity, the son of Zeus, in feast, in festival, delights.
He loves the goddess Peace, generous of good,
preserver of the young.
To rich and poor he gives the simple gift of wine,
the gladness of the grape.

(trans. W. Arrowsmith)

Imagery on a squat lekythos by the Eretria Painter, a contemporary of the Dinos Painter who painted mainly cups, helps to clarify the imagery on the Vienna krater (Pl. 40A).[90] As in the Dinos Painter's scene, the ground lines suggest a hilly, rural setting with figures sitting at different levels. Beardless Dionysos, naked to the waist, sits holding a thyrsos, his legs crossed at the ankles. Long curls come down over his collar bones. Though his pose might be deemed effeminate, his torso is well muscled. Around him on the hillside are women and satyrs, all labelled with careful inscriptions: *chrysis* (golden) holds pipes, *kisso* (ivy) sits holding a thyrsos as does *antheia* (blossom); *periklymene* (honeysuckle) beats a tympanon, *makaria* (happiness) reclines, a nebris over her chiton; *phanope* (bright-eyed) dances and *nymphe* holds *naia* who has swooned into her arms and dropped her thyrsos; *chora* (dance) reclines, with her arms over her head, and *kale* watches. The satyrs are *silenos* and *komos*. The scene is one of undifferentiated Dionysian bliss.[91]

A different Dionysos appears on the obverse of the krater in Bologna with the Return of Hephaistos on the reverse (Pl. 40B).[92] There the beardless god, naked to the waist, sits to the far right beside a woman who gazes at him as she plays small cymbals. In front of them, to the left, three women dance wildly, one swinging a thyrsos, one beating a tympanon, and one baring her right breast. Above them are half-figures above a ground line of a satyr conversing with a woman with a tympanon. A woman with a child riding on her shoulders walks on the base line by a tree toward the dancing women, and above her a seated satyr plays pipes. To the left a woman with a thyrsos looks casually toward a satyr who gestures toward the left.

The tone of this scene is noticeably different from the tone on the Vienna krater. These are wild dancing women, not peaceful attendants of the god. To the music of the tympanon and pipes has been added the sound of cymbals, which the Dinos Painter has given to the woman seated beside Dionysos.[93] Beazley calls the woman Ariadne, but this is probably not who

---

[90] Once Berlin F 2471, *ARV* 1247.1, Lezzi-Hafter (1988: pls. 143D, 144–5).

[91] See Henrichs (1990: 269–71); Burn (1987). [92] Bologna 283, see above, n. 82.

[93] In a heavily restored scene by the Dinos Painter on a krater in Paris (Louvre G 488, *ARV* 1154.27, *CV* 5 pl. 33. 1–3, 5) one of four dancing women on one side has cymbals and the names Semele and Thyone(?) may appear beside her. I have not seen this vase, but given the painter's tendency to sprinkle

the painter had in mind. There is no clear erotic element, and it is difficult to imagine why Ariadne would be playing cymbals. Rather, lines from Pindar (*Isth.* 7. 3–5), albeit referring to Thebes, may help to clarify the meaning. There Dionysos is said to be enthroned beside Demeter 'of the clashing cymbals' (*kalkokrotou*) an epithet that seems to depend on an identification of her with Kybele.[94]

Cymbals are quite rare in Attic vase painting. In red-figure they first appear as much as a decade before the Bologna krater, on a vase from the Group of Polygnotos in a depiction of some form of ecstatic worship.[95] As discussed in the previous chapter, the lion with the enthroned woman on that Ferrara krater connects her with Kybele, and it is worth noting that not only the cymbals and tympana from the earlier vase appear on the Bologna krater, but in the Return frieze on the obverse, a lion inexplicably stands beside the enthroned Hera, whose throne itself has the same griffin-head finial.[96]

Still another Dionysos appears on a dinos in Athens (Pl. 41).[97] There the beardless god dances in a rowdy procession that circles the vase. He wears an elaborately decorated *ependytes* that ends at his knees, Thracian boots, and a cloak over his left arm. He holds a thyrsos and and kantharos (?); his hair is short and he wears a wreath of some sort. On either side of him a woman beats a tympanon. The rest of the procession comprises satyrs and women with thyrsoi, more tympana, a cup, and an oinochoe.

This is the young Dionysos with his companions, the satyrs and the nymphs his nurses. Dancing here, one of very few examples, he is probably to be understood as the mad (*mainomenos*) god who dances with or without the halves of a rent fawn earlier in the century.[98] Thus, this vase seems to be connected with the narrative sequence about the youthful Dionysos that can be traced back to the beginning of the fifth century. Myth, not cult, is the inspiration.

The question remains, what allowed the breaking of the old and very tenacious convention of always representing Dionysos as a bearded figure on

Dionysian names into scenes without much care on whom they fall, not too much should be made of the names.

   [94] See Moreux (1970: 1–14). See also, Euripides, *Helen* 1301–68.

   [95] For a discussion of cymbals in Dionysian scenes, see above, Ch. 5.

   [96] Ferrara 2897, see above, Ch. 5 n. 2.

   [97] Athens 14500, *ARV* 1152.4, *MemAmAc* 6 (1927) pl. 19. 2–3; cf. Athens 1488, *ARV* 1152.5 (unpublished) where the god is bearded, wearing ependytes and Thracian boots, carries a thyrsos and kantharos in a procession of satyrs and women with thyrsoi, torches, and tympanon.

   [98] e.g. London E 439, *ARV* 298, *LIMC* III pl. 312, Dionysos 151; Private, *ARV* 605.65*bis*, T. Carpenter (1993: 186 fig. 7); London E 75, *ARV* 406.2, *LIMC* III pl. 355, Dionysos 470. See above, Ch. 3.

Attic vases, a convention which I have suggested was initially adopted by vase painters from rural masks connected with the god as bringer-of-wine? The answer cannot be a simple one. The last quarter of the fifth century was a time of political and social instability for Athens. Perikles was dead, the plague had decimated and demoralized the population, and the war with Sparta continued. Does the change represent a change in religious outlooks, or only a change in tastes? Does it reflect a different market or perhaps different uses for the vessels? Is there sufficient evidence to read social or religious implications into the change?[99] Once again we have questions that require the joint efforts of philologists, historians, and archaeologists.

Suffice it to say here that the change may say as much about vase painting in late fifth-century Athens as it does about Dionysos. The truly creative periods ended before the middle of the fifth century, an end that was signalled by the appearance of multiple ground lines borrowed from monumental painting showing vase painters' unwillingness to accept the limitations of their form—figures silhouetted against the surface of undifferentiated black. The techniques of fifth-century monumental painting are surely inappropriate for the curved surface of a vase. With the decline in the quality and ingenuity of drawing went the strength of the iconographic conventions that had governed the choice of imagery. This new-found freedom led to a brief period of splendid innovations in the works of the Meidias Painter and his followers, as Lucilla Burn has shown, but beyond that it produced a disintegration of a coherent visual language.[100] The Dionysos of vases gave way to the Dionysos of monumental art, who is different again from the Dionysos of tragedy, of satyr plays, or of comedy. Ultimately the Dionysos of fourth-century Attic vases is a saccharin figure who has lost, with his ambiguity, his divinity.

[99] Mikalson (1984: 219), discussing the effects of the plague on Athenian religion has written: 'to judge from Thucydides, their society as a whole reached a depth of religious despair unparalleled in the records of ancient Greek civilization.' Such turning from traditional cults as Thucydides describes (2. 47. 4) fits nicely with the passing of a venerable image on vases, but even so this could only be a small part of an explanation.

[100] Burn (1987).

7

Bacchae *and* Frogs

AFTER vase painting, Euripides' *Bacchae* is the richest source of Dionysian imagery to survive from fifth-century Athens. When the play was produced, Dionysian narratives had already appeared on Attic vases for more than a century and a half, and the death of Pentheus itself had appeared on them for nearly a century. Presumably an Athenian attending the performance would have been familiar with other images connected with the god and might also have seen other versions of the Pentheus story in the theatre. He might recently have attended the performance of Aristophanes' *Frogs* where Dionysos was also a central character.[1]

While much effort has been put into searches for later vase paintings influenced by the *Bacchae* either by illustrating it or alluding to it,[2] curiously little attention has been paid to the relation between the vivid imagery of the play and the images on earlier vases that contemporary Athenians might have known.[3] What follows here is a comparative review of imagery in the *Bacchae*, in the *Frogs*, and on Attic vases in an attempt to address the ways in which Athenians' prior awareness of Dionysian imagery might have affected their understandings of the plays.

As in earlier chapters, I start with the assumption that in the beginning there was a body of traditional tales to which the Pentheus story belonged. Both poets and painters (of vases and presumably of monumental works as well) drew on these traditional tales for their narratives. That the vase painter occasionally borrowed details from a poetic description is clear; that the poet occasionally borrowed details from the painter is also possible. Visual elements from productions of satyr plays and tragedies did work their way onto vases, but this type of influence is relatively rare. The *Bacchae*, with its vivid imagery comes at the end of a long visual tradition of which the playwright could not have been ignorant. That Euripides would have been aware of the three depictions of Dionysos on the Parthenon goes

---

[1] For recent discussions of other 5th-cent. plays in which Dionysos appeared, see Dover (1993: 39–40); Oranje (1984: 124–30).

[2] Most recently, March (1989). See also Dodds (1960: xxxiii–xxxvi and bibliography there).

[3] Cf. Philippart (1930) for a catalogue of monuments (mostly dating later than the *Bacchae*) in some way connected with the play. Fol (1993: 433–5) implies that Euripides was influenced by visual imagery.

without saying. His use in *Ion* of images from the Gigantomachy on the temple of Apollo at Delphi (184–218) shows at the least an awareness of sculpted narratives, and his description of the pavilion erected in the same play (1132–65) suggests an awareness of woven imagery as well.[4]

In fifth-century Athens there seem to have been three distinct traditions for representing Dionysos which I have called the mythic, the comic and the cultic. In the mythic the god is a beardless youth, which is appropriate since most myths about him deal with his childhood and youth. In the comic he is a buffoon, probably beardless, who wears female clothing. The saffron robe (*krokotos*) usually associated with women, is worn by Dionysos only in comedy. In the cultic he is a mature male, distinguished by his full beard, long hair, and dignified mien as on the marble statue from Ikaria or the mask-idols on vases.[5] Until the last quarter of the fifth century vase painters mixed traditions by using the cultic form of the god in mythic narrations;[6] however, they never seem to have drawn on the comic tradition, never dressing the god in explicitly female clothing.[7]

In the *Bacchae* Dionysos is on stage for much of the play, yet at least until his reappearance after the death of Pentheus he is disguised as an effeminate oriental youth. Euripides has the god repeat three times (4, 53, 54) that he comes to Thebes in disguise, and presumably his costume would have made that clear to the audience as well. When the god reappeared, he may have had a different form, but no indication survives of exactly what that form was.[8] However, the chorus of Lydian women provides images of the god himself in the choral songs, which allow Euripides to play on the ambiguity of his 'true' form, thus emphasizing the significance of the disguise. In the parodos, describing his birth, the chorus calls him the 'bull-horned god' (100) and tells of his crown of snakes. This connection with the bull is made explicit later in the play when a dazed Pentheus who sees two suns and two Thebes as he follows the stranger says (920–2):

[4] See also the woven cloth by which Creusa recognizes her child (*Ion* 1420–5). For a recent discussion of the iconography of classical textiles, see Barber (1991: ch. 16) and Vickers (forthcoming).

[5] See also the late 5th-cent. relief on the round altar from Brauron, Vikelas and Fuchs (1985: pls. 2–5). Alkamenes chryselephantine statue of Dionysos in the sanctuary by the theatre mentioned by Pausanias (1. 20. 3) was probably bearded if evidence from coins is reliable, see *LIMC* III pl. 309, Dionysos 133.

[6] See above, Ch. 3.

[7] For a unique Attic representation of Dionysos (named) in a comic scene, see Athens, Agora P23907, one of four late 5th-cent. unglazed water pitchers with figures from comedy painted in polychrome published by Crosby (1955: 81–2, pl. 34C). The fat figure is poorly preserved but seems to wear a short chiton over padded tights.

[8] The cultic form would seem to have been the most appropriate for this final epiphany.

> And you—you are a bull
> who walks before me there. Horns have sprouted
> from your head. Have you always been a beast?
> But now I see a bull.

And Dionysos answers, 'It is the god you see.' (923)

In the fourth stasimon the chorus calls to the god and urges him to reveal himself as a bull, a snake, or a lion (1017–18). And in the final choral ode it tells that Pentheus had a bull to lead him to his death (disaster) (1159).

In the *Homeric Hymn to Dionysos* (VII, 44–8) Dionysos turns himself into a lion and creates a bear, and in Kratinos' comedy, *Dionysalexandros* (*PCG* 142 frag. 40), he seems to have turned himself into a ram. However, in fifth-century visual narratives neither Dionysos nor any other deity aside from Zeus takes on an animal form, in part, no doubt, because of the problem of making a metamorphosed god recognizable.[9] Dionysos on vases always has a wholly human form; however, lions, leopards, and snakes are associated with him in some scenes, particularly the Gigantomachy. Associations between Dionysos and bulls on Attic vases are rare, and the god (young or old) is never shown with snakes in his hair.[10]

The Dionysos who appears on three of the ten surviving depictions of the death of Pentheus on Attic vases has nothing to do with the oriental stranger of the *Bacchae*.[11] On one side of a cup from the first quarter of the century the god sits on a stool in the midst of women who rush about with pieces of Pentheus' body in their hands (Pl. 42A & B).[12] He is a dignified figure wearing a himation over a long chiton and an ivy wreath on his head. He holds a kantharos with his right hand, ivy sprigs with his left. This is the canonical Dionysos of non-narrative scenes.[13] A figure from the cultic

---

[9] Transformations can only be indicated as on Thetis or Nereus, e.g. Berlin F 2279, *ARV* 115.2, Boardman (1975: fig. 214.1); Louvre CA 823, *ABV* 12.23, Boardman (1974: 16. 2). Gods retain human forms on vases. On one side of a black-figure amphora, Würzburg HA 146, *LIMC* III pl. 350, Dionysos 435, Dionysos rides on the back of a bull, on the other side Poseidon rides on a similar bull.

[10] Cf. Villaneuva-Puig (1983), particularly 247–52; *LIMC* III Dionysos K, 3,157. See above, Ch. 5 for discussion of a seated deity with a snaky fillet sometimes said to be Dionysos.

[11] Three from the last quarter of the 6th cent.: Boston 10.221, *ARV* 16.14, *LIMC* VII pls. 256–7, Pentheus 39; Louvre G 69, *ARV* 133.21, *LIMC* VII pl. 257, Pentheus 41; Berlin 1966.18, *LIMC* VII pl. 257, Pentheus 40. Three from the first quarter of the 5th cent.: Oxford 1912.1165, *ARV* 208.144, *LIMC* VII pl. 258, Pentheus 42; Kiel B 500, *Para* 357.19*bis*, *LIMC* VII pl. 65, Orpheus 66 (Schauenburg (1975) suggests a maenad with the head of Pentheus, Beazley identifies her as a Thracian with the head of Orpheus); once Toronto, Borowski, *LIMC* VII pl. 259, Pentheus 43. Four from the last quarter of the 5th cent.: Athens, Kerameikos, *ARV* 1313.6, *LIMC* VII pl. 254, Pentheus 25; Louvre G 445, *LIMC* VII pl. 254, Pentheus 24; Villa Giulia 2268, *LIMC* VII pl. 259, Pentheus 44; once Heidelberg, private, *LIMC* VII 308, Pentheus 1.

[12] Once Toronto, Borowski, see above, n. 11.

[13] For sculptural representations of the god in a similar form see Schuchhardt (1967: 7–20); Pochmarski (1974: 24–8).

tradition, he intrudes on the mythic. In the other two scenes, both from the last quarter of the century, the god is a naked, beardless youth as he often is on vases from that period.[14] He stands casually, holding a thyrsos while the women attack Pentheus.

The Dionysos who is on stage throughout Aristophanes' *Frogs* stands in sharp contrast to the polymorphous Dionysos of the *Bacchae*. From Herakles' comments (45–8) we know that he wears a yellow gown (*krokotos*) and soft boots (*kothornoi*). From Charon's comment (200) we know that he is fat. As in the *Bacchae* he wears a disguise, but here it is only a lion skin to make him look like Herakles.

That the krokotos is explicitly female dress is made clear by many other passages in Aristophanes' surviving plays.[15] Kothornoi, too, are associated with women there, but can be worn by men as well.[16] The mistaken conclusions that the krokotos is a regular attribute of Dionysos and that kothornoi are 'characteristic of Dionysos in vase painting' have recently been repeated in Dover's new edition of *Frogs*.[17] In literature the krokotos is worn by Dionysos almost exclusively in comedy, and in vase painting there would be no way to indicate the color, its defining characteristic. The long chiton he often wears on vases is not exclusively female dress but is also worn 'by senior males of myth or contemporary society'.[18] Zeus, Poseidon, and Apollo are all depicted wearing it at one time or another (Pl. 43).[19] When Dionysos wears boots on Attic vases they are usually Thracian riding boots, not kothornoi.[20] In short, the Dionysos of *Frogs* has little or nothing to do with representations of the god in fifth-century sculpture or vase painting, and by his dress alone he would have been recognized as a figure quite distinct from the mythic or cultic manifestations of the god.[21]

The most vivid imagery in the *Bacchae* is used to describe the mad women and their actions, but before turning to them a word should be said about the peculiar geography of the play. As I have suggested above, Thrace seems to be the locus of many Dionysian narratives on vases from the end of the sixth century on through the fifth century.[22] Aeschylus made much

---

[14] Athens, Kerameikos 2712 and Louvre G 445, see above, n. 11. For a recent discussion of the Kerameikos scene, see Schöne (1990: 163–78).

[15] e.g. *Women at the Thesmophoria* 138, 253, 941, 945, 1220; *Lysistrata* 44, 47; *Women in Assembly* 332, 879.   [16] e.g. *Women in Assembly* 346, 657 (women) and *Birds* 994 (men).

[17] Dover (1993: 40 and 195 note on l. 47).

[18] Kurtz and Boardman (1986: 58); T. Carpenter (1993: 204).

[19] e.g. Basle Lu 39, Berger and Lullies (1979: 110–11. 39), a stamnos attributed to the Berlin Painter illustrates this well by showing Zeus, Poseidon, Apollo, and Dionysos in similar dress. See also London E 140, *ARV* 459.3.

[20] See above, Ch. 2.

[21] In Kratinos' *Dionysalexandros* (*PCG* 142, fr.40) Dionysos was also dressed in a krokotos.

[22] See Chs. 2 and 3

of the Thracian side of Dionysos in his Lykourgos tetralogy, and vase
painters, particularly during the first half of the century, often give the god
and his companions elements of Thracian dress. Euripides himself refers to
the Thracian Dionysos in both his *Rhesus* (972) and his *Hecuba* (1267) and
probably in *Hypsipyle* (frag. 64, 50 f.). In the *Bacchae*, however, there is no
reference to Thrace whatsoever, an exclusion that must be intentional and
must have had a purpose.[23]

Euripides is explicit in tracing the travels of Dionysos, and the route he
describes is as interesting for what it excludes as for what it includes.
Dionysos himself tells of his premature birth from Semele (1–3), and the
chorus adds the story that he was then sewn into the thigh of Zeus until he
came to full term (88–98). Neither Dionysos nor the chorus refers to any of
the traditional tales of his upbringing. Rather, Dionysos tells of his travels
(13–22), starting in Lydia and Phrygia. First he headed south-east to the
Persian steppes, then north-east to Bactria. He then reversed direction and
headed back west to Media, then further west to Arabia and finally up the
coast of Asia Minor 'where Greeks and foreign nations mingle'. After estab-
lishing his mysteries and rites there, he came to Thebes. What is striking
here is the complete absence of any reference to Thrace. What route did he
take from Asia Minor to Thebes? After the explicit details about the rest of
his travels, the vague 'and thence to Thebes' is curious. That Thebes would
be the first city he visited in Greece is also hard to imagine in geographical
terms even if he travelled by boat.

The geography of the epode of the second stasimon is particularly noteworthy in this context. The Lydian women of the chorus list the mountains
in which Dionysos can be found leading his thiasos—Nysa, Parnassos,
Olympos, and Pieria—and they specifically mention the route to Pieria
across the rivers Axios and Lydias in Macedonia. Just what an Athenian
would have understood by Nysa is unclear; Dodds suggested Euripides
might mean Thracian Pangaeum 'which might be expected to figure in the
play',[24] but there are many other possibilities. The route west to Pieria
across the two Macedonian rivers suggests a journey from Thrace and
makes the absence of that name (and the exclusion of the Strymon) all the

---

[23] Part of the purpose for the exclusion of Thrace may have been to highlight the play's exclusively
oriental travels for Dionysos, an idea that would have been unfamiliar to an Athenian audience. Parallels
between Dionysos' description of his journey and the account of the sources of Xerxes, army by the
chorus in Aeschylus' *Persians* (12–64), particularly the emphasis on Tmolus, may be worth noting. Part
of the motive for this peculiar emphasis on the east may have been what Versnel (1990: 99) calls the
poet's deliberate presentation of 'Dionysiac religion as one of the new "sects" that invaded Greece and
especially Athens at this time'.

[24] Dodds (1960: note on 556–9); Cf. Seaford (1984: note on 68). For ancient locations for Nysa see
Hesychius s.v. Nysa (742)

more odd.[25] Finally, the placing of Orpheus on Olympos rather than in Thrace is a deliberate change in the fifth-century story as told on vases and, usually, in the theatre. In his own *Hypsipyle* written a few years before the *Bacchae* he explicitly links Orpheus with Thrace (frags. I iii. 10 and 64. 98), as did Aeschylus.[26]

There are two distinct groups of women in the play: the Lydian women of the chorus who are on stage throughout the performance and Theban women about whom we hear much but do not see, except for Agave at the end of the play. All are mortal. Dionysos tells us that he has driven mad all of the women of Thebes as a punishment (32–3), and he also tells us that the Lydian women are worshippers who have come with him specifically from the area around Tmolus in Lydia (55–6).

The play is set in the heroic past, before the Trojan War, when Cadmus was still alive and Dionysos and his cousin Pentheus were young. The Theban women belong to this myth-time, the Lydian women do not. The women who usually accompany Dionysos in literature and on vases are nymphs, often his nurses.[27] Euripides has replaced the traditional nymphs with women from a clearly defined geographical location—not just the east, but the region around Mt. Tmolus in Lydia. At the same time the Lydian women are problematic. Surely they are not to be seen simply as 'missionaries'[28] who have come with their priest to introduce a new religion. They are 'detached from any normal human environment',[29] their entire existence is in their association with the god. When the madness passes, the women of Thebes will return to their homes, but the women of the chorus will not. In short, they maintain the traits of traditional nymphs in spite of their mortal label.

There is a standard costume or livery for all of the followers of Dionysos in the play (34, 180) including the Lydian and Theban women, Cadmus, and Teiresias, and even Pentheus. The essential elements are a nebris, a thyrsos, and an ivy wreath.[30] Only Pentheus wears a mitra. Women in Dionysian scenes on Attic vases sometimes wear a nebris from the middle of the sixth century down to the end of the fifth. Of skins, however, the leopard is more common during the first half of the fifth, and more often than not in all periods the women do not wear skins at all over their peploi

---

[25] J. E. Harrison (1903: 373), noting the absence of references to Thrace in the *Bacchae* concludes that Euripides knew perfectly well that Dionysos was from Thrace but 'as poet can afford to contradict himself. He accepts popular tradition, too careless of it to attempt an irrelevant consistency. It matters nothing to him *whence* the god came'.

[26] Bond (1963: 144). For Orpheus in Macedonia see Graf (1987).   [27] See above, Ch. 4.

[28] Cf. Winnington-Ingram (1969: 32, 37).   [29] Ibid. 41

[30] For a nebris with curls of braided wool somehow attached to it, see 111 and Dodds' note. Bryony, oak, and fir are also associated with maenads. See Dodds on 108–10.

or chitons. The nebris is also common apparel for other female figures, most notably Artemis, on both black and red-figure vases.[31] To say that the nebris is a principal attribute of 'maenads' in the fifth century is to depend on Euripides rather than on visual evidence.[32]

The thyrsos first appears on red-figure vases before the end of the sixth century and continues to be a Dionysian attribute throughout the fifth.[33] On vases it clearly consists of a narthex to which ivy leaves have been attached at the top, and this is in keeping with the references to the thyrsos (and narthex) in the *Bacchae*.[34] From the start it is frequently carried by female companions of the god. The thyrsos does not appear on black-figure vases before the first half of the fifth century nor in literature before the second half.[35] The ivy wreath, on the other hand, is almost always worn by Dionysos and often by his companions in sixth- and fifth-century vase paintings.

In the play snakes are also a part of the costume of some followers of Dionysos. The Herdsman tells that snakes serve as girdles for some of the Theban women (695) and, later, that they lick the blood from their cheeks (767–8). Also, the chorus tells an etiological tale about snakes worn by 'maenads' in their hair in recognition of a crown of snakes Zeus put on the head of Dionysos (101–4).

Three points should be made about these snakes. (1) It is highly unlikely that anyone in the audience had ever worn or seen anyone else wear snakes as they worshipped Dionysos. (2) During the second half of the sixth and first half of the fifth century female companions of Dionysos on Attic vases often wear or carry snakes. (3) The women with snakes on these vases need not imply that followers of Dionysos in Athens or anywhere else ever wore or carried snakes outside of myth.[36]

---

[31] e.g. *LIMC* II s.v. Artemis nos. 353–95.   [32] Cf. Schlesier (1993: 110).

[33] See above, Ch. 1

[34] For Theban women mending their thyrsoi see 1054–5. On black-figure vases and occasionally on later vases Dionysos or his companions can carry a leafing staff instead of the thyrsos (e.g. Naples 128333, *ABV* 367.93, RM 27 (1912) pl. 8; Harvard 1960.343, *ARV* 1042.2, *CV* Robinson 2, pl. 46; Louvre G 33, *ARV* 14.4, *CV* I pl. 1. 2, 6; 2, 4), which may be the image Euripides had in mind with *kladon* (308). See also London E 140, *ARV* 459.3 (pl. 43A), where Dionysos holds a fennel staff (note the diagonal markings) and an unconnected ivy bunch.

[35] See Henrichs (1987: 121 n. 71).

[36] See below, n. 41, also Henrichs (1982: 140–4) and (1990: 264). Cf. Dodds (1960: 79 on ll. 101–4), Winnington-Ingram (1969: 151), and Oranje (1984: 110–11). For similar uses of snakes by mortal (?) women in the Bronze Age Aegean world see the 'Priestess' from Thera with a large snake in her hair, S. Immerwahr (1990: 186 AK no. 8); Doumas (1992: figs. 24–5); also the more familiar figurines of a 'goddess' holding snakes. There need be no connection between the Minoan and the Greek images, rather they might most appropriately be seen as independent developments. E. R. Dodds, in his essay on maenadism (1951: 275–6) describes snake-handling accompanied by ecstatic dancing that forms part of religious services of the Holiness Church in remote parts of Appalachia. This 'ritual' was only

A snaky fillet worn by a woman on her head appears in the white ground tondo of a cup in Munich by the Brygos Painter from early in the fifth century.[37] There she runs with a leopard skin tied at her throat, a thyrsos in her right hand and a leopard held by a hind leg with her left. A woman wearing such a snake is a relatively rare image, and on a white ground lekythos in Basle before the middle of the fifth century it is a winged Fury rather than a companion of Dionysos who wears one (Pl. 30A).[38]

One of the earliest depictions of snakes with companions of Dionysos is on a black-figure krater by Lydos from the middle of the sixth.[39] The subject is the Return of Hephaistos, but most of the scene is occupied by a lively procession of satyrs and nymphs. Most of the women wear nebrides, and a snake has wrapped itself around the waist of one, a satyr holds another by the tail. These, like the snakes in the early Gigantomachy, are large and frightening reptiles with beards. The beards, it has been convincingly shown, are borrowed from Egypt where they are associated with tutelary spirits that accompany the dead, and in Greece they are not limited to Attica nor to vase painting.[40] These are snakes from the world of myth, not from nature—no Greek had ever seen such a snake—and they continue to appear on Attic vases at least until the middle of the fifth century. Nymphs frequently hold snakes (often as weapons) on vases from the sixth century and from the first half of the fifth, but snakes are unusual in Dionysian scenes after the middle of the fifth century when they become common attributes of the Furies.

The snakes in the *Bacchae*, like those on vases, are not from nature. In fact, they behave in ways very similar to those on vases, and it is entirely possible that Euripides' inspiration for them came from earlier visual images. The fact that there is no surviving literary source aside from the *Bacchae* that mentions snake handling as part of mortal maenadic ritual supports this suggestion.[41]

Though pipes (*auloi*) are mentioned (380)[42] and called Phrygian (127–28), the tympanon is the principal musical instrument in the play. At the end of the prologue Dionysos calls to the Lydian women of the chorus and urges them to come to the palace door bringing with them their Phrygian drums (*tympana*), which he says is his invention and Rhea's (58–9).

introduced in 1909 and is based on a passage in Mark (16: 18): 'They shall take up serpents.' The ritual appears to have been a spontaneous invention in rural areas where poisonous snakes are commonly encountered. See Kane (1974).

[37] Munich 2645, *ARV* 371.15, Boardman (1975: fig. 218).
[38] Basle Lu 60, *LIMC* 3, pls. 595, Erinys 1. See above, Ch. 5.
[39] New York 31.11.11, *ABV* 108.5
[40] Guralnick (1974: 184); see also T. Carpenter (1986: 71–3).   [41] Bremmer (1984: 269–9).
[42] The music of pipes is also mentioned at the end of the epode (156) though the term there is *lotos*.

Pentheus' comment about silencing the drums when he threatens to have the women sold as slaves (513) suggests that they carry tympana throughout the play. In the epode of the parodos the chorus tells the history of the drum, which is described as hide stretched over hoops of wood (120–34). First used by the Curetes (who are equated with the Corybantes) in Crete to hide the cries of the infant Zeus, then adopted by Rhea for her rites, it was borrowed by the satyrs to celebrate a festival of Dionysos (*trieteris*).

References to tympana in fifth-century literature are relatively rare; the earliest are in Pindar (*Pythian* 2. 9) where it is linked to Bacchic rites of Meter on Olympus, and Aeschylus (*Edonians* frag. 57 *TrGF* 3) where it is linked to the Thracian goddess Kotys, again in a Dionysian context.[43] Outside of the *Bacchae*, Euripides associates the tympanon with Meter and with Dionysos;[44] in both *Cyclops* and *Herakles*, in fact, its absence is used to indicate the absence of Dionysos himself (64–5, 204–5).[45] Aristophanes' use of the tympanon to refer to ecstatic cults implies that the instrument was actually in use in Athens, at least during the last quarter of the century.[46]

The tympanon first appears on Attic vases around the middle of the fifth century and becomes increasingly common during the second half;[47] until the fourth century it is almost always associated there with Dionysos and his companions. Prior to its appearance, *krotala*, castanet-like clappers made of wood or metal, and pipes usually provide the music in Dionysian scenes.[48] Though Meter has not been recognized on vases, she is depicted with a tympanon in fifth-century sculpture, most notably in the seated statue of her by Pheidias or his pupil Agorakritos in the Athenian Agora.[49]

The connection between Dionysos and Meter, implied by Pindar and by Euripides in *Helen*, and explicitly stated in *Bacchae*, deserves some comment here. Dodds saw the explanation for this in cult practices, and particularly in the introduction of the cult of 'Asiatic Cybele' to Greece in the fifth century.[50] I suggest, however, that the answer is to be found in the literary rather than in the religious traditions.[51] Apart from poetic references, we

---

[43] I am assuming, with West (1992: 124), that *Homeric Hymn* 14. 2 is later.

[44] *Herakles* 891, *Helen* 1346 (where Aphrodite holds it), *Cyclops* 64–5, 204–5.

[45] Seaford (1984, nn. on 65 and 205).

[46] *Wasps* 119; *Lysistrata* 3, 388. At the end of the 5th cent. and on into the 4th cent. Eros sometimes carries a tympanon on Attic vases.   [47] See above, Ch. 5 n. 26.

[48] e.g. Munich 2344, *ARV* 182.6, Arias, Hirmer, and Shefton (1962: pls 122–3, xxx–xxxi); Munich 2645, see above, n. 37.

[49] Following Lynn Roller (forthcoming) I use the name Meter in what follows for the various Greek manifestations of the Phrygian Mother goddess: Mother of the Gods, Mountain Mother, Great Mother, Kybele, and Rhea. In Euripides' *Helen* she is Demeter.

[50] Dodds (1960: 76–7 nn. on 78–9). Cf. Kannicht (1969: ii. 331–2).

[51] Caveats by Mikalson (1991: 5, 227) on the differences between 'literary fantasy and genius' and 'the Greek religious spirit' are particularly important here.

have no evidence for any connection between their cults in fifth-century Athens, but a much earlier link seems to be established in myth.[52]

The chorus of the *Bacchae*, in its description of the happy man, speaks of his participation in mystic rites made lawful by the Great Mother Kybele, which are then linked to the worship of Dionysos (78–82). Rather than being an example of 'syncretism', this may refer to an old poetic tradition summarized by Apollodorus (3. 5. 1–3) that the young Dionysos, maddened by Hera, was purified by Rhea at Kybela and learned from her the rites of initiation.[53] Both the purification of Dionysos by Rhea at Kybela in Phrygia and her teaching of the mysteries to him are repeated in a passage attributed to Eumelos, and while there is no way to confirm its antiquity, there is no reason to dismiss it out of hand. West has recently argued that the passage in Apollodorus is a combination of different versions including the one related by Eumelos.[54] Kallixeinos alludes to the purification of Dionysos in his description of the grand procession of Ptolemy Philadelphus in Alexandria, which is dated to the first half of the third century. There, in one of the cart-borne tableaux, Dionysos appears 'having fled to the Altar of Rhea when he was pursued by Hera'.[55]

In the Return of Hephaistos frieze by Kleitias on the François Vase, one of the earliest depictions of Dionysos in Greek art, a nymph playing small cymbals accompanies the god (Pl. 12B).[56] Cymbals do not appear again on Greek vases for over a century, and when they do, the scenes are usually Dionysian.[57] In literature the instrument, which is of oriental origin, is associated with orgiastic cults.[58] The instruments themselves 'were devoid of musical value for the Greeks'.[59] The inclusion of the cymbals in the depiction of the Return on the François Vase suggests that the connection between Dionysos and Eastern orgiastic rites was already a part of Dionysian narratives before the middle of the sixth century—part of a mythic tradition.[60]

Kleitias' depiction of the Return is both the earliest and the most complete version of the story on Attic vases.[61] The version common on later vases is almost always in an abbreviated form which usually excludes any reference to orgiastic rites. The vast majority of Dionysian scenes on Attic

---

[52] A 6th-cent. shrine from Sardis (S63.51:5677) provides evidence for some sort of cultic link between Meter and Bacchus (Baki) in Lydia. See Hanfmann and Ramage (1978: 43–51, figs. 20–50). Also, Hanfmann (1983: 90–3).

[53] See above, Ch. 3.   [54] West (1990: 26–7).

[55] Athenaeus 5.201c. Rice (1983: 19 and 99–102). For an altar on Cos said to represent this scene see Benndorf and Niemann (1884: 13–14 and pl. II; Rice (1983: 101 n. 201) and Burkert (1993: 270–5).

[56] Florence 4209, *ARV* 76.1.   [57] See above, Ch. 5.   [58] West (1992: 125).

[59] Michaelides (1978: 70).   [60] See above, Ch. 3

[61] See T. Carpenter (1986: 13–29) and above, Ch. 3.

black-figure vases are not recognizable narratives but simply show the god standing or sitting amongst his companions, satyrs and nymphs. When nymphs dance on black-figure vases those dances could hardly be called ecstatic. When new narratives about the god appear with the red-figure painters at the beginning of the fifth century, they seem to be localized in Thrace, and while wild dancing becomes common, the music remains Greek with pipes, lyre, and krotala.[62]

In the middle of the fifth century the focus of Dionysian scenes on Attic vases changes when the orgiastic dimension is reintroduced, signalled by the inclusion of foreign instruments—cymbals and tympana. That a fifth-century Athenian would have known well the connection between Dionysos and Meter in the mythic tradition seems likely. The reappearance of imagery on Attic vases related to the orgiastic dimension of Dionysos may have been inspired by increased significance given to the cult of Meter in Athens implied by the installation of her statue (with tympanon) in the Metroon in the Agora.[63] In any case, Dionysos' connection with Meter (and probably with cymbals and krotala) belonged principally to the mythic tradition; that an Athenian present at the first production of the *Bacchae* would have known that tradition seems likely.

The extraordinary behaviour of the Theban women on the mountain is recounted in two messenger speeches. The imagery of the first (677–774) which is our principal literary account of the behavior of 'maenads', has many parallels in red-figure imagery. The imagery of the second (1043–152), which describes the death of Pentheus, has parallels in a group of red-figure depictions of that subject.

The activity of the women described in the first speech has three stages. In the first stage the sound of cattle wakes the sleeping women, who nurse young animals and relax in a land flowing with milk, honey, and wine. In the second stage they are suddenly and mysteriously aroused to violent activity, where they tear live cattle to pieces and raid villages, and in the third stage they return to the idyll of the first. These opposite extremes of behaviour are indicated by red-figure vase painters when they show nymphs in some scenes destroying the same kinds of animals they fondle in others.

A woman suckling an animal (or a child) is not an image that ever appears on Attic vases, so the visual contrast on vases lacks the brutal balance of Euripides' nurture and destruction; none the less, the effect is similar. On a

---

[62] On krotala West (1992: 123): 'It is in popular, festive music-making that they have their place, not in the theatre, in professional contests or in cult.' On krotala in early literature see Hall (1989: 46–7). See also van der Weiden (1991: 71). See also Dover (1993: 351) on l. 1305.

[63] See Thompson and Wycherley (1972: 31).

mid-fifth-century amphora in Brussels a nymph wearing an ivy wreath and animal skin and holding a snake and thyrsos looks down at a fawn that jumps up toward her like a pet dog (Pl. 44A).[64] The opposite extreme is depicted on several roughly contemporary vases where a nymph holds the halves of a rent fawn in her hands as she dances (Pls. 11A, 44B).[65] These scenes parallel another group in which Dionysos himself dances with a rent animal in his hands, which show the god in the throes of the madness inflicted on him by Hera (Pls. 9B, 10A & B).[66] The god or the nymph in this pose unequivocally shows Dionysian madness in its most destructive and terrifying,[67] which literary sources describe as explicitly pathological for both the god and the women of Thebes—both are driven mad. The torn animal had stood as a visual symbol of this terrible madness for more than half a century when Euripides used it.[68]

The messenger tells that the Theban woman snatched children from the homes in the villages they raided (754), but he does not say what they did with them. Given the violence of the moment, it is unlikely that they cuddled them or carried them gaily on their shoulders.[69] At the beginning of the fourth century a woman with a child flung over her shoulder appears in a Dionysian scene on the lid of an Attic pyxis (Pl. 45A).[70] A very similar figure appears on a fragment of a contemporary krater in Samothrace and on the bronze Derveni krater from the mid-fourth century in Salonica.[71] Other women on the pyxis prepare to rend a fawn, and this image is repeated on a related pyxis once in Heidelberg,[72] on the Derveni krater, and on an early fourth-century bronze krater in Berlin.[73] All three of these works seem to draw on a common model, and late fifth-century paintings

---

[64] Brussels R 255, *ARV* 670.4, *RA* 1983, 245, fig. 7

[65] Newcastle, *ARV* 587.1; Syracuse 24554, *ARV* 649.42, *RA* 1982, 243, fig. 6; Paris, Cab.Méd 357, *ARV* 987.2, Bérard, Bron, *et al.* (1989: 149 fig. 204); Athens, Acr. 717, Graef and Langlotz (1933: pl. 54).

[66] See above, Ch. 3.

[67] For late 5th cent. depictions of women about to rend a fawn see London E 775, *ARV* 1328.92, *LIMC* VII pl. 264, Pentheus 68; Odessa, Metzger (1951: pl. 1. 38); and once Heidelberg, see above, n. 11. For a woman having cut an animal in two with a sword, see Kavalla 1937, *ARV* 1691, *Deltion* 19.1 (1964) 74 fig. 1, pls. 45.1–2, 46–9.

[68] The memorable image of a maenad or the god holding up the halves of a rent fawn with either hand calls to mind Euripides' curious wording in his description of one of the two women tearing a calf in two *echousan en cheroin dicha* (738). Dodds, in his note on the line, writes that it 'can only, I think, mean "holding apart", but the sense required is surely "wrenched asunder" '. It is conceivable that it was just such an image that Euripides (and his audience) would have had in mind, whatever its original source might have been.

[69] e.g. Bologna 283, *ARV* 1151.1, *CV* 4 pls. 68. 3–5, 69, 70. 9. See also Dodds's notes on 754, 755–7.

[70] London E 775, *ARV* 1328.92, see above, n. 67.

[71] Samothrace 65.1041. See Green (1982: 237–48). Salonica, see Gioure (1978).

[72] Once Heidelberg, private, see above, n. 11.   [73] Berlin inv. 30622, Züchner (1938).

described by Pausanias (1. 20. 3) in a temple of Dionysos in Athens have been proposed as a possible source.[74]

A messenger tells of the women sleeping where they fell on boughs of fir or oak leaves;[75] he insists on their modesty and sobriety and denies that they were 'led astray by wine or the music of the flute, to hunt through the woods for sex' (683–8). As mentioned earlier, nymphs in red-figure scenes (as opposed to those on black-figure vases) are often hostile to the erotic advances of satyrs, and they often use their thyrsoi to defend themselves (Pl. 45B).[76] When the herdsmen try to ambush them, Agave cries to her companions (731–3):

> Hounds who run with me
> men are hunting us down! Follow, follow me!
> Use your wands (*thyrsoi*) for weapons.

Which recalls many early fifth-century depictions of maenads using their thyrsoi to defend themselves from satyrs.[77]

Of the second messenger's speech, only the ultimate destruction of Pentheus has parallels in Attic art.[78] The earliest depictions appear on three vases from before the end of the sixth century, a century before Euripides' *Bacchae* and several decades before Aeschylus' *Pentheus*.[79] Pentheus' name appears above the torn torso with head attached held by two women—the principal one labelled *Galene*—on fragments of a psykter in Boston (Pl. 46A). His head is bearded, two of the women may have thyrsoi, and one carries a severed leg. On a hydria in Berlin three women carry body parts, including a bearded head. On one side of a cup in the Louvre, four maenads with thyrsoi also carry body parts, and a rabbit runs into the scene from under one handle, ivy grows under the other (Pl. 46B). None of the women on any of these vases wears an animal skin of any sort. The scene on the Louvre cup is of particular interest because the scene on the other side, a generic fight amongst warriors, has nothing to do with it. The satyr in the tondo with bunches of grapes and a thyrsos is only tangentially related. The implication is that conventions were well established for the scene and that it was simply a part of the repertory.

On two vases from the first quarter of the fifth century the scene has

---

[74] Robertson (1972: 38–48); Burn (1987: 78–80).

[75] For a group of more than twenty red-figure vases from the end of the 6th to the end of the 5th cent. on which a sleeping maenad is molested by satyrs, see Schöne (1987: 137–40, 297–9). See also Caskey and Beazley (1954: 95–9).

[76] For a discussion of this change see McNally (1978).

[77] e.g. Munich 2344, ARV 182.6, see above, n. 48; Munich 2654, *ARV* 462.47, Boardman (1975: fig. 313.

[78] See above, n. 11.   [79] Boston 10. 221, Berlin 1966. 18, Louvre G 69: see above, n. 11.

changed slightly.[80] On both Pentheus is now a beardless youth. All three scenes on the Borowski cup are related. On one side two women wearing leopard skins hold Pentheus' upper torso with head attached, while women to the left hold a severed leg and a himation, and a satyr to the right raises his hands in horror (Pl. 42A). On the other side, a bearded Dionysos holding a kantharos and ivy sprigs sits on a stool while a satyr plays pipes and women dance about him with various body parts (Pl. 42B). In the tondo a woman with a thyrsos carries a leopard by the tail. The scene on the fragmentary stamnos in Oxford, which went right around the vase, is the bloodiest (Pl. 47A & B). On one side three women move to the right, on the other to the left, and between them is a small roaring lion. All the women, who wear ivy wreaths but no animal skins, wave dripping body parts and thyrsoi; one holds a mass of entrails, as if about to throw it, recalling the lines in the *Bacchae* (1135–6):

> and every hand
> was smeared with blood as they played ball with scraps
> of Pentheus body.

The death of Pentheus is also the subject of Attic vases from the end of the fifth century, and of South Italian vases from the fourth. It is difficult to tell whether some of these were made before or after the *Bacchae* was first produced in Athens, but in any case, the imagery is not closely connected with the play, nor is it related to the earlier scenes. On two, maenads use swords in their attack.[81] On another, two maenads pull at the arms and legs of a struggling, but still whole, Pentheus.[82]

The comic Dionysos of Aristophanes' *Frogs* has little or nothing to do with the mythic or cultic Dionysos, nor with any surviving depictions of the god on vases or in sculpture.[83] He wears the dress of a contemporary Athenian woman, a stock comic device, and has no other distinctive attributes. He carries neither wine vessel nor thyrsos, nor is he accompanied by nymphs or satyrs. Aristophanes gives no indication he is aware of the comic potential of donkeys in Dionysian scenes so exploited by generations of vase painters, nor that he is aware of another trip Dionysos took to the underworld to retrieve his mother. [84] A comparison between the imagery of the *Frogs* and on vases serves only to emphasize how separate the comic Dionysos is from other perceptions of him.

---

[80] Oxford 1912. 1165; once Toronto, Borowski. See above, n. 11.

[81] Athens, Kerameikos 2712; Rome, Villa Giulia 2268. See above, n. 11.

[82] Louvre G 445, see above, n. 11.   [83] For one exception, see above, n. 7.

[84] Cf. M. I. Davies (1990), who suggests a link between Bdelykleon's donkey in *Wasps* (169–97) and Dionysian imagery.

Euripides, on the other hand, borrows heavily from the mythic tradition and also from visual imagery for the *Bacchae*. The behaviour and the appearance of the women of Thebes could have been well known to Athenians from visual images as well as from performances of other tragedies. They would have known of the connection between Dionysos and Meter, but they might have found surprising the strong emphasis on the east, particularly Lydia and Phrygia, to the exclusion of Thrace. They might also have known that it was only in the last decade of Euripides' life that he showed an interest in ecstatic cults, to the extent of describing ecstatic behaviour and orgiastic instruments.[85] So too, they might also have remembered that Euripides seemed less interested in the names of the deities than in the types of behaviour, a lack of precision that may have been shared by many of them as well.

[85] For dates of the plays, see Seaford (1984: 48); Dale (1967: xxiv); Bond (1981: xxx–xxxii); Bond (1963: 144).

8

Conclusion

FOR fifth-century Athenians the name Dionysos would have had a multitude of associations coming from many sources: from poetry, the theatre, traditional tales, vases, sculpture, monumental painting, and cult to name a few of the more tangible ones. The incarnate Dionysos who appears in images usually has a human form, and extant evidence (literary and archaeological) allows the conclusion that some Athenians might have recognized three broad categories into which representations of the anthropomorphic Dionysos fit: the mythic, the comic, and the cultic. Failure to recognize the differences between these forms has led to much scholarly confusion in the past as attempts have been made to patch together a whole Dionysos from contradictory bits of evidence.

The mythic Dionysos (of hymns, epic, tragedy, and folklore) seems usually to have been perceived as a youth or adolescent. The comic Dionysos (of the theatre) appeared as an effeminate fop, and the cultic Dionysos was known (in cult images) as a bearded mask or a stately, bearded adult usually holding a kantharos as his principal attribute. Until the last quarter of the century vase painters used the bearded, cultic form of the god, with an emphasis on his role as wine god, to represent him in mythic narratives that often recounted events from his youth. Ironically, even though they used the cultic form in these scenes, they rarely if ever depicted cultic events associated with his worship by mortals. Though humour can certainly be an element in many of their scenes, vase painters never represented the foppish Dionysos of Attic comedy.

Painted vases are by far the richest source of Dionysian imagery from fifth-century Athens, but there is reason to think that the imagery on them is in ways unique to vase painting and thus not necessarily representative of other lost forms. Though we know little about the potters, painters, or patrons, we are probably safe in assuming that the painters' ultimate purpose was to please the patrons with the hope that they would buy the pots. Unlike architectural sculpture and probably monumental painting, the primary purpose of most Dionysian scenes on Attic vases, at least during the first half of the fifth century, seems to have been to entertain. Preconceptions derived from familiarity with Christian religious art have often obscured this perspective and have led to attempts to see some images as didactic or 'sacred'. As in the Christian story, Dionysos is the son of a god who takes on human form, but there is a fundamental difference in the nature of his incarnation, which makes Dionysian imagery radically different from Christian art. In the Christian story the son of God took on human form to save mankind, with terrible consequences for himself. In Greek stories, Dionysos takes on human form as one of several disguises, often with more than a hint of humour, and the form has nothing to do with his divinity.[1] In other words, there is nothing inherently important about his human form and nothing inherently admirable about his human behaviour. Thus the form can be a vehicle for a vast range of activities from the truly terrible to the absurdly comic, which provide neither models nor lessons and carry with them no demands for religious awe.

Depictions of Dionysos in the Gigantomachy on red-figure vases illustrate this point well. Though the battle itself, which appeared on the Panathenaic peplos and in architectural sculpture on numerous temples, was a serious matter or at least a significant metaphor, elements of imagery or juxtapositions of images in many depictions of Dionysos in the battle are undeniably humorous. Though the form used for him in his fight with a giant on the Parthenon metope is essentially the same as the form used on earlier vases, details on the vases make the effect of the scenes quite different. Dionysos on the vase could mock the civic form, even of himself. Dionysos the mock-hero fights giants with the help of satyrs, or better yet, with the help of his nurses. Like Achilles he receives armour (which he never wears in battle) from nymphs. As parodies, the humour comes from visual parallels too subtle to depend on literary forms or theatrical performances. But these Dionysian scenes enlivened by wit seldom if ever appear after the middle of the fifth century.

The nature of imagery on vases changes with each new generation of vase painters. This is, of course, true of Dionysian imagery, and its development during the century and a quarter of this study is most usefully seen as the product of specific painters and groups of painters. Dionysos seems to have been born anew with early red-figure painters—Oltos, Epiktetos, and the Pioneers—who used new imagery to define him more sharply than black-figure painters ever did and who introduced a range of new stories for him. Once the new imagery and subjects were established, other painters took them up and their development can be traced through the works of related 'mainstream' painters starting with the workshop of the Niobid Painter in the 470s and continuing into the second half of the century with Polygnotos and

---

[1] Orphic myths of Dionysos-Zagreus and the Titans do not appear in 5th-cent. Attic imagery.

his group including the Kleophon and Dinos Painters who take it down nearly to the end of the century.

In general the vitality of early scenes fades as the new imagery becomes canonical. Lively, focused narratives tend to give way to staid tableaux. The rough and tumble of the early scenes is replaced by what might be called a new self-consciousness where, for example, the randy satyrs of the beginning of the century are, by the end, more like court eunuchs chaperoning swooning nymphs.

The god's fight with giants is one of several Dionysian subjects to appear on early red-figure vases with a distinctly Thracian flavour. These stories, which include the god's madness, his confrontation with Lykourgos, and the Return of Hephaistos in addition to the Gigantomachy, seem to form a group of narratives about the god linked visually by Thracian attributes, and there is reason to think that most Dionysian narratives were, in fact, about the god's infancy and youth. This Thracian emphasis fades toward the middle of the century.

The use of the term 'maenad' for the female companions of Dionysos on red-figure vases with its implication that they are, or at least reflect, mortal votaries of the god, has led some to see maenadism as an important aspect of the worship of Dionysos in archaic and classical Greece, making it part of a continuous tradition for which the evidence is all much later. In fact, these women on vases are more appropriately called 'nymphs' and are connected with him in both literature and visual imagery through the Thracian narratives of his childhood and youth where they serve as his nurses. In early scenes, participating in the god's madness induced by Hera, they dance wildly and sometimes tear live animals apart with their bare hands. Toward the middle of the century their behaviour mellows and in depictions of the god's infancy stately nymphs are sometimes given appropriately Dionysian labels like *mainas* (mad-woman) and *methuse* (drunken woman) in place of actions. Then during the second half of the century the narrative focus tends to blur and these female companions of the god take on quite different labels like *chrysis* (golden) and *oinanthe* (grape bloom) which seem to be sprinkled on them in a random way. There is, however, no convincing reason to see any of these women with the god as mortals. They are not different in kind from the earlier, more clearly defined nymphs.

Semele and Ariadne are the two identifiable women from myth who appear with the god on fifth-century vases. Semele, his mother, appears only as a bystander, but her presence presupposes his rescue of her from the underworld. Ariadne first appears with Dionysos during the last quarter of the sixth century in scenes on black-figure vases that imply marriage (but not romance). On red-figure vases, most of which come from the first half of the century, the god joins her in narrative scenes depicting her rescue from Naxos. These scenes do not seem to be connected in any way with the Thracian narratives. During the second half of the century a distinctly romantic element is introduced into depictions of the couple, and by the last quarter this has developed with the young god into a veiled eroticism of a type that permeates much Attic vase painting of that period.

One of the more puzzling problems in the study of fifth-century Dionysian imagery is the persistent use of the bearded cultic form of the god in depictions of stories that must have taken place during his youth. He is almost always bearded on vases until the last quarter of the century when there is a sudden change, seen most clearly in the works of the Dinos Painter. Of extant monuments, the sculpted figure of the beardless god at the Birth of Athena in the east pediment of the Parthenon (Figure D) marks the change. That he should appear beardless there is appropriate for what I have called the mythic form. However, it is another decade before the Dinos Painter adopts this beardless form for vase painting, after which it quickly becomes canonical.

The bearded form seems originally to have been borrowed from traditional masks connected with Dionysos' function as wine god. Hung on pillars, if vase paintings are to be believed, masks formed idols probably not dissimilar in function to herms. The unkempt state of Dionysos' beard on vases (by comparison with other Olympians) is from the start one of its characteristics, hinting at the rural and uncivilized rather than the urban and cultivated. The tenacity of the bearded form on vases probably resulted from the ancient roots that the mask had in popular religion of the countryside. The eventual change to the appropriately beardless form for poetic scenes on vases could reflect social turmoil in Athens during the Peloponnesian Wars but must in large part be explained by changes in the nature of Greek vase painting after the middle of the century and the concomitant tendency toward the romantic in Dionysian scenes. Saccharin romanticism is hardly possible with an older bearded figure heavily draped in chiton and himation.

Before the last quarter of the fifth century the Dionysos on vases is preeminently a wine god; it his connection with wine, usually indicated by his kantharos, that provides the continuity for the different representations of him on vases. When, after the middle of the century, tympana and cymbals are introduced into Dionysian scenes—instruments usually associated with orgiastic cults of foreign gods—the bearded Dionysos continues to carry his kantharos. The appearance of those instruments in the scenes may, in fact, result from a narrative connection between Dionysos and the Great Mother (Meter) rather than from far-reaching changes in perceptions of the god.

One of the stories from his youth, which was probably known in Athens by the early sixth century has the god cured of his Hera-induced madness by Rhea (Meter) in Kybela, and in his *Bacchae*, Euripides explicitly links Dionysos with Kybele (Meter). There is no evidence (aside from the vases and the *Bacchae*) for such syncretism in fifth-century Attic cults of Dionysos.

The vivid imagery in Euripides' *Bacchae*, which had such a profound influence on later perceptions of the god and his followers, reflects the traditional visual imagery we know from earlier fifth-century vases. By way of contrast, Aristophanes' *Frogs* depends upon it not at all. A new interest in the trappings of ecstatic cults appears on vases during the second half of the fifth century, though vase painters seem to be more interested in presenting the general idea in an entertaining way than in giving accurate accounts. It seems that it was during the last decade of Euripides' life that he too took a particular interest in ecstatic cults and it also seems that he, like the vase painters, may have been more interested in the general idea than in the specific reality. On the whole, vases and Euripides prove unreliable sources for specific and detailed knowledge of cult in fifth-century Athens. The irony is that with changing times and needs the lively stories and images from the beginning of the fifth century ultimately took on cultic trappings that obscured the lines demarcating the mythic, the comic, and the cultic dimensions of the anthropomorphic Dionysos.

Works Cited

ALFIERI, N. (1979), *Spina: Museo archeologico nazionale di Ferrara*, I (Bologna).

ANDERSON, J. K. (1974), *Xenophon* (London).

—— (1991), 'Hoplite Weapons and Offensive Arms', in V. Hanson, (ed.), *Hoplites: The Classical Greek Battle Experience* (London), 15–37.

ANDERSON, J. K., and WEST, R. (1982), *Poseidon's Realm: Ancient Greek Art from the Lowie Museum of Anthropology, Berkeley* (Sacramento).

ARAFAT, K. (1986), 'A Note on the Athena Parthenos', *BSA* 81: 1–6.

—— (1990), *Classical Zeus: A Study in Art and Literature* (Oxford).

ARAFAT, K., and MORGAN, C. (1989), 'Pots and Potters in Athens and Corinth: A Review', *Oxford Journal of Archaeology* 8 (1989), 311–46.

—— (1994), 'Athens, Etruria and the Heueneburg: Mutual Misconceptions in the Study of Greek–Barbarian Relations', in I. Morris, (ed.), *Classical Greece: Ancient Histories and Modern Archaeologies* (Cambridge), 108–34.

ARIAS, P. E., HIRMER, M., and SHEFTON, B. B. (1962), *A History of Greek Vase Painting* (London).

AURIGEMMA, S. (1960), *La necropoli di Spina in Valle Trebba* (Rome).

AVAGIANOU, A. (1991), *Sacred Marriage in the Rituals of Greek Religion* (Bern).

BARBER, E. (1991), *Prehistoric Textiles* (Princeton).

—— (1992), 'The Peplos of Athena', in Neils (1992), 103–17.

BARRETT, W. (1964), *Euripides: Hippolytos* (Oxford).

BEAZLEY, J. D. (1928), *Greek Vases in Poland* (Oxford).

—— (1929), 'Notes on the Vases in Castle Ashby', *Papers of the British School at Rome* 11: 1–29.

—— (1933), 'Narthex', *AJA* 37, 400–3.

—— (1955), 'Hydria-Fragments in Corinth', *Hesperia* 24: 308–15.

—— (1986), *The Development of Attic Black-figure*, revised by D. von Bothmer and M. Moore (Berkeley).

BEAZLEY, J. D., and PAYNE, H. (1929), 'Attic Black-Figured Fragments from Naucratis', *JHS* 49: 253–72.

BELL, E. (1978), 'Two Krokotos Mask Cups at San Simeon', *California Studies in Classical Antiquity* 10: 1–15.

BENNDORF, O., and NIEMANN, G. (1884), *Reisen in Lykien und Karien, Reisen im süd-westlichen Kleinaisen*, i (Vienna).

BÉRARD, C. (1976), 'Le Liknon d' Athéna', *AK* 19: 101–14.

BÉRARD, C., and BRON, C. (1989), 'Satyric Revels', in Bérard, Bron, *et al.* (1989), 131–49.

BÉRARD, C., BRON, C., *et al.* (1989), *A City of Images: Iconography and Society in Ancient Greece* (Princeton).

BERGER, E. (ed.) (1984), *Parthenon-Kongress Basel* (Mainz).

—— (1986), *Der Parthenon in Basel, Dokumentation zu den Metopen* (Mainz).

BERGER, E., and LULLIES, R. (1979), *Antike Kunstwerke aus der Sammlung Ludwig*, i (Basel).

BEST, J. (1969), *Thracian Peltasts and their Influence on Greek Warfare* (Groningen).

BIERS, W. (1992), *Art, Artefacts, and Chronology in Classical Archaeology* (London).

BOARDMAN, J. (1972), 'Herakles, Peisistratos and Sons', *RA* 57–72.

—— (1974), *Athenian Black Figure Vases* (London).

—— (1975), *Athenian Red Figure Vases: The Archaic Period* (London).

—— (1984), 'The Parthenon Frieze', in Berger (1984), 210–15.

—— (1990a), 'The Greek Art of Narrative', in J. Descoeudres (ed.), *Ceramic and Iconographic Studies In Honour of A. Cambitoglou* (Sydney), 57–62.

—— (1990b), 'Symposion Furniture', in Murray (1990), 122–31.

—— (1992), 'The Phallos-Bird in Archaic and Classical Greek Art', *RA* 227–42.

BOND, G. W. (1963), *Euripides: Hypsipyle* (Oxford).

—— (1981), *Euripides: Herakles* (Oxford).

BOTHMER, D. VON (ed.) (1990), *Glories of the Past: Ancient Art from the Shelby White and Leon Levy Collection* (New York).

BOULTER, C. G. (ed.) (1985), *Greek Art: Archaic into Classical* (Leiden).

BOVON, A. (1963), 'La Représentation des guerriers perses et la notion de barbare dans la 1er moitié du Ve siècle', *BCH* 87: 579–602.

BOWIE, T., and THIMME, D. (1971), *The Carrey Drawings of the Parthenon Sculptures* (Bloomington).

BOWRA, C. M. (1963), 'Two Lines of Eumelus', *The Classical Quarterly* NS 13: 145–53.

BREMMER, J. (ed.) (1984), 'Greek Maenadism Reconsidered', *Zeitschrift für Papyrologie und Epigraphik* 55: 267–86.

—— (1987), *Interpretations of Greek Mythology* (London).

BRIJDER, H., DRUKKER, A., and NEEFT, C. (1986), *Enthousiasmos: Essays on Greek and Related Pottery Presented to J. M. Hemelrijk* (Amsterdam).

BRINKMANN, V. (1985), 'Die aufgemalten Namensbeischriften am Nord- und Ostfries des Siphnierschatzhauses', *BCH* 109: 77–130.

BROMMER, F. (1937), *Satyroi* (Würzburg).

—— (1959), *Satyrspiele*, 2nd edn. (Berlin).

—— (1961), 'Die Geburt der Athena', *Jahrbuch des Römische-Germanischen Zentralmuseums Mainz* 8: 66–83.

—— (1963), *Die Skulpturen der Parthenon-Giebel* (Mainz).

—— (1967), *Die Metopen des Parthenon* (Mainz).

—— (1977), *Der Parthenonfries* (Mainz).

—— (1978), *Hephaistos: der Schmiedegott in der antiken Kunst* (Mainz).

—— (1979), *The Sculptures of the Parthenon* (London).

—— (1980), *Göttersagen in Vasenlisten* (Marburg).

—— (1983), 'Satyrspielvasen in Malibu', *Greek Vases in the J. Paul Getty Museum* 1: 114–20.

BRON, C., CORFU-BRATSCHI, P., and MAOUENE, M. (1989), 'Hephaistos bacchant ou le cavalier comaste: simulation de raisonnement qualitatif par le langage informatique LISP', *Annali Istituto Orientale Napoli, Archeologia e Storia Antica* 11: 155–72.

BROUSKARI, M. (1974), *The Acropolis Museum: A Descriptive Catalogue* (Athens).

—— (1985), *The Paul and Alexandra Canellopoulos Museum* (Athens).

BRUHN, A. (1943), *Oltos and Early Red-Figure Vase Painting* (Copenhagen).

BUITRON-OLIVER, D. (1972), *Attic Vase Painting in New England Collections* (Cambridge).

—— (1995), *Douris: A Master-Painter of Athenian Red-Figure Vases* (Mainz).

BURKERT, W. (1966), 'Greek Tragedy and Sacrificial Ritual', *GRBS* 7: 87–121.

—— (1983), *Homo Necans: The Anthropology of Ancient Greek Sacrificial Ritual and Myth* (Berkeley).

—— (1985), *Greek Religion* (Oxford).

—— (1993), 'Bacchic Teletai in the Hellenistic Age', in Carpenter and Faraone (1993), 259–75.

BURN, L. (1987), *Meidias Painter* (Oxford).

—— (1991), 'A Dinoid Volute Krater by the Meleager Painter', *Greek Vases in the J. Paul Getty Museum* 5: 107–30.

BUROW, J. (1989), *Der Antimenesmaler* (Mainz).

BURROW, E. (1817), *The Elgin Marbles* (London).

BUSCHOR, E. (1943), *Satyrtänze und frühes Drama* (Munich).

BUXTON, R. (1994), *Imaginary Greece: The Contexts of Mythology* (Cambridge).

CAHN, H. (1944), *Die Münzen der sizilischen Stadt Naxos* (Basel).

—— (1973), 'Dokimasia', *RA* 3–15.

CARPENTER, R. (1962), 'On Restoring the East Pediment of the Parthenon', *AJA* 66: 265–8.

CARPENTER, T. (1986), *Dionysian Imagery in Archaic Greek Art* (Oxford).

—— (1991), *Art and Myth in Ancient Greece* (London).

—— (1993), 'On the Beardless Dionysus', in Carpenter and Faraone (1993), 185–206.

—— (1995), 'A Symposion of Gods', in O. Murray (ed.), *In Vino Veritas* (Rome), 145–63.

—— (forthcoming), 'Harmodios and Apollo, What's in a Pose?', in Oakley (forthcoming).

CARPENTER, T., and FARAONE, C. (eds.) (1993), *Masks of Dionysus* (Ithaca: NY).

CASKEY, L., and BEAZLEY, J. D. (1954), *Attic Vase Paintings in the Museum of Fine Arts, Boston* ii (Oxford).

CASTRIOTA, D. (1992), *Myth, Ethos and Actuality: Official Art in Fifth-Century B.C. Athens* (Madison).

CHRISTOPULU-MORTOJA, E. (1964), *Darstellungen des Dionysos in der schwarzfigurigen Vasenmalerei* (Berlin).

COCHE DE LA FERTÉ, E. (1951), 'Les Ménades et le contenu réel des représentations de scènes bachiques autour de l'idole de Dionysos', *RA* 12–23.

CONNOR, P. (1981), 'Replicas in Greek Vase-Painting: The Work of the Painter of Louvre F 6', *BABesch* 56: 37–42.

Cook, R. (1983), 'Art and Epic in Archaic Greece', *BABesch* 58: 1–10.

Corbett, P. (1949), 'Attic Pottery of the Later Fifth Century from the Athenian Agora', *Hesperia* 18: 298–351.

Crosby, M. (1955), 'Five Comic Scenes from Athens', *Hesperia* 24: 76–84.

Cultrera, G. (1938), *Hydria a figure rosse del Museo di Villa Giulia* (Rome).

Dale, A. (1967), *Euripides: Helen* (Oxford).

Dasen, V. (1993), *Dwarfs in Ancient Egypt and Greece* (Oxford).

Davies, M. (1988), *Epicorum Graecorum Fragmenta* (Göttingen).

Davies, M. I. (1990), 'Asses and Rams: Dionysiac Release in Aristophanes' *Wasps*', *Metis* 5: 169–83.

Dentzer, J.-M. (1982), *Le Motif du banquet couché dans le proche-orient et le monde grec du VIIᵉ au IVᵉ siècle avant J.-C.* (Rome and Paris).

Dodds, E. R. (1951), *The Greeks and the Irrational* (Berkeley).

—— (1960), *Euripides: Bacchae*, 2nd edn. (Oxford).

Doumas, C. (1992), *The Wall-Paintings of Thera* (Athens).

Dover, K. (1993), *Aristophanes: Frogs* (Oxford).

Dugas, C. (1928), *Les Vases de l'Héraion: Exploration archéologique de Délos* X (Paris).

Durand J.-L., and Frontisi-Ducroux, F. (1982), 'Idoles, figures, images: autour de Dionysos', *RA*, 81–108.

Edwards, M. (1960), 'Representation of Maenads on Archaic Red-Figure Vases', *JHS* 80: 78–87.

Ehrhardt, W. (1993), 'Der Fries des Lysikratesmonuments', *Antike Plastik* 22: 7–67.

Eisman, M. (1978), 'Robertson's Kiln Skyphos', *AJA* 82: 394–9.

Faraone, C. A. (1992), *Talismans and Trojan Horses* (New York).

Felten, F., and Hoffelner, K. (1987), 'Die Relieffriese des Poseidontempels in Sunion', *AM* 102: 169–84.

Ferrari-Pinney, G. (1983), 'Achilles Lord of Scythia', in W. Moon (ed.), *Ancient Greek Art and Iconography* (Madison), 127–46.

—— (1986), 'Eye-cup', *RA*, 5–20.

—— (1988), *I vasi attici a figure rosse del periodo arcaico* (Rome).

Fol, A. (1993), 'Thrace and Macedonia in the 6th–4th Century B.C. in Euripides *Bacchae*', in *Ancient Macedonia* v (Thessaloniki), 433–41.

Fränkel, C. (1912), *Satyr- und Bakchennamen auf Vasenbildern* (Halle).

Frel, J. (1967), 'Dionysos Lenaios', *Anz* 28–34.

Frontisi-Ducroux, F. (1989), 'In the Mirror of the Mask', in Bérard Bron, *et al.* (1989), 151–65.

—— (1991), *Le Dieu-Masque: une figure du Dionysos d'Athènes* (Paris and Rome).

Fuchs, W. (1993), *Die Skulptur der Griechen* (Munich).

Fuhrmann, H. (1950/1), 'Athamas: Nachklang einer verlorenen Tragödie des Sophokles auf dem Bruchstück eines 'Homerischen' Bechers', *JdI* 65/6: 103–34.

Furtwängler, A. (1883–7), *La Collection Sabouroff* (Berlin).

Furtwängler, A., and Reichhold, (1904–32), *Griechische Vasenmalerei* (Munich).

Gerhard, E. (1840), *Auserlesene griechische Vasenbilder*, i (Berlin).

GERHARD, E. (1843), *Etruskische und kampanische Vasenbilder des Königlichen Museums zu Berlin* (Berlin).

GETTY MUSEUM (1980), *Stamnoi: An Exhibition at the J. Paul Getty Museum* (Malibu).

GILL, D., and VICKERS, M. (1990), 'Reflected Glory: Pottery and Precious Metal in Classical Greece', *JdI* 105: 1–30.

GIOURE, E. (1978), *O krateras tou Derveniou* (Athens).

GNADE, M. (ed.) (1991), *Stips Votiva: Papers Presented to C. M. Stibbe* (Amsterdam).

GOLDMAN, H. (1942), 'The Origin of the Greek Herm', *AJA* 46: 58–68.

GRAEF, B., and LANGLOTZ, E. (1925), *Die antiken Vasen von der Akropolis zu Athen*, i (Berlin).

—— (1933), *Die antiken Vasen von der Akropolis zu Athen*, ii (Berlin).

GRAF, F. (1984), 'The Arrival of Cybele in the Greek East', Proceedings of the 7th Congress of Int. Fed. of Societies of Classical Studies (Budapest), i. 117–20.

—— (1987), 'Orpheus: A Poet Among Men', in Bremmer (1987), 80–106.

GREEN, J. (1982), 'Dedications of Masks', *RA* 237–48.

—— (1991), 'On Seeing and Depicting the Theatre in Classical Athens', *GRBS* 32: 15–50.

GREIFENHAGEN, A. (1966), 'Der Tod des Pentheus', *Berliner Museen* 16: 2–6.

GRIFFIN, J. (1983), 'The Myth of Lykourgos, King of the Edonians', in A. Poulter (ed.), *Ancient Bulgaria*, i (Nottingham), 217–32.

GURALNICK, E. (1974), 'The Chrysapha Relief and its Connection with Egyptian Art', *Journal of Egyptian Archaeology* 60: 175–88.

HÄGG, R. (1992), *The Iconography of Greek Cult in the Archaic and Classical Periods*, *Kernos* Supplement 1 (Athens).

HALL, E. (1989), *Inventing the Barbarian: Greek Self-definition through Tragedy* (Oxford).

HALLAGER, E., VLASAKIS, M., and HALLAGER, B. (1992), 'New Linear B Tablets from Khania', *Kadmos* 31: 61–87.

HALM-TISSERANT, M. (1986), 'La Représentation du retour d'Héphaïstos dans l'Olympe', *AK* 29: 8–22.

HAMILTON, R. (1992), *Choes and Anthesteria: Athenian Iconography and Ritual* (Ann Arbor).

HAMPE, R. (1936), *Frühe griechische Sagenbilder in Böotien* (Athens).

HANFMANN, G. (1983), *Sardis from Prehistory to Roman Times* (Harvard).

HANFMANN, G., and Ramage, N. (1978), *Sculpture from Sardis* (Harvard).

HARRISON, E. (1967), 'Athena and Athens in the East Pediment of the Parthenon', *AJA* 71: 27–58.

HARRISON, J. E. (1903), *Prolegomena to the Study of Greek Religion* (Cambridge).

HARTWIG, P. (1893), *Die griechischen Meisterschalen* (Stuttgart).

HAWKINS, E. (1842), *Description of the Collection of Ancient Marbles in the British Museum* (London).

HEDREEN, G. (1992), *Silens in Attic Black-figure Vase-painting* (Michigan).

—— (1994), 'Silens, Nymphs, and Maenads', *JHS* 114: 47–69.

HENDERSON, J. (1975), *The Maculate Muse* (New Haven).

HENRICHS, A. (1978), 'Greek Maenadism from Olympias to Messalina', *Harvard Studies in Classical Philology* 82: 121–60.

—— (1982), 'Changing Dionysiac Identities', in B. Meyer and E. Sanders (eds.), *Jewish and Christian Self-Definition*, 3, 137–60, and 213–36.

—— (1987), 'Myth Visualized: Dionysos and His Circle in Sixth Century Attic Vase Painting', in *Papers on the Amasis Painter and His World* (Malibu), 92–124.

—— (1990), 'Between Country and City: Cultic Dimensions of Dionysos in Athens and Attica', in M. Griffith and D. Mastronarde (eds.), *Cabinet of Muses: Essays on Classical and Comparative Literature in Honor of Thomas G. Rosenmeyer* (Atlanta), 257–77.

HEUBECK, A., and HOEKSTRA, A. (1989), *A Commentary on Homer's Odyssey*, ii (Oxford).

HEYDEMANN, H. (1880), *Satyr- und Bakchennamen* (Halle).

HOFFMANN, H. (1983), 'Ubrin orthian knodalon' in D. Metzler, B. Otto, and C. Müller-Wirth (eds.), *Antidoron, Festschrift für Jürgen Thimme* (Karlsruhe), 61–73.

—— (1988), 'Why Did the Greeks Need Imagery? An Anthropological Approach to the Study of Greek Vase Painting', *Hephaistos* 9: 143–62.

HÖLSCHER, T. (1973), *Griechische Historienbilder des 5. und 4. Jahrhunderts v. Chr.* (Würzburg).

HOUSER, C. (1979), *Dionysos and His Circle* (Cambridge).

IMMERWAHR, H. R. (1990), *Attic Script: A Survey* (Oxford).

IMMERWAHR, S. (1990), *Aegean Painting in the Bronze Age* (University Park).

ISLER-KERÉNYI, C. (1977), *Stamnoi* (Lugano).

JAMESON, M. (1993), 'The Asexuality of Dionysus', in Carpenter & Faraone (1993) 44–64.

JEANMAIRE, H. (1951), *Dionysos: Histoire du culte de Bacchus* (Paris).

JENKINS, I. (1994), *The Parthenon Frieze* (London).

JEPPESEN, K. (1984), 'Evidence for the Restoration of the East Pediment', in Berger (1984), 267–77.

JOHNS, C. (1982), *Sex or Symbol: Erotic Images of Greece and Rome* (London).

JOHNSON, S. E. (1984), 'The Present State of Sabazios Research', *Aufstieg und Niedergang der Römischen Welt* II.17.3: 1583–613.

JOHNSTON, A. W. (1979), *Trademarks on Greek Vases* (Warminster).

—— (1987), '*IG* II² 2311 and the Number of Panathenaic Amphorae', *BSA* 82: 125–9.

—— (1991), 'Greek Vases in the Marketplace', in Rasmussen and Spivey (1991), 203–31.

KAEMPF-DIMITRIADOU, S. (1979), *Die Liebe der Götter in der attischen Kunst des 5. Jahrhunderts v. Chr. AK* Beiheft 11 (Bern).

KAMERBEEK, J. C. (1984), *The Plays of Sophocles: Commentaries, vii The Oedipus Coloneus* (Leiden).

KANE, S. (1974), 'Holy Ghost People', *Appalachian Journal* 3: 255–64.

KANNICHT, R. (1969), *Euripides: Helena* (Heidelberg).

KAROUZOU, S. (1956), *The Amasis Painter* (Oxford).

KAROUZOU, S. (1972), 'Saturoi Purrichistes', in *Kernos, Festschrift Bakalakis* (Thessaloniki), 58–71.

—— (1983), 'Zur Makron-Schale von der Akropolis', *AM* 98: 57–64.

KASSEL, R., and AUSTIN, C. (eds.) (1983), *Poetae Comici Graeci*, iv (Berlin).

KERÉNYI, C. (1976), *Dionysos: Archtypal Image of Indestructible Life* (London).

KIRK, G. S. (1970), *The Bacchae by Euripides* (Englewood Cliffs).

—— (1990), *The Iliad: A Commentary*, ii (Cambridge).

KOKKOROU-ALEWRAS, G. (1975), *Archäische naxische Plastik* (Munich).

KORSHAK, Y. (1987), *Frontal Faces in Attic Vase Painting of the Archaic Period* (Chicago).

KOSSATZ-DIESSMANN, A. (1991), 'Satyr- und Mänadennamen auf Vasenbildern des Getty-Museums und der Sammlung Cahn (Basel) mit Addenda zu Charlotte Fränkel, *Satyr- und Bakchennamen auf Vasenbildern* (Halle, 1912)', *Greek Vases in the J. Paul Getty Museum* 5: 131–99.

KRAAY, C. M. (1976), *Archaic and Classical Greek Coins* (London).

KRAAY, C. M., and HIRMER, M. (1966), *Greek Coins* (London).

KURTZ, D. C. (1985), 'Beazley and the Connoisseurship of Greek Vases', *Greek Vases in the J. Paul Getty Museum* 2: 237–50.

KURTZ, D. C., and BOARDMAN, J. (1986), 'Booners', *Greek Vases in the J. Paul Getty Museum* 3: 35–70.

KURTZ, D. C., and SPARKES, B. A. (1982), *The Eye of Greece: Studies in the Art of Athens* (Cambridge).

LANE, E. N. (1989), *Corpus Cultus Iovis Sabazii*, iii (Leiden).

LAWLER, L. (1927), 'The Maenads: A Contribution to the Study of Dance in Ancient Greece', *Memoirs of the American Academy in Rome* 6: 69–112.

LEAKE, W. M. (1841), *The Topography of Athens with Some Remarks on its Antiquities*, 2nd edn. (London).

LEIPEN, N. (1971), *Athena Parthenos: A Reconstruction* (Toronto).

—— (ed.) (1984), *Glimpses of Excellence: a Selection of Vases and Bronzes from the Elie Borowski Collection* (Toronto).

LÉVÊQUE, P. (1949), 'Héra et le lion d'après statuettes de Délos', *BCH* 73: 125–32.

LEZZI-HAFTER, A. (1988), *Der Eretria-Maler* (Mainz).

LISSARRAGUE, F. (1987), 'Dionysos s'en va-t-en guerre', in C. Bérard (ed.), *Images et société en Grèc ancienne* (Lausanne), 111–18.

—— (1990a), 'Why Satyrs are Good to Represent', in J. Winkler and F. Zeitlin (eds.), *Nothing To Do With Dionysos?* (Princeton), 228–36.

—— (1990b), 'The Sexual Life of Satyrs', in D. Halperin, J. Winkler, and F. Zeitlin (eds.), *Before Sexuality: The Construction of Erotic Experience in the Ancient Greek World* (Princeton), 53–81.

—— (1990c), *The Aesthetics of the Greek Banquet* (Princeton).

—— (1990d), *L'Autre Guerrier: archers, peltastes, cavaliers dans l'imagerie attique* (Paris and Rome).

LLOYD-JONES, H. (1970), 'Heracles or Dionysus?', *AJA* 74: 181.

LOEB, E. (1979), *Die Geburt der Götter in der griechischen Kunst der klassischen Zeit* (Jerusalem).

LOUCAS, I. (1992), 'Meaning and Place of the Cult Scene on the Ferrara Krater T 128', in Hägg (1992), 73–83.

MACDOWELL, D. (ed.) (1971), *Aristophanes: Wasps* (Oxford).

McNALLY, S. (1978), 'The Maenad in Early Greek Art', *Arethusa* 11: 101–36.

MANNACK, T. (forthcoming), *The Late Mannerists in Attic Vase-Painting*.

MANSFIELD, J. M. (1985), *The Robe of Athena and the Panathenaic 'Peplos'* dissertation (Ann Arbor).

MARCH, J. (1989), 'Euripides' *Bakchai*: A Reconsideration in Light of Vase Paintings', *BICS* 36: 33–65.

METZGER, H. (1951), *Les Représentations dans la céramique attique du IVᵉ siècle* (Paris).

MICHAELIDES, S. (1978), *The Music of Ancient Greece: An Encyclopaedia* (London).

MICHAELIS, A. (1871), *Der Parthenon* (Leipzig).

MIKALSON, J. (1984), 'Religion and the Plague in Athens, 431–423 B.C.', in *Studies Presented to Sterling Dow*, *GRBS* Monograph 10: 217–25.

—— (1991), *Honor Thy Gods: Popular Religion in Greek Tragedy* (Chapel Hill).

MILLER, M. (1989), 'The Ependytes in Classical Athens', *Hesperia* 58: 313–29.

—— (1991), 'Foreigners at the Greek Symposium?', in W. J. Slater (ed.), *Dining in a Classical Context* (Ann Arbor), 59–81.

MOREUX, B. (1970), 'Dèmèter et Dionysos dans la septième *Isthmique* de Pindare', *Revue des études grecques* 83: 1–14.

MORROW, K. D. (1985), *Greek Footwear and the Dating of Sculpture* (Madison).

MURRAY, O. (ed.) (1990), *Sympotica: A Symposium on the Symposion* (Oxford).

NAUMANN, F. (1983), *Die Ikonographie der Kybele in der phrygischen und der griechischen Kunst* (Tübingen).

NEILS, J. (ed.) (1992), *Goddess and Polis: The Panathenaic Festival in Ancient Athens* (Princeton).

NILSSON, M. (1957), *The Dionysiac Mysteries of the Hellenistic and Roman Age* (Lund).

NOBLE, J. V. (1988), *The Techniques of Painted Attic Pottery*, rev. edn. (London).

NORDQUIST, G. (1992), 'Instrumental Music in Representations of Greek Cult', in Hägg (1992), 143–68.

OAKLEY, J. (1982), 'Athamas, Ino, Hermes and the Infant Dionysos', *AK* 25: 44–7.

—— (1990), *The Phiale Painter* (Mainz).

—— (1992), 'An Athenian Red-figure Workshop from the Time of the Peloponnesian War', in F. Blondé and J. Perreault (eds.), *Les Ateliers de potiers dans le monde grec aux époques géometrique, archaïque et classique* (Paris), 195–203.

—— (ed.) (forthcoming), *Athenian Potters and Painters* (Athens).

ORANJE, H. (1984), *Euripides' Bacchae: The Play and its Audience* (Leiden).

OTTO, W. (1965), *Dionysus: Myth and Cult* (Bloomington).

PALAGIA, O. (1993), *The Pediments of the Parthenon* (Leiden).

PARKE, H. W. (1967), *The Oracles of Zeus* (Oxford).

—— (1977), *Festivals of the Athenians* (London).

PATITUCCI, S. (1962), 'Osservazioni sul cratere polignoteo della tomba 128 di valle Trebba', *Arte antica e moderna* 18: 146–64.

PATTON, K. (1990), 'Gods Who Sacrifice: A Paradox of Attic Iconography', *AJA* 94: 326.

PAYNE, H., and YOUNG, G. (1936), *Archaic Marble Sculpture from the Acropolis* (London).

PEASE, M. (1935), 'The Pottery from the North Slope of the Acropolis', *Hesperia* 4: 214–302.

PELLEGRINI, G. (1900), *Museo Civico di Bologna: Catalogo dei vasi antichi dipinti della collezioni palagi ed universitaria* (Bologna).

PEREDOLSKA, A. (1967), *Krasnofigurnie atticheskie vazi v Ermitaze* (Leningrad).

PERNICE, E. (1898), 'Ein korinthischer Pinax', in K. Masner (ed.), *Festschrift für Otto Benndorf* (Vienna), 75–80.

PHILIPPAKI, B. (1967), *The Attic Stamnos* (Oxford).

PHILIPPART, H. (1930), *Iconographie des Bacchantes d'Euripide* (Paris).

PICKARD-CAMBRIDGE, A. (1988), *The Dramatic Festivals of Athens*, 2nd edn. rev. J. Gould and D. Lewis (Oxford).

PICON, C. (1993), 'The Oxford Maenad', *Antike Plastik* 22: 89–104.

PIPILI, M. (1991), 'Hermes and the Child Dionysos: What Did Pausanias see on the Amyklai Throne?', in Gnade (1991), 143–47.

POCHMARSKI, E. (1974), *Das Bild des Dionysos in der Rundplastik der klassischen Zeit Griechenlands* (Vienna).

—— (1984), 'Zur Deutung der Figur D in Parthenon-Ostgiebel', in Berger (1984), 278–80.

POURSAT, J.-C. (1968), 'Les Représentations de danse armée dans la céramique attique', *BCH* 92: 550–615.

PRAG, A. J. (1985), *Oresteia: Iconographic and Narrative Tradition* (Warminster).

PRANGE, M. (1989), *Der Niobidenmaler und seine Werkstatt* (Frankfurt).

PRASCHNIKER, C. (1928), *Parthenonstudien* (Vienna).

QUEYREL, A. (1984), 'Scènes apolliniennes et dionysiaques du Peintre de Pothos', *BCH* 108: 123–59.

RAECK, W. (1981), *Zum Barbarenbild in der Kunst Athens in 6. und 5. Jahrhundert v. Chr.* (Bonn).

RASMUSSEN, T., and SPIVEY, N. (eds.) (1991), *Looking at Greek Vases* (Cambridge).

RAUBITSCHEK, I. (1969), *The Hearst Hillsborough Vases* (Mainz).

RICE, E. (1983), *The Grand Procession of Ptolemy Philadelphus* (Oxford).

RICHARDSON, N. (1974), *The Homeric Hymn to Demeter* (Oxford).

RICHTER, G., and HALL, L. (1936), *Red-figured Athenian Vases in the Metropolitan Museum of Art* (New Haven).

ROBERTSON, C. M. (1967 review of Aurigemma, *Scavi di Spina* in *Gnomon* 39: 819–25.

—— (1972), 'Monocrepis' *GRBS* 13: 38–48.

—— (1975), *A History of Greek Art* (Cambridge).

—— (1979), 'Two Question-marks on the Parthenon', in G. Kopcke and M. Moore (eds.), *Studies in Classical Art and Archaeology: A Tribute to Peter von Blanckenhagen* (Locust Valley), 75–87.

—— (1986), 'Two Pelikai by the Pan Painter', *Greek Vases in the J. Paul Getty Museum* 3: 71–90.

—— (1992), *Art of Vase-painting in Classical Athens* (Cambridge).

ROBERTSON, C. M., and FRANZ, A. (1975), *The Parthenon Frieze* (London).

ROLLER, L. E. (1991), 'The Great Mother at Gordion: The Hellenization of an Anatolian Cult', *JHS* 111: 128–43.

ROMANO, I. B. (1982), 'The Archaic Statue of Dionysos from Ikarion', *Hesperia* 51: 398–409.

SANZ, F. (1990), 'La falcata Ibérica', *Archivo Español de Arqueología* 63: 65–93.

SCHAUENBURG, K. (1975), 'Zwei Kieler Lekythen mit Seitenpalmetten', in *Festschrift für Erich Burck* (Amsterdam), 546–60.

—— (1977), 'Zu Repliken in der Vasenmalerei', *Anz* 194–204.

SCHEFOLD, K. (1934), *Untersuchungen zu den kertscher Vasen* (Berlin).

SCHEIBLER, I. (1983), *Griechische Töpferkunst, Herstellung, Handel und Gebrauch der antiken Tongefässe* (Munich).

SCHLESIER, R. (1993), 'Mixture of Masks: Maenads as Tragic Models', in Carpenter and Faraone (1993), 89–114.

SCHÖNE, A. (1987), *Der Thiasos: Eine ikonographische Untersuchung über das Gefolge des Dionysos in der attischen Vasenmalerei des 6. und 5. Jhs.v.Chr.* (Göteborg).

—— (1990), 'Die Hydria der Meidias-Malers im Kerameikos', *AM* 105: 163–78.

SCHUCHHARDT, W. H. (1967), 'Sitzender Dionysos', *Antike Plastik* 6: 7–20.

SCHWAB, K. (1989), *The Parthenon Metopes and Greek Vase Painting: A Study of Comparison and Influences*, dissertation (Ann Arbor).

SEAFORD, R. (1984), *Euripides: Cyclops* (Oxford).

—— (1993), 'Dionysus as Destroyer of the Household: Homer, Tragedy, and the Polis', in Carpenter and Faraone (1993), 115–46.

SHAPIRO, H. (1981), *Art, Myth and Culture: Greek Vases from Southern Collections* (New Orleans).

—— (1989), *Art and Cult under the Tyrants in Athens* (Mainz).

SHEAR, T. L. Jr. (1973), 'The Athenian Agora: Excavations of 1972' *Hesperia* 42: 359–407.

SHEFTON, B. (1982), 'A Krater from Baksy', in Kurtz and Sparkes (1982), 149–81.

SICHTERMANN, H. (1966), *Griechische Vasen in Unteritalien aus der Sammlung Jatta in Ruvo* (Tübingen).

SIDOROVA, N., et. al. (1985), *Antique Painted Pottery in the Pushkin State Museum of Fine Arts* (Moscow).

SIMON, E. (1953), *Opfernde Götter* (Berlin).

—— (1963), 'Ein Anthesterien-Skyphos des Polygnotos', *AK* 6: 6–22.

—— (1982), 'Satyr-plays on Vases in the Time of Aeschylus', in Kurtz & Sparkes (1982), 123–48.

—— (1983), *Festivals of Attica: An Archaeological Commentary* (Madison).

—— (1985), 'Early Classical Vase-painting', in Boulter (1985), 66–82.

SIMON, E., and HIRMER, M. (1981), *Die griechischen Vasen* (Munich).

SLATER, W. J. (1971), 'Pindar's House', *GRBS* 12: 141–53.

SMALL, J. P. (1994), 'Scholars, Etruscans, and Attic Painted Vases', *Journal of Roman Archaeology* 7: 34–58.

SMITH, A. H. (1892), *A Catalogue of Sculpture in the Department of Greek and Roman Antiquities, British Museum*, i (London).

SNODGRASS, A. (1967), *Arms and Armour of the Greeks* (London).

SOURVINOU-INWOOD, C. (1989), 'The Fourth Stasimon of Sophocles' *Antigone*', *BICS* 36: 141–65.

—— (1991), *'Reading' Greek Culture: Texts and Images, Rituals and Myths* (Oxford).

SPARKES, B. A. (1985), 'Aspects of Onesimos', in Boulter (1985), 18–39.

—— (1991), *Greek Pottery: an Introduction* (Manchester).

SPARKES, B. A., and TALCOTT, L. (1970), *Black and Plain Pottery of the 6th, 5th and 4th Centuries B.C.: The Athenian Agora*, xii (Princeton).

SPIER, J. (1990), 'Emblems in Archaic Greece', *BICS* 37: 107–29.

SPIVEY, N. (1991), 'Greek Vases in Etruria', in Rasmussen and Spivey (1991), 131–50.

STROCKA, V. M. (1987), *Griechische Vasen zur Ausstellung: Alltag und Fest in Athen* (Freiburg).

SUTER, P. (1975), *Das Harmodiosmotiv*, dissertation (Basel).

SUTTON, D. F. (1980), *The Greek Satyr Play* (Meisenheim).

SUTTON, R. F. Jr. (1992), 'Pornography and Persuasion on Attic Pottery', in A. Richlin (ed.), *Pornography and Representation in Greece and Rome* (New York), 3–35.

SVORONOS, J. (1919), *L'Hellénisme primatif de la Macédoine prouvé par la numismatique et l'or du Pangée* (Paris and Athens).

TAPLIN, O. (1993), *Comic Angels: And Other Approaches to Greek Drama through Vase-paintings* (Oxford).

TAYLOR, M. (1981), *The Tyrant Slayers* (New York).

THOMPSON, H., and WYCHERLEY, R. (1972), *The Agora of Athens:The Athenian Agora*, xiv (Princeton).

TRENDALL, A. D., and WEBSTER, T. B. L. (1971), *Illustrations of Greek Drama* (London).

VAN DER WEIDEN, M. (1991), *The Dithyrambs of Pindar: Introduction, Text and Commentary* (Amsterdam).

VERMASEREN, M. J. (1977–89), *Corpus Cultus Cybelae Attidisque* (Leiden).

VERSNEL, H. (1990), *Ter Unus: Isis, Dionysos, Hermes: Three Studies in Henotheism* (Leiden).

VIAN, F. (1951), *Répertoire des gigantomachies* (Paris).

—— (1952), *La Guerre des géants* (Paris).

VIKELAS, E., and FUCHS, W. (1985), 'Zum Rundaltar mit archaistischem Götterzug für Dionysos in Brauron', *Boreas* 8: 41–8.

VICKERS, M. (forthcoming), 'Images on Textiles: the Weave of Fifth-Century Athenian Art and Society', *Xenia: Konstanter Althistorische Vorträge und Forschungen*.

VILLANEUVA-PUIG, M. (1980), 'A propos du nom de "bacchante" attribué par les auteurs ancien à la figure artistique de la compagne de Dionysos: un point du vocabulaire de la critique d'art dans l'Antiquité', *Revue des études anciennes* 82: 52–59.

—— (1983), 'A propos d'une ménade aux sangliers sur une oinochoé a figures noires du British Museum: notes sur le bestiaire dionysiaque', *RA* 229–58.

VON SALIS, A. (1940), 'Die Gigantomachie am Schilde der Athena Parthenos', *JdI* 55: 90–169.

WALTER, H. (1985), *Die Gestalt der Frau* (Stuttgart).

WEBSTER, T. B. L. (1966), 'The Myth of Ariadne from Homer to Catullus', *Greece and Rome* 13: 22–31.

—— (1970), *Greek Theatre Productions*, 2nd edn. (London).

—— (1972), *Potter and Patron in Classical Athens* (London).

WEGNER, M. (1963), *Musikgeschichte in Bildern Bd.2 Musik der Altertums, 4, Griechenland* (Leipzig).

WEHGARTNER, I. (1983), *Attische Weissgrundige Keramik* (Mainz).

WELCKER, F. (1851), *Alte Denkmäler* (Göttingen).

WEST, M. L. (1966), *Hesiod: Theogony* (Oxford).

—— (1990), *Studies in Aeschylus* (Stuttgart).

—— (1992), *Ancient Greek Music* (Oxford).

WIESNER, J. (1969), 'Über den Gott auf dem Esel', *Anz* 531–45.

WILAMOWITZ-MOELLENDORFF, U. von (1932), *Der Glaube der Hellenen*, ii (Berlin).

WILLIAMS, D. (1976), 'The Ilioupersis Cup in Berlin and the Vatican', *Jahrbuch der Berliner Museen* 18: 9–23.

—— (1990), 'Euphronios: du peintre au potier', in *Euphronios, peintre à Athènes av VIᵉ siècle avant J.-C.* (Paris), 33–7.

WINNINGTON-INGRAM, R. P. (1969), *Euripides and Dionysos: An Interpretation of the Bacchae* (Amsterdam).

WREDE, W. (1928), 'Der Maskengott', *AM* 53: 66–95.

ZANKER, P. (1965), *Wandel der Hermesgestalt in der attischen Vasenmalerei* (Bonn).

ZEITLIN, F. I. (1993), 'Staging Dionysus between Thebes and Athens', in Carpenter and Faraone (1993), 147–82.

ZIMMERMANN, K. (1980), 'Thraker-Darstellungen auf griechischen Vasen', in *Actes du IIe Congres International de Thracologie*, i (Bucarest), 429–46.

ZÜCHNER, W. (1938), *Der Berliner Mänadenkrater* (Berlin).

Index of Vases

General Index

Achilles 32–3, 41 n. 33, 88 n. 21
Achilles Painter 74
Adonis 77
Aeschines 77, 79
Aeschylus 35
  Bassarai 53
  Edonians
    (fr. 57) 78, 98, 112
    (fr. 61) 36
  Lykourgos tetralogy 35–7, 108
  Nereids 32
  Oresteia 75 n. 32
  Pentheus 116
  Persians (12–64) 108
  Seven Against Thebes (387–676) 8
Agave 109, 116
Agrigento Painter 74
Aithra 59
Alkamenes 105 n. 5
alopekis 19, 33, 49, 50 n. 83
  see also Thracian dress
Altamura Painter 30–2, 39, 40, 47, 54, 98
Amasis Painter 45, 52–3, 63, 93
Amphitrite 55
Andokides Painter 13
Anthesteria 11 n. 29, 66, 94 n. 55
Aphrodite 61, 62 n. 63, 67, 91
Apollo 18, 20–4, 59, 91
Apollodorus:
  (1. 6. 1–2) 16, 21
  (3. 4. 3) 53
  (3. 5. 1–3) 35, 53, 63, 113
  (3. 17) 41 n. 33
  Epitome (1. 8) 65 n. 79
Arabia 108
Arcadia 16 n. 5
Ares 23, 29, 91
Argos 35
Ariadne 31, 59, 62, 64–9, 101–2
Aristophanes:
  Birds
    (823–31) 22 n. 32

(873) 77 n. 42
(994) 107
Clouds (889–1106) 10
Frogs 63, 104–7
  (45–8) 107
  (200) 107
  (336) 63
Horae (fr. 566) 77 n. 42
Knights (566) 22 n. 34
Lysistrata
  (3) 112 n. 46
  (44, 47) 107
  (387–9) 77 n. 42, 112 n. 46
Wasps
  (8–10) 77
  (119) 112 n. 46
  (169–97) 117 n. 84
  (1215) 22 n. 32
Women in Assembly (332, 346, 657)
  107
Women at the Thesmophoria (138, 253,
  941, 945, 1220) 107
Aristotle:
  Poetics (1451) 65
arming:
  Achilles 32
  Dionysos 32
  satyr 33
Arrian:
  Periplus ponti Euxini (9) 76
Artemis 20, 21, 64, 91
Atalanta 20 n. 20
Athamas 53–7
Athena 31, 55, 91
  birth 84–90
  gigantomachy 17, 24–6, 33
Athenaeus:
  (3. 78c) 93 n. 51
  (5. 201c) 113
  (9. 407a) 25
aulete 71, 73, 78
Axios 108

Plates

PLATE 1A Parthenon metope E II (Praschniker reconstruction)

PLATE 1B London, British Museum E 8

PLATE 2A London, British Museum E 443

PLATE 2B London, British Museum E 443

PLATE 3A Parthenon metope E IX (Praschniker reconstruction)

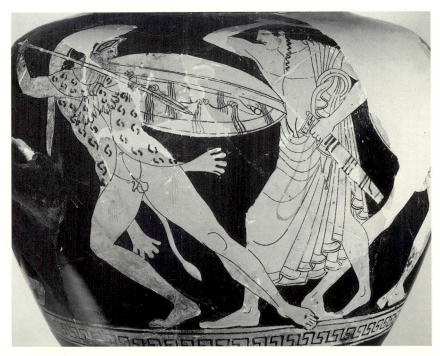

PLATE 3B Paris, Louvre C 10748

PLATE 4A Athens, from Marathon Street

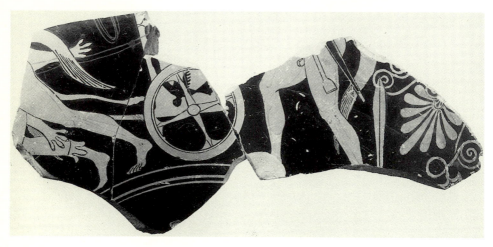

PLATE 4B Athens, from Marathon Street

PLATE 5A Florence, Museo
Archeologico 4209

PLATE 5B Malibu, J. Paul Getty
Museum 86.AE.1109.6

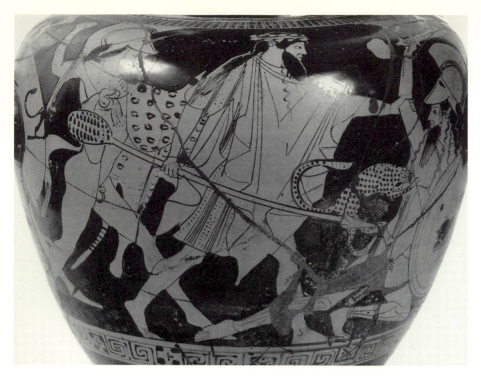

PLATE 6A Orvieto, Museo Civico 1044

PLATE 6B Orvieto, Museo Civico 1044

PLATE 7A St Petersburg, Hermitage 765

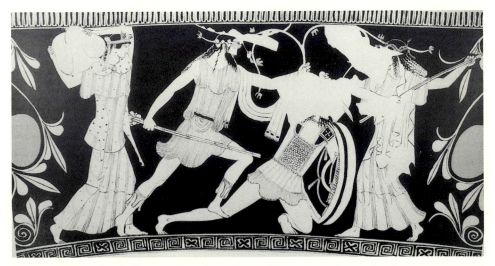

PLATE 7B Boston, Museum of Fine Arts 00.342

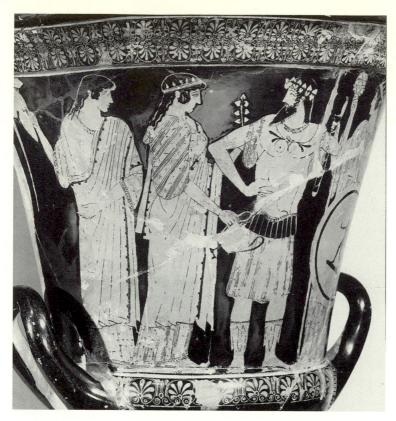

PLATE 8A St Petersburg, Hermitage 638

PLATE 8B Bologna, Museo Civico Archeologico 291

PLATE 10A London, British Museum E 75

PLATE 10B Private collection

PLATE 11A Newcastle-upon-Tyne, Shefton Museum

PLATE 11B Newcastle-upon-Tyne, Shefton Museum

PLATE 12A Florence, Museo
Archeologico 4209

PLATE 12B Florence, Museo
Archeologico 4209

PLATE 12C Thasian stater

PLATE 13A Munich, Antikensammlungen 2606

PLATE 13B Geneva, Musée d'Art et d'Histoire HR 85

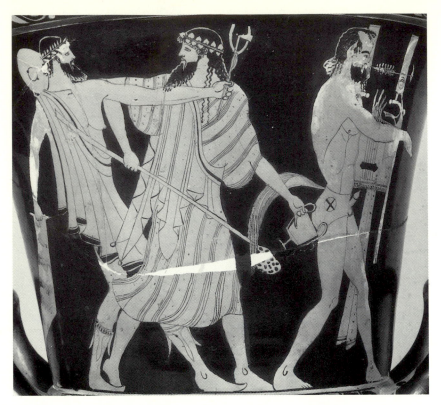

PLATE 14A Vienna, Kunsthistorisches Museum 985

PLATE 14B Naples, Museo Archeologico Nazionale Stg. 701

PLATE 15A Harvard, Fogg Museum 1960.236

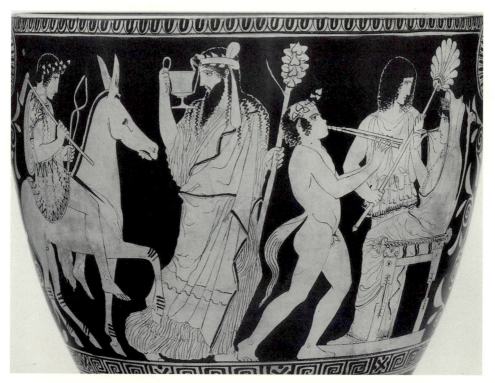

PLATE 15B Toledo, Museum of Art 82.88

PLATE 16a London, British Museum E 768

PLATE 16b Boston, Museum of Fine Arts 03.788

PLATE 17A Sarasota, Ringling Museum 1600.G5

PLATE 17B Paris, Louvre G 185

PLATE 18A Paris, Cabinet des Médailles 222

PLATE 18B Tarquinia, Museo Nazionale RC 6848

PLATE 19A Ferrara, Museo Archeologico 2737

PLATE 19B Ferrara, Museo Archeologico 2738

PLATE 20A Athens, Acropolis Collection 325

PLATE 20B Berlin, Staatliche Museen F 2290

PLATE 21 Berlin, Staatliche Museen F 2290

PLATE 22A Paris, Cabinet des Médailles 440

PLATE 22B Athens, Kryou Collection

PLATE 23A London, British Museum E 492

PLATE 23B New York, Metropolitan Museum of Art x.313.1

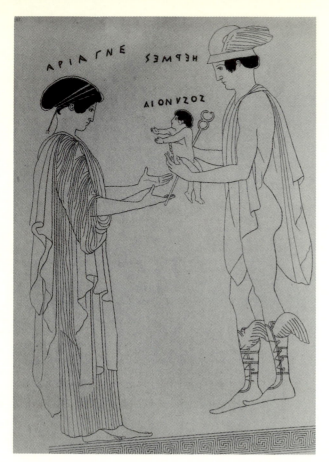

PLATE 24A Palermo, Museo
Nazionale 1109

PLATE 24B Syracuse, Museo
Nazionale 22177

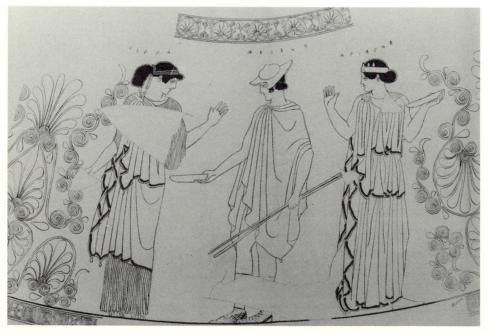

PLATE 25A Karlsruhe, Badisches Landesmuseum 208

PLATE 25B Naples, Museo Archeologico Nazionale 2419

PLATE 26A Oxford, Ashmolean Musem 524

PLATE 26B Oxford, Ashmolean Musem 524

PLATE 27A Warsaw, National Museum 142355

PLATE 27B New York, Metropolitan Museum of Art 1986.11.12

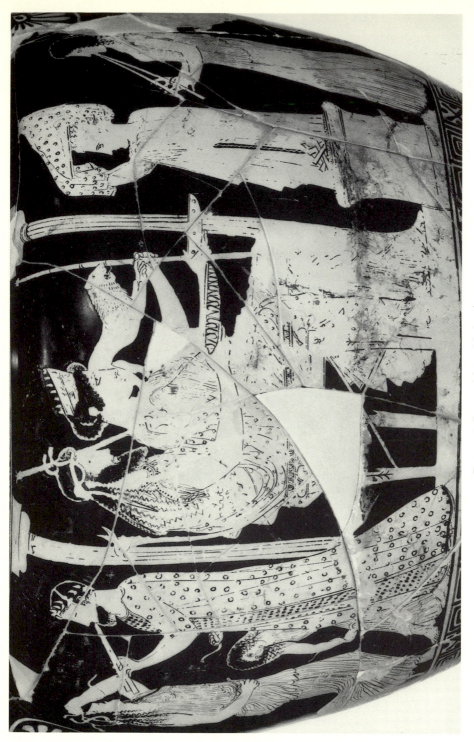

PLATE 28 Ferrara, Museo Nazionale 2897

Plate 29 Ferrara, Museo Nazionale 2897

PLATE 30A Basle, Antikenmuseum
Lu 60

PLATE 30B Harvard, Fogg
Museum 1960.343

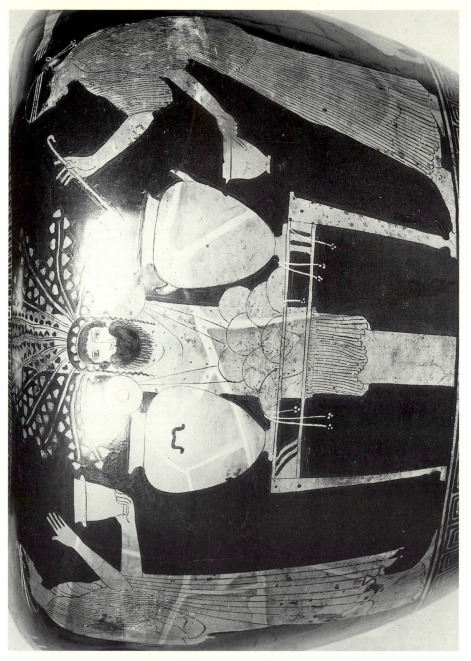

PLATE 31 Boston, Museum of Fine Arts 90.155

PLATE 32A Warsaw, National Museum 142465

PLATE 32B Paris, Louvre G 532

PLATE 33A Munich,
Antikensammlungen 2344

PLATE 33B New York, Metropolitan
Museum of Art 56.171.38

PLATE 34A Paris, Cabinet des Médailles 576

PLATE 34B Paris, Cabinet des Médailles 576

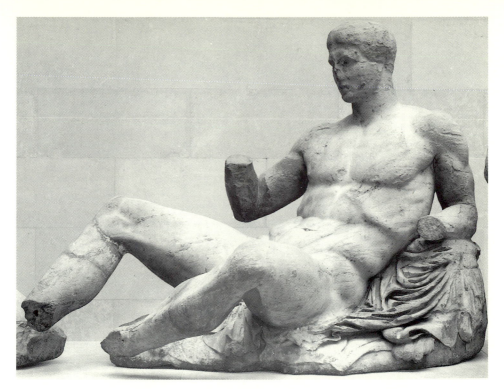

PLATE 35A Parthenon, E. Pediment, Figure D

PLATE 35B Berlin, Staatliche Museen 2401

Plate 36a Cast of frieze from the Lysikrates Monument

Plate 36b Vienna, Kunsthistorisches Museum 1024

PLATE 37A Parthenon, E. Frieze, IV, 24–27.

PLATE 37B London, British Museum E 503

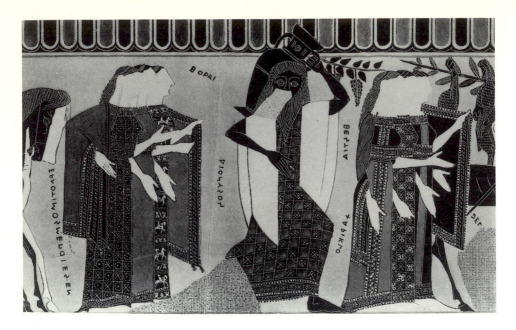

PLATE 38A Florence,
Museo Archeologico
4209

PLATE 38B Athens,
Agora Museum S 2485

Plate 39a Athens, Agora Museum
P 24472

Plate 39b Malibu, J. Paul Getty
Museum 88.AE.150

PLATE 40A   Once Berlin, Staatliche Museen F 2471

PLATE 40B   Bologna, Museo Civico Archeologico 283

PLATE 41 Athens, National Museum 14500

PLATE 42A Once Toronto, Borowski

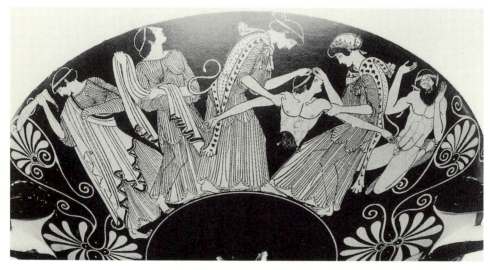

PLATE 42B Once Toronto, Borowski

PLATE 43 London, British Museum E 140

PLATE 44A Brussels, Musée Royaux d'Art et d'Histoire R 255

PLATE 44B Paris, Cabinet des Médailles 357

PLATE 45A London, British Museum E 775

PLATE 45B Munich, Antikensammlungen 2654

PLATE 46A Boston, Museum of Fine Arts 10.211

PLATE 46B Paris, Louvre G 69

PLATE 47A Oxford, Ashmolean Museum 1912.1165

PLATE 47B Oxford, Ashmolean Museum 1912.1165